LIBERALISM AND LIBERAL POLITICS IN EDWARDIAN ENGLAND

LIBERALISM AND LIBERAL POLITICS IN EDWARDIAN ENGLAND

George L. Bernstein
Department of History, Tulane University

Boston
ALLEN & UNWIN
London   Sydney

Allen & Unwin, Inc.,
8 Winchester Place, Winchester, Mass. 01890, USA

George Allen & Unwin (Publishers) Ltd,
40 Museum Street, London WC1A 1LU, UK

George Allen & Unwin (Publishers) Ltd,
Park Lane, Hemel Hempstead, Herts HP2 4TE, UK

George Allen & Unwin Australia Pty Ltd,
8 Napier Street, North Sydney, NSW 2060, Australia

First published in 1986

Library of Congress Cataloging-in-Publication Data

Bernstein, George Lurcy, 1947–
   Liberalism and Liberal politics in Edwardian England.
Bibliography: p.
Includes index.
1. Great Britain – Politics and government – 1901–1910.
2. Great Britain – Politics and government – 1910–1936.
3. Liberalism – Great Britain – History – 20th century.
I. Title.
DA570.B47   1986   941.082   85–22877
ISBN 0–04–942198–0 (alk. paper)
ISBN 0–04–942199–9 (pbk.: alk. paper)

British Library Cataloguing in Publication data

Bernstein, George L.
   Liberalism and Liberal politics in Edwardian England.
1. Liberalism – England – History – 19th century
2. Liberalism – England – History – 20th century
I. Title
320.5'1'0942   JC599.G7
ISBN 0–04–942198–0
ISBN 0–04–942199–9 Pbk

Set in 10 on 12 point Palatino by Computape (Pickering) Ltd.,
North Yorkshire
and printed in Great Britain by
Anchor Brendon Ltd, Tiptree, Essex

To Emmet Larkin and Bill Heyck

Table of Contents

List of Tables and Figures

Acknowledgements

The sinews of scholarship, like those of war, are measured in dollars and cents (in the United States). A dissertation-year grant from the Ford Foundation helped finance the initial research for this book. A grant from the Primrose Fund of the American Philosophical Society helped enable me to do the research necessary for revising it. The Murphy Institute of Political Economy at Tulane University paid for typing the final manuscript. I thank all of these institutions for their generous support. My greatest debt, however, is to my father and mother. Our profession, like the rest of the world, is weighted in favour of those with resources of their own. The unstinting generosity of my parents assured that the means always were available for me to complete my education, wait out the job market, and travel to Britain to do research. I am eternally grateful.

Many people made contributions to improving this book. Bill Heyck, Pat Auspos, Claire Lennox and Joel Wolfe all made specific methodological or analytical suggestions which have made the final product far superior to what it otherwise would have been. I am particularly grateful to Pat Auspos, who, as my companion and colleague in the study of Liberal politics between 1870 and 1914, deeply influenced my thinking on the subject. I owe a special debt to P. F. Clarke, H. V. Emy, D. A. Hamer and H. C. G. Matthew. While I have sought to revise some of their conclusions, their work in the early 1970s has defined the framework for the historical debate over the nature of Edwardian Liberal politics. Professors Emmet Larkin, Bill Heyck, William McNeill, Lloyd Rudolph, Radomir Luza and Jon Sumida have read all or part of the manuscript at different stages of its evolution. Their comments and suggestions have been invaluable in improving it. Elaine Siverio, Cathy Edwards, Maureen Kelleher and, most of all, Mildred Covert have been wonderfully patient and efficient in preparing and typing the manuscript in various incarnations.

Several people have given me moral support and encouragement during my career: my brothers Daniel and Alan, their wives Ann and Jayusia, my cousins Jane and Jim Rhodes, Henry Rosovsky, Al Moss, Lindsay and Ann Waters, and my colleagues Rick Teichgraeber, Larry Powell and Ken Harl. Theirs was the kind of help which cannot be defined, merely gratefully acknowledged. Even more, it is impossible adequately to express my gratitude to Emmet Larkin and Bill Heyck. Without them this book would not exist. I dedicate the book to them.

Finally, I want to thank many people and institutions for permission to quote from copyrighted material. I thank the following institutions and trustees for permission to quote from material in collections in their care: the British Library Board (Campbell-Bannerman Papers, Viscount Gladstone Papers, J. A. Spender Papers); the House of Lords Record Office, the Beaverbrook Foundation and Mr A. J. P. Taylor (Lloyd George Papers); Mr B. C. Bloomfield, Director, India Office Library and Records, British Library (letters of John Morley as India Secretary); Liverpool Record Office (diary of Richard Holt); Trustees of the National Library of Scotland (Rosebery Papers, Haldane Papers, diary of A. C. Murray). I thank the Controller of Her Majesty's Stationery Office for permission to quote from Crown-copyright records in the India Office Records (letters of John Morley as India Secretary) and in the Public Record Office (letters of Sir Edward Grey as Foreign Secretary). I thank the following publishers for permission to quote from books which they have published: Oxford University Press (H. H. Asquith, *Letters to Venetia Stanley*, selected and edited by Michael and Eleanor Brock [1982]; H. C. G. Matthew, *The Liberal Imperialists: The Ideas and Politics of a Post-Gladstonian Elite* [1973]; Peter Stansky, *Ambitions and Strategies: The Struggle for the Leadership of the Liberal Party in the 1890s* [1964]); Cambridge University Press (Stefan Collini, *Liberalism and Sociology: L. T. Hobhouse and Political Argument in England 1880–1914* [1979]; H. V. Emy, *Liberals, Radicals and Social Politics, 1892–1914* [1973]); Harvester Press (Patricia Jalland, *The Liberals and Ireland: The Ulster Question in British Politics to 1914* [1980]; R. T. Shannon, *Gladstone and the Bulgarian Agitation, 1876* [1963, originally published by Nelson & Sons]); Rowman and Littlefield (Kenneth D. Brown, *Labour and Unemployment 1900–1914* [1971]); Batsford (Maurice Bruce, *The Coming of the Welfare State* [1966]); John Murray and St Martin's Press (Edward David, editor, *Inside Asquith's Cabinet: From the Diaries of Charles Hobhouse* [1977]); Methuen London and University of California Press (John Grigg, *Lloyd George: The People's Champion, 1902–1911* [1978]); Yale University Press (Stephen E. Koss, *John Morley at the India Office, 1905–1910* [1969]); George Weidenfeld & Nicolson and St Martin's Press (John P. Mackintosh, editor, *British Prime Ministers in the Twentieth Century*, Vol. I: *Balfour to Chamberlain* [1977]); Frank Cass & Co. (Lucy Masterman, *C. F. G. Masterman: A Biography* [1968, originally published by Nicholson and Watson]); Macmillan Publishing Company and Curtis Brown Ltd. (Keith Robbins, *Sir Edward Grey: A Biography of Lord Grey of Fallodon* [1971, originally published by Cassell and Co. Ltd.]); Newnes Books (Lord

Riddell, *More Pages from my Diary 1908–1914* [1934]); Macmillan Publishing Company (A. P. Ryan, *Mutiny at the Curragh* [1956]); Basil Blackwell and University of California Press (Geoffrey R. Searle, *The Quest for National Efficiency: A Study in British Politics and Political Thought, 1899–1914* [1971]); Longman (George M. Trevelyan, *Grey of Fallodon: Being the Life of Sir Edward Grey, Afterwards Viscount Grey of Fallodon* [1937]); Havard University Press (Samuel R. Williamson, Jr., *The Politics of Grand Strategy: Britain and France Prepare for War, 1904–1914* [1969]). Lastly, I thank the following individuals for permission to quote from letters or other material for which they hold the copyright: Mr Mark Bonham Carter (letters of H. H. Asquith); Dr Pauline Dower (letter of Charles P. Trevelyan); Lady Alethea Eliot (letter of Sydney Buxton); Lord Gainford (letters of J. A. Pease); Sir William Gladstone (letters of Herbert Gladstone); Oron J. Hale (his book *Publicity and Diplomacy, with Special Reference to England and Germany 1890–1914* [1940, originally published by Appleton-Century]); Mr N. C. Masterman (diary of Lucy Masterman); Dr Mary C. Moorman (letters of George M. Trevelyan); Mrs Mary Sinclair Rothenberg (letters of Sir Henry Campbell-Bannerman); Mary Duchess of Roxburghe (letter of Lord Crewe); Lord Shuttleworth (letters of Sir Ughtred Kay-Shuttleworth); Warren Murton, Solicitors (letter of James Bryce). I have made every effort to identify and contact copyright holders. I have not, however, always succeeded, and I hope all those whom I have been unable to locate will accept this acknowledgement for their kindness in allowing me to quote from the material for which they own the copyright.

A Note on the Use of Newspapers

It was crucial to the purposes of this book to attain some sample of the views and attitudes of the Liberal rank and file. Too often, historians have taken the *Daily News*, the *Manchester Guardian*, the *Nation* and the *Westminster Gazette* as representative of Liberal opinion as a whole. The first three were the self-conscious exponents of the new liberalism. The last was treated at the time as the voice of official liberalism. Three of the four were based in London, while the *Guardian* was based in a region where the Liberals had been weak during the first twenty years of the third Reform Act. None directly reflected the views of the Liberal activists in those regions of the country which were the centres of the party's strength.

In order to get at those views, I have examined the Liberal newspapers of Leeds, Leicester and Norwich. The West Riding of Yorkshire and the East Midlands were staunchly Liberal. East Anglia was a swing area, with the Norfolk county divisions providing the Liberals with one of their bases in the region. The newspapers of Leicester and Norwich served their respective counties, providing links to rural and small town liberalism in their regions. All three cities were included in the Gladstone–MacDonald agreement, and so offered a test of the effectiveness of the progressive alliance in regions (unlike Lancashire) where the Liberals would have to make substantial concessions to Labour. Finally, from the autumn of 1901, the *Leeds Mercury* offered a means of testing the distinctiveness of liberal imperialism. (In 1909 the *Mercury* began to describe itself as independent and seemed about to break with the Liberals. Once it was clear, however, that the Budget would lead to a crisis with the House of Lords, it reverted to a conventionally liberal position on most issues. I have therefore treated it as liberal throughout.) In order to check the congruence of Liberal and Nonconformist opinion, I also examined the principal Congregationalist newspaper (as most likely to be Liberal), plus the *Methodist Recorder* (the least likely to be Liberal).

When, in the course of the narrative, I refer to the views of the Liberal and Nonconformist rank and file, or of the provincial Liberal press, those views are based on the editorial opinions expressed in these newspapers, the speeches of local Liberals, and articles by Nonconformist spokesmen. Obviously, they cannot provide a large enough sample in a statistical sense. None the less, the extent to which these sources agreed was impressive. When such a consensus existed on an issue, usually I have not provided specific references, although I have sometimes done so when the consensus view was unexpected or was of unusual importance to my argument (for example, during the international crisis of July 1914). When there were disagreements or divergences from the norm, I have indicated so in the notes.

Introduction

Why did the Liberal Party collapse after the First World War, to be replaced as the principal party of the left by a socialist Labour Party? In trying to answer this question, historians since Elie Halévy and George Dangerfield have been investigating the condition of Edwardian liberalism to see if decay had set in before the war.[1] For a generation, the debate has centred around whether the Liberal Party had resolved the problem of retaining the support of working-class voters in a new era of class politics. In this book, I argue that the new liberalism and the progressive alliance which had evolved by 1914 did not offer a long-term solution to this problem. As a result, the Liberals remained vulnerable to a challenge from a party committed to promoting the interests of the working class. This is not to say that the Liberal Party was in danger of immediate collapse. Without the war, the process of decline surely would have been gradual and uneven. Nor does it mean that the Labour Party was on the verge of replacing the Liberals as the predominant party of the left. On the contrary, Labour had much work to do before it would have the constituency organizations to enable it to mount such a challenge. What does seem clear is that Labour finally was facing this reality before the war and had started on the task at hand. An aggressive Labour Party would create trouble for the Liberals, for a prolonged division of the forces of the left would almost surely have led to a period of Conservative domination – as it did between the wars and as it may do again in the 1980s.

This argument represents, in an updated form, the orthodoxy which has predominated for years among historians of the Labour Party. Henry Pelling, for example, argued in the 1960s that a Liberal Party whose local caucuses were dominated by the middle class was losing touch with a working class which was increasingly insistent upon asserting its independence of its 'betters' and shaping its own political destiny. The Labour Party was the vehicle which enabled the workers to break with middle-class tutelage, and Labour historians such as Roy Gregory and Ross McKibbon have sought to show the slow and hesitant process by which workers came to accept the necessity of such a break before the First World War.[2]

Two seminal books in the early 1970s challenged the interpretation

1

of the Liberal Party implicit in the analysis of the Labour historians. Peter Clarke and H. V. Emy denied that the Liberal Party was a nineteenth-century middle-class anachronism, unable to adapt to the needs of the working class.[3] Both men pointed to the evolution, beginning around 1890, of a new liberalism. This was the product of an attempt by liberal intellectuals (and some politicians) to modify traditional liberal ideology, so that state intervention to promote social reform policies in the interest of the poor and the working class would be central to the mission of the Liberal Party.[4] Emy showed how the social policies pursued by the Liberal governments of 1905–14 were in part a response to pressures exerted by 'new Liberals'. Clarke showed that in Lancashire the new liberalism came to be accepted by most of the party's rank and file. Furthermore, it provided the basis for a progressive alliance with the Labour Party which successfully contained any challenge Labour might have mounted against the Liberals as the predominant party of the left. Emy was more doubtful than Clarke that the Liberal rank and file had accepted either the partnership with Labour or the redirection of liberalism, for he saw the possibility of eroding organizational strength at the constituency level. None the less, historians of the Liberal Party quickly accepted that the new liberalism and the progressive alliance had enabled the Liberal Party to consolidate its role as the party of the working class; therefore, the party was not facing the prospect of decline prior to the First World War.[5]

In reassessing this orthodoxy, I have sought to reintegrate the new liberalism and the progressive alliance into a broader analysis of liberalism and liberal politics. First, I have tried to reestablish the connection between liberal politics at the national and local levels. Both Clarke and Emy recognized that if the intellectuals and political leaders were to succeed in redirecting the Liberal Party, they had to carry with them the rank and file – the activists in the constituencies whose enthusiasm and labour were essential if elections were to be won. Yet neither author was primarily concerned with examining the relationship between the leaders and the rank and file. One of the central themes of this book is the importance of the dynamics of that relationship to an understanding of the Liberal Party. In order to identify the views of the Liberal activists, I have chosen for investigation three constituencies – Leicester, Leeds and Norwich. Unlike Clarke's Lancashire, these were in regions where the Liberal Party was strong and had something to lose by co-operating with Labour. I have not, however, limited my inquiry to the local response to the new liberalism and the progressive alliance, as important as both are to this book. A proper understanding of the strength of the Liberal Party requires an assessment of the local reaction to all that was being done

2

by the party at Westminster, including traditional domestic policies and foreign and defence policies as well as new social policies. Only then can a judgement be arrived at concerning how the relationship between the leadership and the rank and file affected the party's policies and priorities.

My concern with the interaction between liberalism at the top and at the bottom also has led me to adopt a broader approach to ideology than that of the historians of the new liberalism. I argue that there was a liberal ideology which united Liberals at all levels. Furthermore, I argue that this liberalism encompassed all liberal policies – new and traditional, domestic and external. The attempt to define this ideology is another unifying theme of this book. In claiming that there was an identifiable liberal ideology apart from that of the intellectuals, I differ with the conclusions of D. A. Hamer. Hamer argued that the Liberal Party was little more than an alliance of dissident groups, each pursuing its own sectional interest. Since there was no common ideology uniting the sections, the challenge facing Liberal leadership was to induce them to act together – a challenge met alternatively by formulating a programme which incorporated all of the sectional issues or by identifying an overriding issue which would subordinate the sectional issues.[6] While Hamer's model is essential for understanding the ebbs and flows of Liberal Party politics, I believe that he underestimates the extent to which there was a liberalism which incorporated the sectional issues, and which was expressed in a fundamental way by the overriding issues.

Thus, it is only by understanding what a liberalism which encompassed all issues meant to Liberals at all levels, and how it affected the relationship between the leaders and the rank and file, that a proper assessment can be made of the impact of the new liberalism and the progressive alliance. Such an integrated approach is especially important when trying to judge the ability of the Liberals to adapt to a new class politics. It is central to Clarke's argument that by 1910, the votes of both the working class and the middle class were determined according to an assessment by each of its class interests. If this were so, then the Liberal victories in the general elections of that year would have proved the party could win the support of workers whose votes were determined by class considerations. While class clearly was an important factor influencing pre-war voters, I argue that the Edwardian Liberal Party did not and could not direct its electoral appeal along such class lines. It could not do so for the reason identified by the Labour historians – the party's rank and file were primarily middle-class Nonconformists. A class appeal, based on the claim that the working class had an identifiable interest which needed to be promoted in opposition to the interest of the middle class, could only

3

repel such people, for it challenged the fundamental tenets of their liberalism. For generations, liberalism had attacked the Conservative Party as the representative of the interest of a class – the landlords. While this attack itself had an obvious class basis, Liberals had justified their effort to unite the middle and working classes against the landed classes by arguing that it was wrong to promote the interest of a class in opposition to that of the community as a whole. They had identified the enemies of that larger community interest – landowners, vested interests, the privileged, the rich – in terms which had obscured possible divisions along class lines between the party's middle-class activists and working-class voters. Any appeal to the workers on the basis of their own class interest would have had the opposite effect, with potentially disastrous consequences for the unity of the party.

The middle-class activists were not, however, indifferent to the concerns of the working-class voters. On the contrary, like Clarke, I found that by 1909, most Liberals were using language derived from the new liberalism and could accept the government's social reform policies with little difficulty. None the less, these were never the priorities of the rank and file. It the party activists were to mobilize, they would do so only in support of traditional Liberal causes like land, education, temperance and the House of Lords. Nor were the rank and file ever very comfortable with the progressive alliance, for they perceived the Labour Party to represent a class interest. Even more, they hated the socialists who were part of the political labour movement, not only because their policies challenged the principles of liberalism, but also because they asserted the necessary opposition of capital and labour. As a result, in the absence of pressure from above, the progressive alliance in most cities was not extended to municipal politics. Furthermore, after 1910 it began to break down at the parliamentary level as the Liberal rank and file insisted on fighting socialism. The socialists were equally indifferent to the progressive alliance. At the same time, working people most often were indifferent, and occasionally even hostile, to Liberal social reforms.

Thus, I argue that the Liberal Party's success before the war was possible because the new class politics had not yet fully taken hold. As a result, the working class was still attracted by the Liberal attack upon privilege and wealth. The failure of the land campaign to interest urban workers, however, may have presaged a change. If that change was towards an increased importance of class issues in determining the votes of labouring men then neither the new liberalism nor the progressive alliance provided the Liberal Party with a long-term basis for competing effectively. The former represented no fundamental reorientation of Liberal priorities towards working-class concerns, and consequently met with little positive response from workers. The latter was in imminent danger of being repudiated by both the Liberal and the Labour rank and file.

1

The Foundations of
Edwardian Liberalism

THE GLADSTONIAN TRADITION

When making his contribution to the party fund for the general election of 1900, William Mather wrote to Herbert Gladstone, 'My devotion to our Liberal principles (I mean the Gospel according to your revered Father) makes a great pleasure giving gifts to that cause.'[1] For most Liberals at the turn of the century, the name of William Ewart Gladstone was synonymous with their party and their creed. Most of them had entered politics between 1866 and 1894, the years when he had led the party in the House of Commons. Four times he had been Prime Minister, and he had led them on many crusades for righteousness and justice. Gladstone had been a messianic figure for the Liberals of his generation – the embodiment of their liberal ideology.

Gladstone was a disciple of Sir Robert Peel, himself one of Britain's greatest Prime Ministers. The Peelite philosophy was a progressive conservatism; the Peelites were committed to preserving and strengthening the existing social order. Like the Whig aristocracy, however, they recognized the need to correct the abuses in the institutions which were the bulwarks of that social order. Both Peelites and Whigs were acutely aware of the threat which class conflict posed to social stability. The objective of reform was to eliminate grievances which might accentuate class hostility and foment revolution. While the Whig approach to reform tended to be pragmatic, however, the Peelites pursued an ideal of rational, efficient and just administration. At the same time, they were guided by a sense of high moral purpose which was alien to the more worldly Whigs.

The Peelite concern for morality and reason was shared by the middle-class radicals of the Manchester School. One result was a common approach to public finance. Both believed the classical economists had proved that free trade promoted national prosperity. They supported retrenchment in government spending to assure efficient administration. Government should balance its budget each year as a safeguard against irresponsible policies which later gener-

6

ations would have to pay for. None the less, the Peelites were not as single-mindedly opposed to all government intervention as were the Manchester School radicals. While the Peelites opposed government interference with the economy and preferred to minimize the role of the state, they could justify intervention to remove legitimate griev-ances and promote social harmony.[2]

By 1900, the Peelite heritage was an integral part of the 'Gospel' of Gladstonian liberalism. One contribution to the liberal tradition, however, was uniquely Gladstone's – his approach to foreign policy. R. T. Shannon has summarized Gladstone's guiding principles: 'that states are bound by the same moral laws as individuals; and that it is not merely desirable but essential that decisions of policy should conform strictly and directly to absolute definitions of righteousness.'[3] By these criteria, British intervention in the affairs of others could be justified only to uphold the cause of morality and justice. When intervention was necessary, it should be by the joint action of the European powers rather than the unilateral action of Britain, and, whenever possible, moral force and persuasion rather than physical force should be employed.

This Gladstonian outlook was quite different from the pragmatic approach to foreign policy of the Whig leaders. They believed that those who engaged in agitations based upon moral considerations displayed a dangerous ignorance of practical difficulties and a naive belief in the righteous motives of other European states. They recog-nized the national interest as a proper basis upon which to conduct a foreign policy; therefore, they were reluctant to engage in criticism that might restrict a Conservative government's freedom of action at a time of crisis.

Opposition to this Whig-Conservative approach to foreign policy was crucial in binding British Nonconformists to the Gladstonian Liberal Party. Gladstone recognized that Nonconformists provided a necessary basis of support for the party.[4] Yet some of the legislation of his first ministry of 1868–74 had alienated that support. Most important was W. E. Forster's Education Act of 1870. This measure created a system of elementary education based upon both privately supported voluntary schools and publicly supported state schools. The former, which were primarily Anglican, Catholic and Wesleyan, continued to receive Exchequer grants but not rate aid. They were left free from public control and free to give denominational religious instruction. The latter were to be established by popularly-elected school boards in areas where the voluntary schools were insufficient to meet the demand. They were to be supported out of the rates as well as by Exchequer grants, and they had the option (by the Cowper-Temple clause) of giving nondenominational religious instruction.

7

Nonconformists opposed the continued existence of the voluntary schools because they objected to the use of public money for the propagation of sectarian religious beliefs. For the same reason, they opposed the government's unsuccessful effort in 1873 to establish a university in Ireland acceptable to the Catholic hierarchy. They feared that this would be an indirect endowment of Roman Catholicism. Finally, the temperance advocates among them opposed the government's attempt at liquor licensing reform. They insisted on local option, that is, the right of each community to suppress the liquor traffic if it chose to do so.

The result of the government's policies was Nonconformist disillusionment, which contributed to the Liberal defeat in 1874. The Nonconformists' problem, however, was with the party, and especially the Whigs, rather than with Gladstone. Thus, his condemnation of the indifference of Lord Beaconsfield's government to the massacre of Bulgarian Christians by the Turks in 1876 merely reaffirmed Nonconformist confidence in Gladstone as the one truly Christian statesman. The result was an agitation against the Bulgarian atrocities and Beaconsfield's immoral foreign policy in general which contributed to a decisive Liberal victory and Gladstone's return to the premiership in 1880.[5]

Gladstone's second ministry was preoccupied with the problem of maintaining the loyalty of the Irish to the union with Britain. In 1869 Gladstone had disestablished the Irish Church. Now, reluctantly, he passed a radical measure of land reform which gave the Irish tenant farmer fixity of tenure and the right to sell his interest in his holding, and which established land courts to fix fair rents. These reforms, however, were not sufficient to satisfy the demands of Irish nationalism. Charles Stewart Parnell created a disciplined Irish Nationalist Party which demanded Home Rule – an Irish parliament and an Irish executive responsible for Irish affairs. After the general election of 1885, Parnell's party comprised 85 of the 103 Irish MPs and held the balance between the Liberal and Conservative Parties in the House of Commons.

Gladstone had been convinced for some time that the Irish must be given a large measure of control over their own affairs if peace was to be restored to the country and the union saved. Following the general election, he saw little alternative to the granting of Home Rule. The large majority of Liberal MPs, as well as most of the constituency organizations, followed their leader. Most of the Whigs, however, after nearly twenty years of fighting with Gladstone over Ireland, foreign policy and religion, finally left the party. They were joined by Joseph Chamberlain and some radicals. These opponents did not think an Irish government responsible for Irish affairs could be reconciled with the ultimate sovereignty of the imperial Parliament. Liberals were never able to allay these fears that Home Rule would lead to Irish separation and thus threatened the security of the empire. Many Nonconformists, who feared Roman Catholic domination of Ireland and resented Irish support of sectarian education in England, also opposed Home Rule. Thus, Gladstone's last crusade divided the Liberal Party and, for the moment at least, weakened it.

The Radical Tradition

Most of Gladstone's followers in the 1890s were radicals, but it is doubtful that he would have recognized radicalism as part of his 'Gospel'. In fact, their radicalism was largely the creation of Joseph Chamberlain. Chamberlain first achieved notoriety as a reforming mayor of Birmingham and leader of the education agitation in the 1870s. He soon recognized, however, that a movement based on Nonconformist grievances was too narrow to have a national appeal. In order to broaden the base of radicalism, Chamberlain, John Morley and Sir Charles Dilke developed a radical programme based upon a comprehensive attack on privilege. Chamberlain then organized the National Liberal Federation (NLF) to promote his programme and help transcend radical sectionalism, that is, the tendency of each radical to promote a particular issue to the exclusion of all others. Chamberlain hoped that a national organization, representing the radical rank and file and under his control, would give unity and order to the radical movement. The radical leaders would then have the necessary leverage to force their policy on the Whigs and moderates in the Liberal Party.[6]

Chamberlain was successful in organizing radicalism for two reasons. First, the Nonconformists, who would provide the activists, increasingly recognized that they would have to work within the Liberal Party to achieve their objectives. Second, a new generation was entering the ranks of British radicalism. Typically, they were Non-conformist businessmen or lawyers who had made their own way. All were active in local politics, and because they had similar social or religious grievances, they all tended to support the same causes. Between 1874 and 1885, about one-third of the Liberals in the House of Commons could be identified as radicals by the causes they supported; between 1886 and 1895 the number had increased to more than 70 per cent.[7] Thus, radicals now had enough shared experiences and concerns to make organization feasible.

The agitation against Beaconsfield's foreign policy aborted Chamberlain's attempt to force the Liberal Party to adopt a radical policy. When, however, Gladstone's second ministry enacted only one radical measure – the Reform Act of 1884 – Chamberlain renewed his efforts to mobilize radicalism. The Home Rule crisis of 1886 deprived radicalism of Chamberlain's inspired leadership, but the split merely accelerated radicalism's permeation of the Liberal Party. Not only was the parliamentary party overwhelmingly radical, but the radical NLF became the organization of the party's rank and file, and its ties with official liberalism were strengthened. Between 1886 and 1890, the NLF adopted the bulk of the radical programme as the policy of Liberals in the country. Finally, in 1891 Gladstone apparently accepted the NLF's programme at its annual meeting at Newcastle. Radicalism was officially joined with Gladstonian liberalism.

The Newcastle Programme incorporated a reasonably coherent liberalism which had been evolving over the previous twenty years.[8] It embodied four fundamental principles. The first was the extension of political and religious liberties. Most Liberals recognized this as the principle which had governed liberal reform since 1832. The Newcastle proposals included a variety of reforms of the electoral system, the limitation of the powers of the House of Lords, the payment of Members of Parliament (MPs) and the disestablishment and disendowment of the established churches in Wales and Scotland. A second set of proposals sought to give communities greater power to manage their own affairs. Among them were Irish Home Rule, increased powers to the London County Council and the creation of elected parish and district councils. Other proposals for greater community control involved interference with the rights of private property. These included local control of the liquor traffic (local option), popular control of all schools receiving public money, and powers to local authorities for compulsory purchase of land needed for public purposes. These three policies embodied a third liberal principle: the ending of those privileges enjoyed by vested interests which were in opposition to the interest of the community at large. Local option attacked the privileges of the liquor trade; disestablishment and education reform attacked the privileges of the Church of England; and land reform, including measures to force land to bear its fair share of taxes and rates, attacked the privileges of the landed aristocracy. Finally, the Newcastle Programme recognized the principle of social reform to improve the condition of the working class. Temperance reform and land reform; the removal of duties on sugar, tea and other articles of consumption; and the extension of the Factory Acts all were perceived by Liberals to be social reform policies. Another was urban housing reform. Chamberlain devoted a chapter of *The Radical Programme* to the subject, and it was included in the resolutions adopted at the NLF's annual meeting in 1895.[9]

During these years when radicalism was being absorbed into the Liberal Party, a new interpretation of liberalism was emerging which provided an intellectual justification for the radical programme. According to this 'new liberalism', the state best promoted individual liberty when it created the conditions which allowed each individual to develop his or her abilities fully. Only when the state had removed the obstacles to individual development would each member of society be able to cultivate those qualities of self-help and self-reliance which were valued by Liberals. Society in turn would benefit from an independent and moral citizenry, each contributing to the best of his or her ability to the general welfare. The new liberalism was an expression of the growing concern among educated Britons for the conditions of life among the poor. It sought to justify, within the context of traditional liberal values, state intervention to improve those conditions.

Those young Liberals who first espoused the new liberalism in the 1880s were primarily concerned with combatting the negativism of older radicals like Sir William Harcourt and Henry Labouchère. The policies they turned to, however, were radical policies. The new Liberals and the radicals both were interested in social reform as a means of reducing class divisions and class hostility. Both used the language of humanitarianism, social obligation and public duty to encourage social reform. Both sought to justify social reform by claiming for the state the right to interfere with individual interests for the benefit of society as a whole. Finally, both believed in the policies of the Newcastle Programme as the best means of reducing class tensions and promoting the interest of the community at large.

THE LEADERSHIP CRISIS

During the 1890s, radical sectionalism emerged with new vigour, leaving the parliamentary Liberal Party in disarray. All parties, however, are beset by internal divisions; one of the functions of responsible leadership is to overcome such centrifugal forces. Gladstone had achieved this with his moral conviction and crusading spirit, which were shared by most radicals and helped to transcend their sectional divisions. Such qualities, however, were unique to Gladstone. Neither of his successors, Lord Rosebery and Sir William Harcourt, possessed comparable qualities which would enable them to lead the party effectively. Rosebery was a man of intelligence and taste, but he hated politics. In the face of difficulties he tended to engage in self-pity and retreat from political activity. Thus, he rarely followed a project through to its conclusion. Harcourt, by contrast,

11

enjoyed political combat. He was a fine leader of a parliamentary opposition, but an impossible colleague with no tact or gift for compromise. Both Rosebery and Harcourt were elitists. They expected the party to follow them loyally, without their having to work to win and hold its confidence. Inevitably, both failed as Liberal leaders. Rosebery lacked the diligence and Harcourt the patience and tolerance to hold together a party of sectionalists.

When Gladstone retired in 1894, Rosebery was chosen as his successor. His weaknesses were immediately exposed when he attempted to inaugurate a campaign against the House of Lords. The issue was a popular one with the rank and file, but typically, Rosebery failed to articulate a policy and failed to follow up on his opening speech at Bradford. As a result, the campaign failed. At the same time, Harcourt rendered Rosebery's position in the Cabinet and with the rank and file an intolerable one.[10] Following the Liberal debacle in the general election of 1895, Rosebery retreated from public activity, and a year later he retired from the leadership. Rosebery's friends, however, refused to accept his resignation as final. His supporters in the House of Commons did everything possible to prevent Harcourt from consolidating his own leadership so that the way would be open for Rosebery's return. Finally, in December 1898, Harcourt resigned as leader in the House of Commons, blaming Rosebery and his followers for the party's failure to give him proper support.

There were two candidates for the vacant leadership in the Commons. One was Sir Henry Campbell-Bannerman, who had been Secretary for War twice. Seemingly unambitious, he was conscientious so long as work did not interfere with his annual trips to Marienbad with his wife between August and October. Campbell-Bannerman had two great assets: he was popular with the Liberal back-benchers, and he believed in liberalism and was able to communicate that belief to others. The other possible leader was H. H. Asquith, Gladstone's last Home Secretary. Asquith had the arrogance of a man whose mind was superior to that of those with whom he dealt. His First in Greats at Balliol, his marriage to Margot Tennant, and his political career all had assisted his entry into the upper class, and he enjoyed the life of conversation and drink which came with it. Both his aloofness and his way of life left Asquith more cut off from the Liberal rank and file than Campbell-Bannerman. None the less, his strong intellect and brilliance as a parliamentarian already had marked him as a future leader of the party. Both Campbell-Bannerman and Asquith had other assets. They had been completely loyal to their leaders and their party, and they got along well with their colleagues. Although both were radicals, neither was a controversialist, for they were by temperament men of the centre. In the end, although many of the other leaders preferred Asquith as the weightier person, the party chose Campbell-Bannerman because of his seniority and because Asquith could not afford to give up his legal practice.[11] Three months later, the new leader chose Herbert Gladstone, the youngest son of the former Prime Minister, as Liberal Chief Whip. At last, the Liberal Party had a team of leaders in the House of Commons whose principal objective was the restoration of unity.

Their prospects, however, did not appear promising. Not only was the struggle between the supporters of Harcourt and Rosebery intensifying, but it was becoming identified with the long-standing division in the party over imperial and foreign policy. The little-Englanders, who opposed an interventionist external policy, numbered something over forty in the House of Commons.[12] Yet, until Harcourt's retirement, they remained the kind of faction which, while common in the Liberal Party, was a source of irritation rather than division. In January 1899, however, John Morley joined Harcourt in resigning from the Liberal front bench, and they immediately launched a crusade against imperialism. When Campbell-Bannerman voted with them a month later on a motion condemning the government's policy in the Sudan, they thought they had captured the new leader. In fact, Campbell-Bannerman had no sympathy with the fanatics and factionalists on either side of the imperialism issue. He was especially suspicious, as he had told Rosebery six weeks before the vote, of those 'half a dozen intriguers whose vanity as well as their malice will lead them to make mischief'. In a letter to his cousin, he had identified the intriguers as Harcourt, Labouchère, Philip Stanhope and their supporters – the little-Englanders.[13]

As long as the former leaders insisted on speaking out independently of the official leader, Campbell-Bannerman's task would not be an easy one. If, moreover, the personal vendetta between Harcourt and Rosebery and the power struggle between their supporters was harnessed to an ideological battle over imperialism, there could be no prospect for peace within the Liberal Party. All of this came to pass and caused enormous difficulties for Campbell-Bannerman and the party; yet both survived. For the first time in years, the party had a leader whose principal allegiance was to his party and to liberalism rather than to himself, and the radical centre responded by giving him its unswerving support.

THE PARLIAMENTARY PARTY

The typical radical who entered the House of Commons between 1874 and 1895 had been a Nonconformist businessman who had strong ties

TABLE 1.1

Professions of Liberal MPs, 1895–1914

First entered Parliament	Industry com- merce finance %	Law %	Military; civil or colonial service %	Other profes- sional[a] %	Land %	No obvious profes- sion %
before 1895	41.2	29.3	6.1	11.7	6.1	10.0
1895–1900	43.7	22.9	2.1	16.7	10.4	4.2
1900–5	41.8	22.4	1.5	10.4	8.9	14.9
1906–9	41.4	21.8	10.0	14.6	2.3	10.0
1910–14	34.4	24.4	2.2	24.4	1.1	13.3

[a] Medicine, teaching, journalism, ministry, accountant, author, social work, etc.

with his constituency and was active in the community.[14] The Non-conformist businessman remained the backbone of the Liberal Party in the House of Commons up to the First World War (Table 1.1).[15] For example, Briggs Priestly, the Bradford textile merchant; C. H. Wilson and Sir Christopher Furness, shipowners from Hull and West Hartlepool respectively; Sir John Brunner, the Cheshire chemical manufacturer; and Sir Charles Palmer, the Jarrow shipbuilder, all retired as Liberal MPs between 1899 and 1910. All eventually were succeeded in the House of Commons by their sons or heirs. The foundations of British manufacturing and commercial wealth – the coal, shipbuilding, shipping, engineering, chemical and textile industries – all continued to be well represented on the Liberal side of the House of Commons before the war. In addition, notable representatives of new wealth, such as W. H. Lever, the soap manufacturer, and Alfred Hedges, the tobacco processer, first entered the House as Liberals. None the less, the Liberal business connection was weakening somewhat. This was evident in Yorkshire and the North of England in 1906, and by 1910 the decline was clear for the entire country.[16] Furthermore, the men who were replacing the Liberal businessmen were a miscellaneous group of professionals, among whom journalists, writers, and social workers were prominent. This class of professionals constituted nearly one-fourth of the Liberal MPs first elected between 1910 and 1914, compared to only one-tenth of those first elected between 1900 and 1905.

Other evidence confirms that the ninety Liberals who first entered the House of Commons between 1910 and 1914 broke with traditional patterns. For example, between 1895 and 1909 the percentage of new Liberal MPs who had attended either a public school or Oxford or Cambridge gradually but continuously increased (Table 1.2). Between

TABLE 1.2

Education of Liberal MPs, 1895–1914

First entered Parliament	Public school and/or Oxbridge %	Other universities %	Secondary %	Elementary %	Private or overseas %	Not clear or none %
before 1895	35.2	25.7	15.1	3.4	16.2	4.5
1895–1900	36.2	27.7	19.1	6.4	6.4	4.2
1900–5	40.9	19.7	21.2	3.0	10.6	4.5
1906–9	43.8	20.0	19.6	3.2	12.3	0.9
1910–14	32.2	32.2	17.8	5.6	10.0	2.2

TABLE 1.3

Liberal MPs, 1895–1914: Age When First Elected

First entered Parliament	Under 30 %	Under 40		40–49		50 and over	
		30–39 %	Total %	%	Total %	50–59 %	60 and over %
before 1895	12.3	33.0	45.3	34.6	20.1	15.6	4.5
1895–1900	6.4	31.9	38.3	38.3	23.4	14.9	8.5
1900–5	7.6	27.3	34.9	36.4	28.7	24.2	4.5
1906–9	6.9	23.8	30.7	37.0	32.0	21.5	10.5
1910–14	5.6	33.3	38.9	42.3	17.8	13.3	4.5

1910 and 1914, however, that percentage dropped dramatically in favour of men who had been educated at other universities. Between 1895 and 1909 there was also a rapid increase in the average age of new Liberal MPs (Table 1.3), but between 1910 and 1914 it showed a substantial drop. Thus, the general elections of 1910 and the by-elections of the following years produced a large number of Liberal MPs who, unlike their immediate predecessors, could not be classified as 'solid citizens'. They were younger and thus probably had not so fully established themselves. They were university educated, but were less likely to have attended an elite institution. Finally, they were more divorced from the business world.

All of this evidence suggests that Liberal MPs who were elected after 1909 were less likely than their predecessors to be local notables. Table 1.4 confirms that they were less likely to have a strong connection with their constituencies, although the change was evident by 1906. Similarly, there was a marked decline in participation in local activities by

MPs who were elected after 1905 in comparison with those elected during the preceding decade (Table 1.5). This reduction, however, was in the level of participation in voluntary organizations – organizations to promote land or temperance reform, peace societies, churches, chambers of commerce, etc. – rather than in local government. At the same time, even after 1905 a majority of Liberal MPs continued to be active in their communities, although these were less likely to be the communities they were elected to represent in Parliament.

It is thus apparent that as a group, the Liberal MPs who were elected after 1909 had neither the same status nor the roots in the constituencies of their predecessors. A possible explanation is that some businessmen and other local notables were alienated by the social policies of the Liberal governments of 1905–14. Another is that the generation now reaching middle age was less likely to be Liberal. As a result, constituencies had to rely more on young enthusiasts of eclectic backgrounds who were supplied by the central party organization. The MPs of 1906–9 also had weaker local connections, but many of them probably had contested and won usually hopeless constituencies which had few distinguished Liberals. The high status of these men as indicated by their education, professions and age, clearly distinguished them from the generation that followed.

It is important, however, not to exaggerate the break with the past represented by 1910. A secondary pattern revealed by the data is the

TABLE 1.4
Liberal MPs, 1895–1914: Connection with Constituency

	First entered Parliament				
	Before 1895 %	1895– 1900 %	1900–5 %	1906–9 %	1910–14 %
Home or business in the constituency	33.5	46.8	41.0	36.9	25.6
Home or business in the county or a neighbouring constituency	24.6	23.4	22.7	16.9	20.0
Family or wife's family connected with the constituency	5.6	0.0	6.1	3.7	11.1
None, but Scot in a Scottish or Welshman in a Welsh constituency	11.2	8.5	4.5	7.3	12.2
Fairly strong connection (lines 1 + 2)	58.1	68.2	63.7	53.8	45.6
No evident connection	25.2	29.3	25.8	35.2	31.2

TABLE 1.5
Liberal MPs, 1895–1914: Local Activity

First entered Parliament	Those engaged in some	none	Kinds of local activity (% of those engaged in some) local government	voluntary society
	%	%		
before 1895	53.6	46.4	71.9	64.6
1895–1900	73.3	26.7	64.6	73.5
1900–5	66.7	33.3	65.9	65.9
1906–9	55.3	44.7	72.0	52.1
1910–14	57.7	42.3	67.3	59.6

extent to which those MPs who were elected between 1895 and 1905 differed from both their predecessors and their successors. This fact is most evident in their strong constituency ties and their high level of community activity; however, data pertaining to religion also reveal an exceptionally high percentage of Nonconformists elected between 1895 and 1900 (Table 1.6).[17] It is probable that in these years, when the fortunes of the party were low, those Liberals with strong local connections, high standing in the community and close ties to the Nonconformist rank and file had a significantly better chance of being elected. To a lesser degree, this also was true for the Liberals who were first elected between 1900 and 1905. Thus, another reason that the Liberal MPs who were elected after 1905 were somewhat different from those who were elected during the previous ten years may have been that it was easier for Liberals to win elections.

Despite such variations, it is still possible to identify a typical Liberal MP from 1895–1914. He was middle class and probably a businessman or a lawyer. He was likely to be a Nonconformist with a university or public school education who was over forty at the time of his election. His home or business probably was in the county, if not the constituency, for which he sat. He typically had gained governmental experience sitting on a town or county council, school board, or board of guardians, and he also probably was active in some local voluntary society. A Liberal MP was more likely to be of this type if he was first elected between 1895 and 1905, less likely if he was first elected after 1909.

LIBERALISM IN THE CONSTITUENCIES

There were six general elections between 1892 and 1914. Two of these (1895 and 1900) resulted in sweeping Unionist victories, one (1906)

TABLE 1.6

Religion of Liberal MPs, 1895–1914

First entered Parliament	Anglican %	Non-conformist %	Church of Scotland %	No guess or other %
before 1895	34.7	45.8	(6.7)	12.9
1895–1900	25.5	55.3	(6.4)	12.8
1900–5	38.8	40.3	(10.4)	10.5
1906–9	43.0	40.6	(8.2)	8.2
1910–14	(36.2)	(46.9)	(8.5)	(8.5)

Numbers in parentheses are rough estimates.

resulted in an even more sweeping Liberal landslide, while the other three (1892 and January and December 1910) gave neither the Liberals nor the Unionists a majority in the House of Commons. Figure 1 shows the regional strengths and weaknesses of the two major parties. If a chart is skewed to the left, there were a large number of seats which the Liberals rarely won, and the region was solidly Unionist. If it is skewed to the right, there were a large number of seats which the Liberals usually won, and the region was solidly Liberal. A roughly symmetrical chart indicates a fair balance between the parties and a swing region.

Unionist power was virtually unshakable in two regions – the South and the West Midlands. Only in 1906 were the Liberals able to make any inroads at all in these areas, and such gains were temporary. The only regions which the Liberals dominated as completely were Wales and East Scotland, which comprised only half as many seats. In Yorkshire, the North, and the East Midlands, however, the Liberals controlled about half the seats, while the Unionists had a comparable influence only in London. The four remaining regions were marginal, and these tended to decide elections. The Central and Southwest regions roughly correspond with what Michael Kinnear has identified as an agricultural swing region.[18] If a party captured a substantial majority of these seats, it was likely to win the election. Lancastria and West Scotland, on the other hand, were not swing areas. Each had tended to be Unionist before 1906, and each tended to be Liberal after 1906.

What determined whether a region was Liberal or Unionist? One factor was social class. If a constituency was middle-class, it was almost certain to be Unionist. If it was working-class, it was likely, though by no means certain, to be Liberal or Labour.[19] The strong party allegiance of the middle class and the weaker party allegiance of the working class together help to account for the astonishing weakness of the Liberals in the large cities. The single-member constituencies created by the third Reform Act were drawn to assure class homogeneity whenever possible. This gave the Unionists a solid middle-class base in all of the large urban areas, while the working-class vote was less reliable for the Liberals. As a result, only Edinburgh and Leeds among the largest cities consistently returned a majority of Liberal MPs between 1885 and 1914. On the other hand, the Liberals never won Birmingham after 1885, Sheffield, and Liverpool; they won London only once in eight elections; they won Manchester–Salford three times and Glasgow four times. The Liberal working-class strength was in the smaller cities and industrial towns of the West Riding of Yorkshire, the East Midlands, and the North. Many of the working-class electors in these regions, most notably the miners, voted in county rather than borough constituencies, thus increasing the Liberal strength outside the boroughs. The Liberals probably would have been stronger in urban areas were it not for the fact that the election laws discriminated against the working class. About half of the industrial working class either could not qualify to vote or were disfranchised as a result of the complexities of the registration system.[20]

Class was much less important as a determinant of voting behaviour under the third Reform Act than it has been since the First World War.[21] In part, this was because religion was also a powerful influence on party allegiance. Usually, the greater the concentration of Nonconformists or Irish Catholics, the more likely it was that a constituency would vote Liberal. Nonconformity provided the Liberals with their strength in rural areas. Small, independent farmers and agricultural labourers tended to be Nonconformist and Liberal. Their pervasiveness in the Central and Southwest regions helps account for the success of the Liberals in countering the Unionist landlord interest on large tenanted farms. The predominance of Nonconformists and small farmers also helps explain the Liberal ascendancy in Wales and East Scotland.

Religion was equally important as an influence in urban areas. When the working class was Nonconformist, as in the mining areas, it was almost always Liberal. The only exception was Birmingham, where Chamberlain's enormous influence changed the affiliation of much of the West Midlands. In London, where Nonconformity was weak among the workers, so was liberalism. In Lancashire, the working class was Anglican, anti-Catholic and Conservative. Lancashire swung away from the Unionists after 1906 in part because both Anglican and Irish workers were willing to vote for Labour candidates (see Table 1.7).[22] Finally, Nonconformity helped account for

19

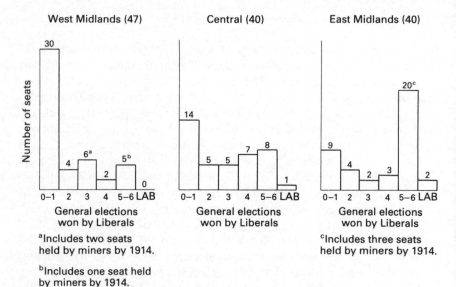

West Midlands (47)

Central (40)

East Midlands (40)

^aIncludes two seats
held by miners by 1914.

^bIncludes one seat held
by miners by 1914.

^cIncludes three seats
held by miners by 1914.

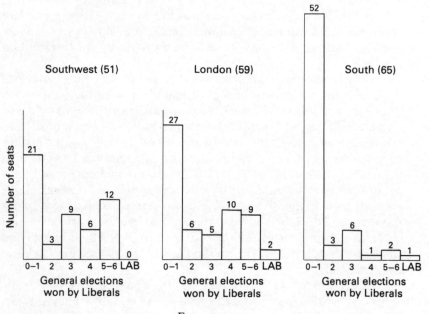

Southwest (51)

London (59)

South (65)

FIGURE 1

Liberal performance in the six general elections between 1892 and 1910.
South: Essex, Hampshire, Hertfordshire, Kent, Middlesex, Surrey, Sussex
Southwest: Cornwall, Devonshire, Dorsetshire, Gloucestershire, Somerset,
Wiltshire
Central: Bedfordshire, Berkshire, Buckinghamshire, Cambridgeshire,
Huntingtonshire, Norfolk, Oxfordshire, Suffolk
East Midlands: Derbyshire, Leicestershire, Lincolnshire,
Northhamptonshire, Nottinghamshire, Rutland

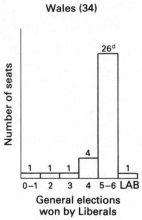
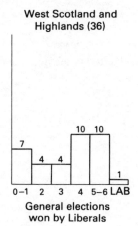

Wales (34)

Number of seats

26[d]

1 1 1 4 1

0–1 2 3 4 5–6 LAB

General elections
won by Liberals

[d]Includes four seats
held by miners by 1914.

West Scotland and Highlands (36)

7

4 4 10 10

1

0–1 2 3 4 5–6 LAB

General elections
won by Liberals

East Scotland (34)

25[e]

3 0 1 4 1

0–1 2 3 4 5–6 LAB

General elections
won by Liberals

[e]Includes one seat held
by miners by 1914.

Lancastria (70)

Number of seats

22

8 8 7 13[f] 12

0–1 2 3 4 5–6 LAB

General elections
won by Liberals

[f]Includes one Irish
Nationalist seat.

Yorkshire (52)

27[g]

14

0 2 5 4

0–1 2 3 4 5–6 LAB

General elections
won by Liberals

[g]Includes two seats
held by miners by 1914.

North (32)

14[h]

2 5 3 4 4

0–1 2 3 4 5–6 LAB

General elections
won by Liberals

[h]Includes three seats
held by miners by 1914.

West Midlands: Herefordshire, Shropshire, Staffordshire, Warwickshire,
Worcestershire
Lancastria: Lancashire, Cheshire
North: Cumberland, Durham, Northumberland, Westmoreland
West Scotland and Highlands: Argyllshire, Ayrshire, Buteshire,
Dumbartonshire, Dumfriesshire, Kirckcudbrightshire, Lanarkshire,
Refrewshire, Wigtownshire, Caithness, Inverness, Orkney and Shetland,
Ross and Cromarty, Sutherland
East Scotland: The remaining Scottish counties

TABLE 1.7

Previous Affiliation of Labour Seats, by Region[a]

	Liberal	Conservative	Marginal
South	0	1	0
London	0	2	0
Southwest	0	0	0
East Midlands	2	0	0
Central	0	0	1
West Midlands	0	0	0
Lancastria	1	9	2
Yorkshire	1	0	3
North	2	1	1
Wales	1	0	0
Scotland	1	0	1
Totals	8	13	8

[a] If the Liberals or Conservatives won the seat in each of the general elections of 1892, 1895 and 1900, the seat is considered affiliated to that party prior to being won by Labour. Otherwise, the seat is considered marginal.

the continued allegiance to liberalism of much of its middle-class support.

The general election of 1906 marked two further developments which benefited the Liberals. One was the final decline of Liberal Unionism, which had been fairly strong in West Scotland, where there was considerable anti-Irish sentiment. By 1906, however, the traditional liberalism of the region had reasserted itself.[23] Also, 1906 was the year in which the Labour Party first emerged as a force in British politics. Labour won twenty-nine seats in at least two of the three general elections of 1906 and 1910; as can be seen from Table 1.7, twenty-one of those seats had been Conservative or marginal in the previous three general elections. This helps to clarify why official liberalism was so eager for an alliance with the Labour Party. The gains in Lancashire alone outweighed any sacrifice the Liberals had to make elsewhere. It is only after 1909, when the Miners' Federation affiliated with the Labour Party, that the threat posed to liberalism becomes clearer (see Figure 1). All but one of the miners' seats had been solidly Liberal, and all but those in the West Midlands were located in regions of Liberal strength.

PARTY ORGANIZATION

The link between the Liberals in the constituencies and the parliamentary party was the party organization. Following the creation of single-member constituencies by the third Reform Act, most parliamentary divisions had a Liberal association. A Liberal association hired the party's election agent, who assumed all responsibilities pertaining to the register, oversaw the canvassing efforts of the ward associations in the boroughs, or the town associations in county divisions, and generally kept the party in a state of electoral readiness. The association also was responsible for maintaining interest in liberalism. It organized meetings to be addressed by the local MP or candidate, one of the more distinguished Liberal back-benchers, or occasionally one of the party's leaders.

In theory, the local associations were democratic and represented all Liberals in the area. In fact, they represented two narrower groups: prominent Liberals of wealth and status in the community and party activists who were prepared to attend meetings and do the work. Political activity required either money and time or unbridled enthusiasm. Money was crucial to the activities of the association. Most associations relied on a few local notables to keep them solvent. Even so, expenditures often exceeded revenues; in both Leeds and Leicester, the Liberal associations finally resorted to bazaars to help pay off their debts.[24] Inevitably, men who provided the money had a central role in directing the affairs of the local parties. They tended to be the same sorts of men who typically represented the party in the House of Commons, that is, Nonconformist businessmen and lawyers. The party activists in the associations represented a different stratum of the middle class – miscellaneous professionals, shopkeepers, tradesmen and non-industrial artisans. For them, political activity was a source of social intercourse, of petty power and of status, as well as a commitment to a cause.

The degree to which local liberalism was dominated by the middle class is underscored by a study of Leeds, Leicester and Norwich (Table 1.8). The working class made little headway in penetrating the local Liberal leadership of the three cities.[25] On the other hand, the principal industries of these cities were well represented among the Liberal leaders. In Leeds, for example, twelve of the fifty businessmen were woollen, cloth, or ready-made clothing manufacturers; six were heavy industrialists; and perhaps another ten were cloth or clothing merchants or in the leather industry. Thus, official liberalism in the cities tended to be a middle-class preserve, run by the leading businessmen and professionals and with the entire spectrum of the middle class making up the rank and file. The vitality of liberalism in a community depended in large part on the degree to which these men were aroused by the party's programme.

The National Liberal Federation (NLF) was the organization of these local activists. Prior to 1886, it had been dominated by Joseph

TABLE 1.8

Occupations of Local Liberals, 1899–1914

	Leicester Town Council	Executive, Leicester Liberal Association 1903–8	Leeds City Council	Executive, Leeds Liberal Federation 1899–1908	Norwich Town Council
Business					
Industry	13	14	19	10	7
Merchant	7	4	7	6	5
Other	2	4	5	3	6
Professional					
Law	2	2	9	4	8
Other[a]	10	19	14	8	3
Shopkeeper, Tradesman, Artisan, etc.[a]	12	8	18	6	12
Gentleman	5	1	2	0	1
Labour	8	4	3	1	2
Totals	59	56	77	38	44

[a] Examples of miscellaneous professionals include accountants, actuaries, teachers, ministers, journalists, salesmen and agents. Examples of non-industrial artisans are tailors, locksmiths, plumbers, a saddle-maker and a monumental mason.

Chamberlain. Between 1886 and 1891, however, its annual resolutions embodied a domestic policy which was representative of the views of the rank and file, and which in large part was agreed upon without guidance from the party leadership. After the Newcastle meeting in 1891, the purpose of the NLF increasingly came to be to express the sense of the party concerning only those policies upon which Liberals were agreed. Contentious issues, such as the eight-hour day for miners, were deliberately avoided at its annual meetings. When the party's leaders were themselves divided, as they were during the Boer War, the NLF naturally tended to support all efforts to promote party unity, for its justification depended upon an identifiable Liberal consensus. By the twentieth century, therefore, the NLF had ceased to be a source of innovation. Instead, it was the custodian of that amalgam of Gladstonian liberalism and radicalism which had become 'traditional liberalism'.

The link between local liberalism and the parliamentary party was the Liberal Central Association (LCA) under the Chief Whip. For the constituency in need, the LCA could be a source of candidates, money, electoral agents to help with organization and registration (especially for by-elections), speakers and literature. Most important was money. A fund for fighting elections depended on the ability of the Chief Whip to persuade wealthy party stalwarts to make large contributions. A few leading businessmen, like Sir John Brunner and W. H. Lever, usually contributed £5,000 to £15,000 to the party funds in the months preceding a general election; many other prominent men contributed £100 to £2,000. These men also gave generously to the campaigns of specific candidates in their regions. As Chief Whip, Herbert Gladstone demonstrated considerable resourcefulness in raising money for the general election of 1906. In addition, he tolerated or even encouraged organizations, such as the Liberal League, the Free Trade Union and the Labour Representation Committee, which might be alternative sources of money for candidates and propaganda. The NLF raised another £46,000 for electoral purposes. This meant Gladstone could use his money more strategically at the general election, spending some £90,000 on 176 out of 518 candidates. Gladstone's successor, George Whiteley, accumulated a war chest of some £515,000 by selling honours. This left his successors more than enough money with which to fight the two 1910 general elections on even terms with the wealthier Unionists.[26]

This money was essential if the party was to field a respectable number of candidates at a general election. Many candidates could not afford the whole of their election expenses, and no candidate would bear that burden for an unwinnable constituency. Thus, if the Liberal Party was to contest the marginal seats which it had to win in Southwest and Central England and in Lancastria, not to mention the usually hopeless seats of the South of England and the West Midlands, the LCA had to provide major financial assistance. If it had the money, the LCA could supply the candidates for those constituencies that were unable to provide their own. From its own list of prospective candidates, it would give a constituency which desired assistance the names of several men who might suit its needs. For these purposes the Chief Whip's knowledge of the peculiarities of the constituencies and the local party leaders was supplemented by that of Robert Hudson, the secretary of both the NLF and the LCA.

The role of the NLF in the organization of the party was not clearly defined. It still functioned as a party propaganda machine, publishing and distributing literature, arranging large demonstrations and supplying speakers for locally organized meetings. Increasingly, however, the organizational initiative was being taken over by the LCA. Gladstone and J. A. Pease, the Chief Whip from 1908–1910, organized most of the regional Liberal federations which, by 1908, covered all of England and Wales. (The autonomous Scottish Liberal Association, under the Scottish Whip, had long been responsible for Scotland.) These federations served as links between the LCA and the local associations. They were especially important for organizing constituencies where liberalism was dormant. Gladstone also organized the National League of Young Liberals, which claimed some 120,000 members by the end of 1911.[27] It and the two Liberal women's organizations were additional sources of volunteers, especially for canvassing and speaking at local meetings. All told, in their efforts to make the Liberal electoral organization more effective, Gladstone and his successors had greatly increased the control of the LCA. One result was to leave the Chief Whip so overworked that by 1914 Asquith was considering dividing his parliamentary and organizational responsibilities between two men.[28] A more insidious effect may have been to dampen party enthusiasm as the central office encroached upon local autonomy.

By 1899, the Liberal Party was faced with two problems. The parliamentary party was in the midst of a prolonged crisis due to a failure of leadership. At the same time, the party in the country was faced with a fundamental contradiction: while the party organization was dominated by Nonconformist men of the middle class who worked to return others like themselves to the House of Commons, its success depended on the party's ability to win the allegiance of the working class in elections. The new leaders had one enormous asset as they sought to resolve these problems. Most politically active Liberals shared a common ideology which was firmly rooted in their Gladstonian and radical past. They also shared a commitment to the Newcastle Programme as the embodiment of their liberal principles. Here was a basis for transcending Liberal sectionalism and restoring the party's unity and direction. It was less clear, however, whether liberal principles and policies also offered a basis for uniting the middle-class activists and the working-class voters in a common cause.

2

The Challenge of
Liberal Imperialism, 1899–1905

For the Liberal Party to be an effective instrument for protecting the interests of its middle-class Nonconformist activists and its working-class voters, it had to act as a reasonably unified whole. If fundamental divisions on matters of principle and policy were to leave Liberals perpetually bickering among themselves, the activists would never be able to mobilize fully and the voters would never accept the party as a viable alternative government. The divisions which existed over imperialism and foreign policy, however, were not fundamental. They could be transcended by any leader who recognized the unifying power of the liberal principles which all Liberals shared and who used those principles to rally the rank and file.

Instead, during the 1890s those divisions had become more acute as they were identified with the power struggle between the supporters of Lord Rosebery and Sir William Harcourt. Each side sought to portray itself as the custodian of the true liberal faith and the other as heretical on external issues. Most Liberals had no sympathy with such views. They saw how much Liberals had in common in their approach to both external and domestic affairs. As a result, they resented the actions of the extremists who divided the party by focusing on the few points of difference. These Liberal centrists were the people whom Sir Henry Campbell-Bannerman spoke for as leader of the Liberal Party. Campbell-Bannerman based his leadership on two propositions: that the antagonism over imperialism obscured the fundamental unity of the Liberal Party, and that the basis of that unity was the traditional liberalism which was enshrined in the policies of the Newcastle Programme. This outlook won him the support of the party rank and file, who provided him with a sufficiently broad and secure political base to render his leadership unchallengeable.

None the less, the Liberal Imperialists sought to challenge it. Campbell-Bannerman's actions during the Boer War convinced them that he was a little-Englander who could not be trusted on matters of external policy. They also thought Liberal domestic policies needed to be modernized, and they claimed to be doing so by offering an innovative approach to social reform. Liberals were not opposed to adapting their principles to deal with new problems. On the contrary, the future would show how flexible they could be in modifying their thinking and adopting new policies. Change, however, could not come at the expense of what they considered to be the essence of their liberalism – the Newcastle Programme. Yet this was precisely what the Liberal Imperialists seemed to be challenging.

In fact, there was little that was distinctive about the liberalism of the Liberal Imperialists. Nothing in their approach to either domestic or external policies broke with the liberal tradition which had evolved over the previous thirty years. By portraying themselves as innovators, however, and appearing to want to discard the Newcastle Programme, they alienated the rank and file who were devoted to the traditional liberalism. They further offended the party activists by forming their own organization to promote their 'distinctive' policy at the very moment when, with the Boer War ending, it seemed that the divisions over imperialism could finally be buried. A group so out of touch with the Liberal rank and file could not mount an effective challenge to Campbell-Bannerman's leadership. On the contrary, by appearing to divide the party and reject traditional liberalism, the Liberal Imperialists reinforced the leader's claim to be the custodian of both Liberal unity and liberal principles. Their weakness was finally exposed in December 1905, when they were forced to enter the new Liberal government on Campbell-Bannerman's terms. At the same time, since they really were well within the liberal tradition, their re-integration represented no long-term threat to the unity and effectiveness of the party.

THE SPLITTING OF THE LIBERAL PARTY[1]

The supporters of Harcourt and Rosebery used the Boer War as a new battleground in their struggle for the soul of the Liberal Party. Harcourt and Morley led the pro-Boers, who believed that the war could have been prevented, was morally wrong and should be stopped. It had been undertaken, they claimed, to promote the interests of financiers, mine-owners and shareholders. Thus, opposition to the war was merely another phase of the great liberal struggle against the power of privilege in the management of the nation's affairs. Rosebery and the Liberal Imperialists denied that any issue of liberal principle was involved. The Boers, they argued, sought to challenge Britain's paramount position in South Africa. The war, therefore, was inevitable, and criticism of the government merely divided the country at a time of crisis. Very few Liberals adhered to either of these extremes. Only seventeen Liberal MPs voted for John

Dillon's pro-Boer amendment to the Address on 17 October calling for a cessation of hostilities; only fifteen voted against Philip Stanhope's amendment criticizing the government's diplomacy.[2] Most Liberals believed that the war must be won, but they were not happy with the government's handling of the crisis and saw no reason why it should not be criticized.

This consensus view provided Campbell-Bannerman and Asquith with a basis for holding the party together during the first year of the war. Their strategy was to emphasize the broad agreement among Liberals on most aspects of the war, as well as on domestic issues. In this way, they hoped to forestall efforts by pro-Boers and Liberal Imperialists to force the party to choose between the extremes. As part of the consensus position, Campbell-Bannerman accepted annexation of the Boer republics. Also, several of the leaders spoke out for a settlement based on a rapid transition to self-government for the new colonies, with full equality between Briton and Boer.

The victory of British arms in the spring and summer of 1900 led to a breakdown of this Liberal consensus. The government insisted upon the unconditional surrender of the republics. When instead the Boer soldiers turned to guerrilla warfare, the British army retaliated by burning Boer farms. Women and children were sent to hastily con- structed concentration camps with inadequate sanitation facilities and insufficient supplies of food and medicine. As a result, by October 1901 the death rate reached an annual equivalent of nearly 35 per cent of all whites in the camps and 60 per cent of the white children.[3]

Heretofore, Campbell-Bannerman and the Liberal centre had sup- ported the war because it was necessary to secure British supremacy in South Africa. Now the Boers had been defeated. Instead of making peace, however, the government was employing methods which most Liberals found repulsive and which made a reconciliation of Briton and Boer in South Africa more difficult. In the winter of 1900–1, therefore, Campbell-Bannerman launched a campaign against the conduct of the war. It was an issue which appealed to traditional Gladstonian opposition to coercion and to immoral acts of policy. None the less, the Liberal Imperialists refused to join in such attacks on the government and the war. Furthermore, when Campbell- Bannerman denounced conditions in the concentration camps as 'methods of barbarism' at a pro-Boer dinner in June 1901, Asquith broke with him and identified himself more openly with the Liberal Imperialists.

Although in July the party unanimously confirmed its confidence in Campbell-Bannerman as leader in the Commons, the gap between the two sides widened during the next six months. Furthermore, with Campbell-Bannerman consolidating a union of the centre and the pro-Boers, it was the Liberal Imperialists who were becoming isolated from the party's mainstream. Ordinary Liberals did not like the way Asquith and Sir Edward Grey always defended the government. Even more, they resented Rosebery's insistence in a letter of 17 July that Liberals must choose between the extreme positions on imperial affairs. They believed that the number of extremists on either side were few, while most Liberals were united by what Arthur Acland called 'a solid Liberalism of a really genuine type'.[4] Votes by the executive committee of the Home Counties Liberal Federation in November and the general committee of the NLF in early December confirmed that the party activists solidly supported the position which Campbell-Bannerman had defined.[5]

Thus, the Liberal Imperialists were in need of help when Rosebery made his first political speech in five years at Chesterfield on 16 December. Without explicitly saying so, he accepted Campbell-Bannerman's position on the war, insisting on a negotiated settlement with generous terms and a rapid transition to self-government for the Boer states. At the same time, however, he implicitly repudiated the Newcastle Programme, calling on the Liberal Party to 'wipe its slate clean' and adopt 'efficiency' as its watchword.[6] During a meeting a week later, Campbell-Bannerman satisfied himself that Rosebery indeed rejected traditional liberalism and had no interest in returning to an active role as a party leader. Most Liberals, however, focused only on what Rosebery had said about the war, which seemed to provide a basis for reuniting the party. For this reason, Campbell-Bannerman's friends insisted, he had to make a friendly response to the Chesterfield speech. Otherwise it would appear that he, not Rosebery, was dividing the party, thus undermining his strength with the rank and file.

On 13 January, while speaking at the inaugural meeting of the London Liberal Federation, Campbell-Bannerman warmly welcomed Rosebery's call for a negotiated peace. A month later, however, Rosebery gave him his opportunity to demonstrate to the rank and file that the former leader could no longer be trusted as a liberal and would not return to the counsels of the party. In two speeches at Liverpool, Rosebery repudiated Irish Home Rule and repeated his argument against the Newcastle Programme. Campbell-Bannerman responded on 19 February while addressing the general committee of the NLF at Leicester. He called on Rosebery to state clearly whether or not he was in the Liberal Party. He then reaffirmed his own position as the custodian of traditional liberalism: 'I am ... wholly opposed to the doctrine of the clean slate ... I am not prepared to erase from the tablets of my creed any principle or measure, or proposal or ideal, or aspiration of Liberalism.'[7] After listing some of the principal measures in the Liberal programme, asking his audience if they wanted to disregard any of them as out of date, he concluded with a vigorous defence of Home Rule as the only Irish policy consistent with liberal principles. Rosebery had little choice but to respond the next day by announcing his 'definite separation' from Campbell-Bannerman and the party he led. A week later, the Liberal Imperialist leaders announced the formation of the Liberal League, with Rosebery as president and Asquith, Grey and Sir Henry Fowler as vice-presidents. The Liberal Imperialist challenge to Campbell-Bannerman's leadership was now open and unambiguous. Furthermore, it was on just the terms which the Liberal leader wanted, with the Liberal Imperialists initiating the split to promote a policy which seemed to be a rejection of the Newcastle Programme. Campbell-Bannerman had forced the Liberal Imperialists to cut themselves off from the party's rank and file.

THE AMBIGUITY OF LIBERAL IMPERIALISM

What was the distinct policy which the Liberal Imperialists were promoting? They were never able to make it clear. They believed that the Liberal Party had lost much moderate middle-class support between 1880 and 1900 because it had become the prisoner of faddists who tied it to irrelevant and unpopular policies, because of its commitment to Home Rule, and because it seemed opposed to imperialism.[8] They used the image of the 'clean slate' to convey their conviction that the party must rethink its policies in order to win back these voters. Most importantly, it must drop the Newcastle Programme, which they viewed as a receptacle of every faddist cause of the previous twenty years. For most Liberals, however, the Newcastle Programme was the embodiment of their liberal principles. For example, following Rosebery's letter of definite separation, Sir Ughtred Kay-Shuttleworth cabled the chairman of his constituency Liberal association 'absolutely declining to turn my back on the policy of Gladstone or on any of the Liberal principles which I have supported during 34 years'.[9] In defending the Newcastle Programme, therefore, Campbell-Bannerman was able to portray himself as the custodian of traditional liberalism, while implying that these principles were threatened by the Liberal Imperialists:

> The real road to success and to duly influencing the opinion and policy of the country lay in adhering to the old principles of the party, and not going about seeking some new forms and theories, which they might perhaps think to have some tinge of novelty and be more attractive to the general feeling of the country ... He did not mean to say that the old

31

things they were anxious about 20 years ago were in themselves all that they need embrace in their policy now; but they must not leave the bedrock of their old principles.[10]

Asquith, who was the only really astute politician among the imperialist leaders, tried to save the situation by arguing that the Liberal Imperialists were merely calling on the party to concentrate its efforts on a few attainable goals. In a speech at Glasgow on 10 March, Rosebery defined these priority issues: education, temperance and housing. All these issues were, however, part of the Newcastle Programme, and even Asquith was not content to concentrate on them alone. In a memorandum stating his proposals for the policy of the Liberal League, he included reform in the areas of education, temperance, housing, the Poor Law, land tenure, local taxation, the relations between the Houses of Parliament and devolution.[11] The Liberal Imperialists thus appeared to be wiping the slate clean merely to write the same items on it again. This gave their opponents ample opportunity to portray them as creating differences in the party when none existed.[12]

The ideal of 'efficiency' got the Liberal Imperialists into as much trouble as the image of a 'clean slate'. As advocates of national efficiency, the Liberal Imperialists were part of a larger movement whose leading intellects were Sidney and Beatrice Webb. The Liberal Imperialist view of efficiency, however, was far vaguer than the Fabian Socialist vision of a bureaucracy of experts who would introduce planning and system into the management of the nation's affairs. According to H. C. G. Matthew, the Liberal Imperialists regarded efficiency as 'a criterion for assessing national and imperial needs and for developing a positive rather than a negative liberalism'.[13] Such a definition clarified nothing for ordinary Liberals. They therefore took efficiency to imply nothing more than the party's traditional commitment to rational and economic government. When, between 1902 and 1905, the Liberal Imperialists joined other Liberals in denouncing the extravagant expenditures of the Unionist government, such an interpretation seemed justified. Thus, once again, the Liberal Imperialists failed to define their terms in such a way as to distinguish themselves from other Liberals.

The social policies of the Liberal Imperialists merely emphasized their kinship with the other Liberals rather than with the 'national efficiency' groups. The Liberal Imperialists were not in advance of the rest of the Liberal Party on questions of social reform. Some contemporaries even perceived them as lagging behind.[14] Like all Liberals, the Liberal Imperialists viewed temperance and housing as the vital issues of social reform. Their temperance policy was to replace local option by more moderate proposals based on the Minority Report of the

Royal Commission on the Liquor Licensing Laws which were published in 1899. Most Liberal temperance reformers had accepted this report by 1900. The Liberal Imperialists, like all Liberals, believed the solution to the housing problem lay in land reform. They supported the standard Liberal proposals: compulsory powers for land acquisition given to local authorities; rating of site values to encourage improvement of land; and rural land reform to stop the depopulation of the countryside.[15]

In policy areas more immediately affecting the working class, the Liberal Imperialists were again conventional in their thinking. They supported extension of workmen's compensation, but were noncommittal on old-age pensions. They supported the rights of trade unions as essential to the stability of the economic system, but they opposed giving trade unions complete freedom from liability for the actions of their members. Their policy for dealing with unemployment included public works and afforestation, but they believed the key to the problem was the old Liberal watchword of 'retrenchment'. If new sources of revenue were needed, they looked to a graduated income tax, which all Liberal MPs had supported in principle in a Commons vote on 11 June 1902, and the taxation of land values. They had nothing to say about sweated industries or reform of the Poor Law, both of particular interest to the Webbs.[16]

The orthodoxy of the Liberal Imperialists was clearly revealed in their response to the two crucial issues of the period: the Education Act of 1902 and Chamberlain's tariff proposals of 1903. In framing the Education Act, Arthur Balfour had been influenced by some members of the 'national efficiency' group. Yet, among the Liberal Imperialists, only R. B. Haldane supported the bill. Like other Liberals, most Liberal Imperialists objected to the lack of public control over denominational schools receiving rate aid, and to the continuation of religious tests for teachers in such schools.[17] One of the leaders of the Nonconformist revolt against the bill was Robert Perks, Rosebery's principal political adviser and treasurer of the Liberal League. At Perks's urging, Rosebery joined in the campaign against the measure. Thus, the Liberal Imperialists had, with the embarrassing exception of Haldane, proved themselves to be far more faithful to traditional Liberal and Nonconformist views on education than to the principles of national efficiency.

When in May 1903, Chamberlain proposed a system of protective tariffs and imperial preference, Rosebery tried to be open-minded. Although he quickly reversed himself, his refusal to join the supposedly non-party Free Trade Union, along with the support some lesser Liberal Imperialists gave to imperial preference, damaged the Liberal League. Most Liberal Imperialists, however, had an orthodox attachment to the sanctity of free trade. Indeed, Asquith led the campaign in the country against Chamberlain. Once again, the deviations by some Liberal Imperialists from traditional liberalism were merely an embarrassment for the majority, who had no interest in defining a distinctive liberal imperialist policy.

Contrary to their claims, therefore, the Liberal Imperialists had no unique approach to domestic policy to offer the Liberal Party. They were equally guilty of exaggerating their differences with the rest of the party on external issues. Reflecting the Whig tradition, they liked to think of themselves as more pragmatic and less moralistic than other Liberals in judging foreign and imperial questions. While this certainly distinguished them from the little-Englanders, most Liberals believed that British policy must involve a responsible pursuit of the nation's legitimate interests as well as what was morally right. Campbell-Bannerman gave voice to their views in his first speech to the NLF as leader in the Commons in March 1899. He recognized that a world power like Britain must maintain a strong defence to protect itself, its trade and its colonies. These necessities might even involve expansion of the empire. Implicitly, however, he warned that power must be exercised with prudence and restraint, for expansion was not an end in itself. On the contrary, the conduct of policy should be directed towards the peaceful resolution of outstanding differences with other nations, and any behaviour which made this more difficult was to be condemned and opposed.[18]

The Liberal Imperialists would have concurred with these sentiments. They were as fierce as any Liberals in their repudiation of jingoism. Like all Liberals, they were repelled by the intolerant and irrational influences on policy-making which that phenomenon embodied. They feared the threat to peace, retrenchment and reform which could result if rational and even moral constraints on policy were removed, and a policy of provocation supported by massive arms expansion were pursued. Thus, in practice, on many matters their views converged with Campbell-Bannerman's. They had been in the forefront of those who had argued that the ultimate settlement in South Africa must be based upon self-government for the Boer colonies and equality between Briton and Boer. These views eventually forced them to break with their friend Lord Milner, as they joined with Campbell-Bannerman and the former pro-Boers in giving the Transvaal responsible government. They believed in continuity in foreign policy. After 1904, this meant supporting the entente with France, which Campbell-Bannerman welcomed and Rosebery criticized. Their defence policy was based upon the preservation of naval supremacy so that Britain would not require a large conscript army like those of the continental powers.[19] This, too, was mainstream liberalism – a view which many Liberals liked to trace back to Richard Cobden of the Manchester School.

With so little separating the Liberal Imperialists from the Liberal centre, why did the former continue to insist that the Chesterfield speech represented a distinctive policy? In part they wanted to continue to distinguish themselves from the little-Englanders, of whom they believed Campbell-Bannerman to be one. But the real purpose of the 'clean slate', of the repudiation of the Newcastle Programme, and of the insistence on a new domestic policy was to enable the Liberal Party to jettison Irish Home Rule as the priority item in the Liberal programme.

RESOLVING THE IRISH QUESTION

There were two aspects of the Irish question which made it very difficult for the Liberals to abandon Home Rule. Ideologically, most Liberals agreed with Campbell-Bannerman's statement at Leicester that a large measure of self-government for Ireland was the only means of ruling that country that was consistent with liberal principles. In addition, as a matter of practical politics, there were many British constituencies where the Irish vote was important to the Liberals. In 1905 Herbert Gladstone estimated that there were ninety-eight seats in England and Wales and twenty-six more in Scotland which had a significant Irish vote. In 1892 the Liberals had won eighty-one of the English and Welsh seats and fifteen of the Scottish seats, whereas in 1900 they had won only forty-two of the former and six of the latter.[20] Irish voters did not automatically support the Liberals because Liberal education policy was vigorously opposed by the Catholic Church. The principal inducement for the Irish to vote Liberal was their desire to promote Irish nationalist aspirations. Thus the Liberal Party would be taking a considerable political risk if it were to abandon Home Rule.

By 1899, however, many Liberals had come to view Home Rule as an election liability. Others were alienated by the Irish MPs' indifference to Nonconformist education grievances and by the Nationalists' enthusiastic championing of the Boer cause when war broke out in South Africa. As a result, on 8 December 1899, Herbert Gladstone sent Campbell-Bannerman a memorandum suggesting that, while the party should remain pledged to Home Rule, the Irish Local Government Act of 1898, which had given Ireland elected county councils, had reduced its urgency. The best route to Home Rule, he argued, was for the Irish to use that Act to demonstrate their capacity for administration. For the moment, the 'Irish question would be in a position analogous to that of Disestablishment. In a general sense it would be before the country, but it would not rank for the time being, as a practical question of politics'.[21] Most of the other Liberal leaders agreed with Gladstone's conclusions. Thus, for the first time since 1885, Liberal candidates in the general election of 1900 were allowed considerable flexibility as to how they dealt with Home Rule.

By the autumn of 1901 the leading Liberal Imperialists were convinced that the policy of the Gladstone memorandum must be stated publicly. With the Irish openly sympathizing with the enemies of the nation, the electorate had to be reassured that the Liberals were not bound to them in any way. For this reason, in their autumn speeches, Asquith, Grey and R. B. Haldane emphasized the complete freedom of the Liberal Party from any Irish alliance. At the same time, they urged that the party must be free to take a fresh look at the Irish problem when it returned to power. Most Liberal Imperialists, however, did not repudiate Home Rule. They were liberals. They opposed coercion, believed Ireland should be governed according to Irish ideas and viewed Home Rule as the only final solution to the problem. They also believed, however, that it should be approached gradually because, as Asquith wrote to his constituency chairman,

> the reconciliation of Ireland to the Empire, and the relief of the Imperial Parliament (not as regards Ireland alone) from a load of unnecessary burdens – can only be attempted by methods which will carry with them, step by step, the sanction and sympathy of British opinion. To recognise facts like these, and to act accordingly, is not apostasy; it is common sense.[22]

A significant minority of Liberal Imperialists, however, including Rosebery, opposed Home Rule. They feared that the Irish viewed Home Rule as preparatory to separation from Great Britain. With the experience of Irish support for the Boers before them, Rosebery argued that it would be folly to give the Irish control of a parliament 'at the very heart of the Empire'. The security of the United Kingdom and of the empire was at stake.[23]

Thus, at the time of Rosebery's letter of definite separation in February 1902, there were three positions on Irish policy in the Liberal Party. Campbell-Bannerman and his supporters remained committed to Home Rule, but recognized that it could no longer be the first article in the Liberal programme. They had not, however, worked out an interim Irish policy to serve until they were prepared to proceed with Home Rule. The body of Liberal Imperialists represented by Asquith went further, insisting that it was essential for the Liberal Party to dissociate itself from the Irish Nationalists. At the same time, they put forward the 'step by step' principle as a means of gradually working towards Home Rule. Finally, Rosebery and his followers rejected

36

Home Rule altogether. They did, however, support 'step by step' as an end in itself, and they enumerated the kinds of reforms they would pursue: the further extension of local government by creating regional councils, and a drastic reform of the Irish administration at Dublin Castle.

Three and a half years of confusion followed as the three sides studiously avoided communicating with each other on the subject. Campbell-Bannerman and his followers acted as if Rosebery spoke for all Liberal Imperialists. They therefore repeatedly reaffirmed their commitment to Home Rule as the only possible solution to the Irish question. They spoke little of the Irish policy of the next Liberal government, and this enabled Roseberyites to portray them as still committed to immediate Home Rule.[24] The Liberal Imperialists, however, refused to recognize their disagreements over Home Rule. They concentrated on the elements of Irish policy on which they were agreed: the end of the Irish alliance and the impossibility of a Home Rule bill being introduced by the next Liberal government. They spoke little of the ultimate solution to the Irish problem, and this gave credence to the belief that they all rejected Home Rule.[25]

Liberals in the country preferred to ignore the Home Rule question. Following Rosebery's letter of definite separation, they were nearly unanimous in condemning him for prolonging party divisions over an issue which was not before the country. Once the split forced them to face the issue, however, they assumed that the Liberal Imperialists were not repudiating Home Rule. At the same time, Irish support of the Education Bill of 1902 was profoundly disillusioning for many Liberals and Nonconformists. Even the staunchest Home Rulers, therefore, were inclined to endorse the Liberal Imperialists' more cautious approach to the Irish question.[26]

It was thus essential for the Liberal leaders to bring themselves into line with the rest of the party. The impetus came from Thomas Lough, a Liberal back-bencher who resided in Ireland. In a November 1904 memorandum to Campbell-Bannerman, Lough argued that much had been done already to give the Irish control of their own affairs. He believed that further administrative reforms, such as the reorganization of Dublin Castle and the devolution of more powers from the Imperial Parliament, could be carried without offending English public opinion the way Home Rule might. Lough admitted to Campbell-Bannerman in a subsequent letter that his proposals were 'step-by-step – a word I hate. But I am forced to the conclusion that nothing else, after *what is done*, is practicable'. Both Gladstone and Campbell-Bannerman accepted Lough's analysis as fundamentally correct, although it was indistinguishable from what many Liberal Imperialists had been saying for the previous three years.[27]

By 1905 Liberals were agreed that Home Rule would not be dealt with in the next Parliament and that the Irish should accept whatever measure of devolution or administration reform the next Liberal government might offer. The 'step by step' policy of Asquith and his friends had been accepted. The real cleavage in the party over Home Rule was finally revealed in November. John Redmond and T. P. O'Connor, two of the Irish leaders, accepted the 'step by step' policy on the understanding that Home Rule remained the policy of the Liberal Party and that some measure which was consistent with and would lead up to Home Rule would be introduced during the next Parliament.[28] After securing the agreement of Asquith and Grey, Campbell-Bannerman stated this policy in a speech at Stirling on 23 November. Rosebery, however, knew nothing of the discussions between his lieutenants and Campbell-Bannerman. In a speech at Bodmin on 25 November, he repudiated the Stirling statement as 'the raising of the banner of Home Rule'. The response to the Bodmin speech was immediate. J. A. Spender, who for six years had been trying to act as a bridge between Rosebery and Campbell-Bannerman, denounced it in a *Westminster Gazette* leader. Liberals of all shades spoke out along the lines of the Stirling speech, emphasizing that no Home Rule bill would be introduced in the next Parliament. Most importantly, Grey rejected Rosebery's interpretation of the Stirling speech at Newcastle-under-Lyme on 27 November.[29]

The Stirling consensus enabled the Liberals to postpone Home Rule while retaining Irish support. As a result, Liberal or Labour candidates won ninety-two of the ninety-eight seats in England and Wales and twenty-two of the twenty-six seats in Scotland which Gladstone had identified as having a significant Irish vote. Formal agreement on the new Irish policy which made this sweep possible had been so long delayed because modification of the Liberals' Home Rule policy had become associated with Rosebery's call for a 'clean slate' and his own rejection of Home Rule. As a result, the difference between Asquith and Campbell-Bannerman (which was insignificant) was magnified, while that between Asquith and Rosebery (which was fundamental) was ignored. As with all other elements of policy, most of the Liberal Imperialists differed little from the rest of the party in their approach to the Irish question. They were responsible for forcing the Liberal leaders to articulate a new approach to Irish problems, and they provided the analysis to support that new approach. When these tasks were accomplished, liberal imperialism could disappear, for it never represented a policy distinct from traditional liberalism.

THE FAILURE OF THE LIBERAL LEAGUE

Like the Chesterfield policy which it was created to promote, the Liberal League was a source of confusion and an object of distrust. The Liberal Imperialists claimed that the purpose of the League was defensive. They insisted that Campbell-Bannerman's Leicester speech was an attempt to proscribe those who held their views; therefore, the League had to be formed to ensure those views a fair hearing and to work for their acceptance by the party. The Liberal League thus was no different from other sectional organizations which worked to promote a particular policy. These assertions, however, were in part a pose. The plans for the League had been proposed by Robert Perks in 1901 and were agreed upon by the Liberal Imperialist leaders in January 1902 – before Campbell-Bannerman's Leicester speech.[30] Nor was the Liberal League like other propaganda societies associated with the Liberal Party. It had all the appearances of a separate electoral organization, hiring election agents to organize constituencies and sponsoring its own candidates.

The Liberal Imperialist leaders were, in fact, uncertain as to what the role of the League should be. Perks wanted to create a compact but elite band of Rosebery's supporters who would have the power to influence Liberal policy. Some organization would be needed to help elect League members to Parliament; however, Perks did not want the League to contribute towards candidates' election expenses, for this might encourage opportunists to join the League in the hope of securing financial backing. The men who created the League's electoral organization, however, recognized that the supply of candidates would be limited unless they could promise some financial assistance. Yet the more the League took on the business of financing candidates, the more it came into conflict with the Liberal Central Association (LCA). Herbert Gladstone, in particular, initially viewed it as a challenge to his authority, and he used all his influence to discourage prospective candidates from joining. Since most candidates could not afford to alienate the Chief Whip, many who were sympathetic to the League's policies and to Rosebery none the less refused to join.[31]

The problems which official opposition and ambiguity of purpose created for the League were illustrated by its unsuccessful attempt to organize in Eastern Scotland. A strong branch of the League in the area was essential. Rosebery's family seat was in Edinburgh, while Asquith and Haldane sat for constituencies in the region. But the influence of the Scottish Liberal Association (SLA), which was dominated by Campbell-Bannerman's supporters, was difficult to overcome. Sympathetic Liberals were fearful of offending the official organization and then being left in the lurch by Rosebery. At the same time, as Thomas Gibson-Carmichael pointed out to Rosebery,

> The general impression among the working classes especially is that the league was mainly called into existence because of the war, & that now that the war is over to start new branches of it will only be interpreted as acting factionally & that will not be at all popular in Scotland.[32]

By encouraging such apprehensions, the SLA was able to appear to be on the defensive and thus to oppose the League with impunity. By early 1903 it was clear that the League had failed to gain a footing in Scotland. Indeed, a year after its formation, Gladstone was confident that it no longer posed a threat to his organization anywhere in the country.[33]

When the Liberal League was organized, Gladstone recognized that the LCA could not oppose a candidate merely because he belonged to the League. Even in 1902, when his hostility was most pronounced, Gladstone displayed a willingness to place League members and sympathizers as candidates. League candidates, moreover, quickly demonstrated their strength as vote-getters. On 29 July, Rowland Barran produced the first Liberal victory ever in North Leeds, converting a Conservative majority of 2,517 in 1900 into a Liberal majority of 758. Although hostility to the Education Bill was probably the decisive factor, Barran was a member of the League, and during his campaign, he had alienated the Leeds Irish by insisting on a step-by-step approach to Irish self-government.[34] His victory, therefore, appeared to be a victory for the policy of the League. A month later there was a by-election in the Sevenoaks division of Kent, which the Liberals had never won. Beaumont Morice, a League sympathizer whose opportunism eventually alienated both sections of the party, reduced a Conservative majority of 4,812 in 1900 to 891.

The relative success of a candidate with even the modest attractions of Morice probably convinced Gladstone that liberal imperialism could be an asset to the party. The Education Act of 1902 and Chamberlain's tariff reform proposals in 1903 gave the Liberals an opportunity to win voters who had not voted Liberal for a generation. Such voters would be more likely to support a Liberal Imperialist who was thought to be safe on Home Rule, the empire and national defence. Thus, once he was convinced that the League could not challenge the LCA, Gladstone worked with it as best he could. He started consulting with the secretaries of the League about the placement of candidates, while the League irregularly kept him informed of its activities. By 1905 co-operation was commonplace. In June of that year, the League went so far as to consult Sir Wilfred Lawson, the former pro-Boer and influential Cumberland Liberal, before it placed F. W. Chance as Liberal candidate for Carlisle.[35] Gladstone not only worked with the League in placing its candidates; he also was willing to encourage it to organize in constituencies where the Liberals traditionally had been weak. His only condition was that the candidates agree to support Campbell-Bannerman as the elected leader of the party in the House of Commons.

Relations between the League and the LCA were not always harmonious. Gladstone was particularly annoyed that the League vice-presidents – Asquith, Grey, Fowler and Haldane – arranged their speaking engagements through the League rather than through the LCA. A more important source of bickering was money. Gladstone believed that the League should contribute to the election expenses of its own members. The League's secretaries were willing to share in the election expenses if they had brought the candidate forward and organized the constituency. Once a candidate was elected, however, they expected his expenses to become the responsibility of the LCA. If, moreover, a Leaguer was placed by Gladstone, then they believed the Chief Whip should bear the cost. There was much room for disagreement, but in general the League appears to have been a useful supplementary source of funds for Gladstone in financing by-elections and preparing for the general election.[36]

The Liberal Leaguers hoped that their organization would attract to the Liberal Party moderate middle-class voters who had been alienated by its policies since 1885. They were at least partially justified in their hopes. Eighty-four Leaguers contested the general election of 1906. Seventeen of these had been elected prior to the formation of the League and thus were fixed in their constituencies. Of the remaining sixty-seven, forty-four were elected in the landslide of 1906. Many of these candidates contested suburban or rural constituencies in the South of England or the West Midlands, regions which traditionally were Unionist strongholds. Forty-eight of the sixty-seven ran in constituencies which the Liberals had lost in the three previous general elections, and twenty-seven of them won. Nine of the victors were strong enough to win in at least one of the 1910 general elections, when the pendulum swung against the Liberals and Home Rule was once again a live issue. Virtually all the losers in 1906 contested hopeless seats.[37]

The League clearly made a significant contribution to the Liberal revival between 1902 and 1905. It could do so, however, only as an adjunct to the LCA. Despite appearances, it probably never was intended to provide the organization for a new Liberal Imperialist party. While the League's organizers expected it to work within the Liberal Party, however, they wanted it to be autonomous. As was so often the case, this showed a lack of appreciation of political realities by the League's leaders. Once the Boer War was over, the pressures for party unity became enormous. If the League was not to appear schismatic, it had to work with the official party in order to have a significant impact. The League's only possible source of independent influence was its association with Rosebery, and the continued prospect that he might return as leader of the party. By 1903 this had become a most tenuous hope.

THE RESOLUTION OF THE LEADERSHIP CRISIS

Rosebery's letter of definite separation greatly complicated the task of those who were working for his return to the leadership of the Liberal Party. Rosebery was not likely to accept a leader of the House of Commons who had repudiated his policies, but Campbell-Bannerman's strength among the rank and file made it virtually impossible to force him out. Campbell-Bannerman's task was nearly as difficult. The rest of the party would not admit the finality of the break with Rosebery. Even an unswerving supporter like Sir Ughtred Kay-Shuttleworth urged Campbell-Bannerman that 'to cling to every *chance* of averting another split & secession, like that of '86, is clearly right. So *we* must avoid closing the door'.[38] Because of Rosebery's continued hold upon the popular imagination, and because the Liberal rank and file desired party unity and could see no insurmountable barrier to it, it was essential that Campbell-Bannerman continue to welcome Rosebery's return to the counsels of the Liberal leadership.

Angered by the apparent revolt of the Liberal Imperialists and the formation of the Liberal League, Campbell-Bannerman's initial response was not to compromise. This brought him into conflict with his Chief Whip. For example, when Rosebery agreed to speak at Leeds on 30 May, Gladstone, who represented a Leeds constituency, felt compelled to speak at the meeting as a demonstration of the party unity which he had been preaching. Campbell-Bannerman was understandably annoyed that 'he who has proclaimed his definite separation from me & my policy is to be supported by the President of the National Liberal Fedn. [Augustine Birrell] & by the Chief Whip of the Liberal Party!'[39] Yet Gladstone's was the sounder judgement. Rank-and-file support could have been shaken if the official leadership had given legitimacy to Liberal Imperialist claims that they were being ostracized.

The standing of the Liberal leaders reached its nadir in 1903. The rank and file were increasingly impatient with their constant bickering when there were no apparent issues to divide them. In May, a series of devastating articles by J. A. Spender in the *Westminster Gazette* exposed the ineffectiveness of the leadership. Spender, who had worked unceasingly for unity, pointed out that there was little consultation and co-operation among the leaders in the House of Commons and insufficient communication between the leadership and the back-benchers. The responsibility for correcting this breakdown clearly rested with Campbell-Bannerman. Spender was equally harsh with Rosebery, who

> is perpetually seeking to combine two things which are essentially incompatible – one, the position of non-political adviser to the public on a platform removed from politics; the other of a politician acting with and speaking on behalf of Liberals and President of a League which claims to represent the most modern Liberal thought.

If Rosebery was to influence the nation's affairs, Spender continued, he must work with the other leaders of the Liberal Party for an agreed policy and be prepared to accept the responsibilities of office when the opportunity came to implement that policy. If he failed to do this, then the party must look elsewhere for its leaders.[40]

The emergence of free trade as an issue increased the pressure for active co-operation by the party's leaders. When the pro-Boer David Lloyd George arranged to have Grey speak with him at Carnarvon, the *Leicester Daily Mercury* asked 'cannot Sir Henry Campbell-Bannerman and Lord Rosebery appear on the same platform?'[41] Finally, speaking at Leicester on 7 November 1903, Rosebery accepted that the defence of free trade was an issue of transcendent importance, which demanded Liberal unity. At Frome on 17 November, Campbell-Bannerman expressed 'cordial satisfaction' that Rosebery again 'was ready to share the labour and responsibility of public life in active co-operation with a united Liberal party'. He tellingly added that all 'true Liberals would welcome Lord Rosebery's appeal for unity, especially at a time when the permanent importance, wisdom, and vitality of the principles of Liberalism were being proved by events'.[42]

By implication, Campbell-Bannerman had set the usual conditions for Rosebery's return. He must work with his former colleagues to promote the traditional principles of liberalism. The Liberal leaders now set out to secure his co-operation upon these terms. On 29 November Augustine Birrell, president of the NLF, invited Rosebery to be the principal speaker at the Federation's annual meeting the following May. The invitation was declined. In December Lord Spencer, whose wife had recently died, asked Rosebery to give the dinner for Liberal peers which would precede the new session of Parliament in January. Rosebery refused, arguing that such an action would be misinterpreted as a renewal of his official relationship with the party. Nor would Rosebery attend the dinner when Lord Ripon agreed to host it. Rosebery also refused to attend a meeting of former cabinet members to discuss strategy concerning fiscal matters for the coming session.[43] Rosebery clearly had no intention of working with the party's leaders, and after January 1904 they made no further effort to conciliate him.

This time there was to be no reprieve for Rosebery. The momentum towards united action which had been growing among Liberals in the country since 1902 finally overwhelmed the parliamentary party in 1904. Liberal Imperialists started to appear at meetings with members of other sections of the party. More importantly, the leaders began to consult again with some regularity. None the less, complete harmony had not been restored, for the leading Liberal Imperialists still believed that Campbell-Bannerman was unreliable on imperial and foreign policy. Once they were convinced that Rosebery would never return, Grey and Haldane began to consider substituting Asquith for Campbell-Bannerman as leader of the House of Commons in a future Liberal government, with Campbell-Bannerman serving as prime minister in the House of Lords. Such a move had much to recommend it. Campbell-Bannerman was considered a weak leader in the House of Commons, while Asquith was a masterful parliamentarian. Campbell-Bannerman's health, moreover, might easily preclude his taking on the strenuous duties of both prime minister and leader of the House of Commons. Campbell-Bannerman himself had recognized this possibility during a conversation with Gladstone in October 1903.[44] His doctor in Marienbad would emphatically press the same view in December 1905.

The logic which supported the Liberal Imperialists' position was undermined by two facts. Although there were good reasons for Campbell-Bannerman to go to the House of Lords, these were not the principal concern of Grey and Haldane. They distrusted Campbell-Bannerman, and the distrust was mutual. The issue thus became an extension of the quarrel between Liberal Imperialists and pro-Boers. The Liberal Imperialist leaders further weakened their position by the means which they chose to achieve their end. In September 1905 Grey, Haldane and Asquith met at Grey's fishing lodge at Relugas. There they agreed that none of them would take office unless Campbell-Bannerman went to the House of Lords, making Asquith chancellor of the Exchequer and leader of the House of Commons. Grey was to be foreign or colonial secretary, and Haldane would become lord chancellor. This had all the appearances of a conspiracy against Campbell-Bannerman, with obvious personal gains for the participants should they succeed.

Asquith, who was given the task of convincing Campbell-Bannerman to accept a peerage, recognized that an ultimatum was impossible. He did his best to secure for his friends the positions they desired. He exerted what pressure he could to persuade Campbell-

Bannerman to go to the House of Lords. But when, on 5 December 1905, the new Prime Minister offered him the chancellorship of the Exchequer, he accepted without making any conditions. Two days later Campbell-Bannerman, having decided to remain in the House of Commons, authorized Asquith to offer Grey the Foreign Office and Haldane the War Office. After two more days of hesitation, on 7 December Grey and Haldane were finally persuaded to accept the positions offered them.

Campbell-Bannerman had, in fact, been most generous to the Liberal Imperialists in the distribution of offices both in and outside the Cabinet. Clearly the new Prime Minister did not fear that liberal imperialism represented a liberalism radically different from his own. The most important exception was Rosebery, and his pronouncement at Bodmin had exposed his isolation and had saved Campbell-Bannerman any embarrassment in not offering him a place in the government. Except for Grey, no one raised a word of protest at his exclusion.

THE FAILURE OF LIBERAL IMPERIALISM

When, in December 1907, Campbell-Bannerman lay dying, Grey wrote him a letter of encouragement. The Foreign Secretary admitted, 'I have felt from the early days of this Parliament that all my forecast before the Elections was wrong & that your presence in the House of Commons has not only been desirable but essential to manage this party & keep it together.' Four months later Haldane wrote his mother on the day after Campbell-Bannerman died, 'He was a loyal leader & I owe a great deal to him for help ungrudgingly given.'[45] Why had men as intelligent as Haldane and as decent and honourable as Grey misjudged their leader for so long? They, like their associates, were the victims of the fundamental misconception upon which liberal imperialism was based: that in imperial and foreign affairs, there were only two positions in the Liberal Party, and those positions were defined during the Boer War. Most Liberals wanted no part of either the power struggle or the concurrent ideological battle which so preoccupied the supporters of Harcourt and Rosebery. They believed that there was an underlying ideology common to all Liberals which transcended differences among them on specific issues. These were the people whom Campbell-Bannerman represented, and this was the message which he preached throughout his seven years as leader of the party in opposition.

The Liberal Imperialists could not recognize this truth about their party because they were political elitists with little respect for and little understanding of the party's rank and file. Campbell-Bannerman, by contrast, 'spoke and acted as if he were always one of the rank and file of Liberalism, well content to do spade work himself and not simply satisfied to call on other people to do it'.[46] These divergent attitudes towards the Liberal activists account for Campbell-Bannerman's strength and the Liberal Imperialists' weakness in the leadership struggle. Not only were the Liberal Imperialists unable to challenge Campbell-Bannerman's base of support, but their very actions alienated it further. For example, their policy objectives were fully consistent with the traditions of liberalism. First, they wanted to convince the public that liberalism did not necessarily imply little-Englandism. Second, they wanted to force the party to modify some of its more unpopular domestic policies, such as local option and immediate Home Rule, and to limit its objectives to the enactment of a few attainable reforms. By cultivating the impression that they stood for radical change, however, they won the distrust rather than the support of the rank and file. Thus, even when events proved that their views were shared by the bulk of the party, it did them little good politically.

The Liberal League similarly was no asset in challenging Campbell-Bannerman. It could only succeed where the party was weak. Elsewhere, it had to come into conflict with the local Liberal associations, and the inevitable result was hostility and suspicion. Perhaps their greatest weakness, however, was the Liberal Imperialists' reliance on Rosebery as a leader. Rosebery still had enormous popular appeal. He despised party politics, however, and this rendered him ineffective as a politician, for he would never sustain work for the policies he believed in. None the less, although Rosebery repeatedly let them down, and frequently reaffirmed his refusal to return as a party leader, the other Liberal Imperialist leaders clung to him as their only hope for capturing the party. It was a forelorn hope once Campbell-Bannerman turned decisively against it in the summer of 1901. His position would never be challenged successfully by a man like Rosebery, who believed neither in traditional liberalism nor in the good sense of the rank and file.

3

The Liberal Revival

On 10 May 1902, George Toulmin, a Nonconformist newspaper proprietor from Preston, won a by-election in the Lancashire cotton-spinning town of Bury. It was the first Liberal victory in Bury since 1885. Two months later, Rowland Barran gave the Liberals their first victory ever in North Leeds. These contests marked the beginning of a Liberal revival which culminated in a landslide victory in the general election of 1906. Between the Bury by-election and the end of 1905, forty-three Unionist seats were contested at by-elections in Great Britain. The Liberals won twenty-two of these contests. During the same period, of the twelve Liberal seats contested, the Unionists won only Devonport – and that was regained by the Liberals in 1904. This remarkable recovery was possible because, despite the quarrels among the leaders, the Boer War had created no fundamental division within the Liberal Party. Thus, when the issues associated with traditional liberalism once again became relevant, it was easy enough for Liberals in the country to rally to the cause.

Two issues were crucial in promoting the Liberal recovery. The Education Act of 1902 provoked a revival of Nonconformist political activity on a scale unknown since the 1870s. Because the Nonconformists were the heart of the Liberal rank and file, there was no surer guarantee of enthusiasm on the part of the constituency activists than a Nonconformist crusade. Even education, however, could be a source of disagreement among Liberals and Nonconformists when they considered how to reform the system. Joseph Chamberlain's tariff reform proposals transcended all divisions among Liberals by challenging one of the sacred principles of their creed. There was no sectional dissent over free trade. At the same time, Chamberlain's policy triggered a struggle at all levels of the Unionist Party which paralyzed the party organization and left it unable to meet the new Liberal challenge. The result was an electoral sweep without precedent since 1832.

LIBERALISM AND NONCONFORMITY

The foundation of liberalism remained, as it had been throughout the nineteenth century, a profound belief in individual liberty. Liberals

47

believed that the welfare of the community was best promoted by assuring freedom for each individual to develop his or her talents to the utmost. They therefore sought to remove all constraints on equality of opportunity, which was the essential prerequisite for individual self-development. During the nineteenth century, Liberals had concentrated their efforts on ending civil and religious disabilities and on rationalizing the institutions of society. They had hoped to minimize direct government intervention, which they feared could in itself be a barrier to individual freedom. By the twentieth century, however, the emphasis of liberalism had changed. Many Liberals were now convinced that state intervention sometimes was necessary to secure the freedom of each individual to realize his or her potential. They saw nothing contradictory to their liberal principles in allowing a more active role for government in creating the conditions for self-development. Even an older generation Liberal like Campbell-Bannerman could speak without embarrassment of a positive role for the state. For example, in a 1901 speech at Peckham, he defined the 'one main principle in all domestic affairs' that motivated Liberals:

> It is that the interest and duty of the State is to secure for every individual among us the opportunity . . . of a healthy, happy, and useful life – the best chance for developing the powers which God has given him . . . We cannot equalize the chances, but we can see that our laws and habits do not aggravate inequalities, and in the pursuit of this purpose we can make, and we ought to make, the interests of individuals and the privileges of classes yield to the general interest of the people at large.[1]

Clearly, by the turn of the century, the logic of the new liberalism of the 1880s had been absorbed into the mainstream of liberal thought.

At the same time, as Campbell-Bannerman's speech makes clear, Liberals perceived the obstacles to individual freedom to be unchanged: those vested interests, in their view supported by the Conservative Party, which set themselves up in opposition to the interest of the community at large. Liberals believed that the best means of thwarting the vested interests was the extension of popular control. If the people, through their elected representatives, were given control over schools, liquor licenses and land, then these by definition would be regulated to serve the people rather than the parsons, the publicans, or the landlords. The most comprehensive statement of the policies by which Liberals intended to limit the power of privilege remained the Newcastle Programme, which most Liberals considered the embodiment of their principles. While priorities would be determined by events, the foremost items of concern to Liberals in 1900 continued to be what they had been in 1891: education, temperance, land and housing reform; registration and electoral reform; the veto of the House of Lords and other constitutional reforms.

Nonconformists shared many of these liberal values. Nonconformity, like liberalism, was rooted in individual liberty. Each conscience must be free to find its own way to Christ and thus the path to salvation. Nonconformists were especially concerned with the moral development of the individual. Just as the liberal believed that society could be served by allowing each member to develop his or her talents, so the Nonconformist believed that society was best served by strengthening the character and moral fibre of each member. Liberals and Nonconformists were especially convinced of the beneficent effects of responsibility on the individual. Indeed, Campbell-Bannerman justified liberalism's belief in popular control, 'not only on grounds of justice and on the grounds of effective administration, but on this ground – that it exercises a wholesome influence on the character of the people who enjoy the privilege'.[2]

Despite the obvious compatibility between Liberals and Nonconformists, Nonconformity was too much divided within itself to provide comprehensive and sustained support for liberalism. In particular, those sects whose roots were in seventeenth-century Puritanism – the Baptists, Congregationalists and Presbyterians – differed in outlook from the Wesleyan Methodists, the largest of the Free Churches. The old dissenter sects tended to be more overtly political, and Liberal, in their outlook. The Wesleyans, on the other hand, struggled mightily to divorce their Church from partisan politics. At the same time, although the Wesleyans shared many of the concerns of the other Nonconformist Churches, their generally more conservative outlook made it far more difficult for Nonconformists to speak with one voice even on those concerns.

The identity of interests between Nonconformists and Liberals was further weakened because the former constituted only one section within the Liberal Party. Like all liberals, the Nonconformists opposed the promotion of sectional interests; they necessarily believed that their policies would benefit the entire community. Therefore, they could not organize, as the Irish Nationalists had done, to promote their particular interest at the expense of the Liberal cause. Any action which injured liberalism threatened the well-being of Nonconformity and of the nation, and was therefore practically inexpedient as well as morally reprehensible. The less the Nonconformists were willing to organize and exert pressure, however, the more the Liberal leaders could afford to take them for granted.

The Free Churches were primarily concerned with three domestic issues, education, temperance and disestablishment of the Church of England. The last illustrates some of the problems which faced the Nonconformists in the political arena. When in 1899, there was a revival of the controversy over ritualism in the Anglican Church, some

Nonconformists wanted to use it to raise disestablishment as an issue of practical politics. The Liberal leaders, however, did not believe the time was ripe to launch a new attack on the Church. They feared that it would merely serve to unite the Anglican factions in support of the government.[3] Furthermore, the Nonconformists themselves were not sufficiently united on the issue to force it upon the Liberal Party, as even the Congregationalist *Examiner* had to admit.[4] This combination of political expediency and lack of consensus among the Free Churches repeatedly hampered the Nonconformists as they pressed their causes on the Liberal leaders.

Liberal Nonconformists looked back with nostalgia upon the years of the Bulgarian agitation when all were united under William Gladstone in a great moral cause. Since then, Ireland, imperialism and the Boer War had created disunity in their ranks. They were waiting for a new leader to rekindle the old enthusiasm which could unite them in a new crusade for righteousness and justice. Neither Campbell-Bannerman nor Rosebery nor Asquith, however, was another Gladstone. Consequently, when the Education Act of 1902 provided the cause, the Nonconformists found that they must lead the campaign for civil and religious liberty themselves.

EDUCATION AND FREE TRADE

Despite their vehement opposition to the Education Act of 1870, Nonconformists found that it served their interests well. Indeed, since the Church was having increasing difficulty in supporting its schools by fees and voluntary contributions, it seemed only a matter of time before many of them would have to be closed down or turned over to the state. In either case, the Nonconformist goal of a national, nondenominational elementary school system would be achieved. Conservative governments, however, insisted on increasing public funding for the Church schools, thus slowing the process of erosion. In the Newcastle Programme, Liberals responded by insisting that all schools supported by public money must be subject to public control.

Quite apart from the contentious issue of denominational schools, there were good educational reasons for seeking revision of the 1870 settlement. The quality of rural education needed to be improved, and some provision had to be made for public secondary and technical education. In an attempt to deal with all of these issues, Arthur Balfour, the Prime Minister, introduced a new education bill in March 1902 which abolished the school boards. Each county, city, or town council was to appoint an education committee responsible for all levels of education. The education committee would oversee secular elementary education given in all the schools, including the denominational schools, which now would be supported with rate aid. A board of six managers was to be appointed to supervise each denominational school, with two of these managers appointed by the education committee and four by the sect. The education committee also would have to approve all teaching appointments, but approval could only be withheld on educational (as opposed to religious) grounds. The denominational schools thus could continue to appoint only teachers of their own denomination.

Virtually every provision of the Bill was offensive to Liberals. A nominated committee was to replace a popularly elected board as the authority responsible for education. Sectarian schools were to be supported by the rates, but the people were to be denied control of the schools. These schools, moreover, could continue to impose religious tests on teachers who were to be paid by the state. The effect was to force Nonconformists to contribute to the propagation of religious doctrines they did not believe in. 'Managers and teachers', the *Eastern Daily Press* complained on 8 April, 'will have their own way in sowing the seeds of religious discord and prejudice in young minds; and they will be enabled to do this work with the rate-payers' money.' The offense was all the greater because nothing was done to relieve the old Nonconformist grievances. There remained some 8,000 school districts where the only available school was Anglican. Nonconformist children were compelled to attend these schools, yet they were denied the right to be pupil-teachers. Nor were the sectarian teacher training colleges opened to Nonconformists.

Despite Nonconformist hostility, however, there were disagreements over how to attack the Bill. Congregationalists could not agree whether their principles were best represented by a secular system of elementary education, by one which continued the Bible teaching provided for under the Cowper-Temple clause of the 1870 Act, or by one which made some provision for denominational teaching.[5] The Wesleyans were not even agreed that the Bill should be opposed outright. Because they had their own schools, the more conservative Wesleyans, represented by the *Methodist Recorder* and Dr D. J. Waller, secretary of the Wesleyan Education Committee, supported rate aid and the schools' right to appoint teachers of their own denomination. On the other hand, the more radical Wesleyans, led by Rev. Hugh Price Hughes and Robert Perks, favoured uncompromising opposition to the Bill. In May, every district synod supported resolutions opposing the Bill; however, in nearly every case there was a small but significant minority which preferred amendment to rejection. In July, the Wesleyan Methodist Conference, by a vote of 454 to 68, adopted resolutions condemning the Bill.[6] Thus, although the opponents of the Bill were in control, the Wesleyans clearly would have difficulty uniting behind a single education policy.

Despite some wavering among the Wesleyans, most Nonconformists and Liberals in the country were fully aroused by their hostility to the Bill. It is indicative of the degree to which the Liberal leaders were absorbed in their own struggle that they appear not to have appreciated the intensity of rank-and-file opposition. The parliamentary party was equally unresponsive to the feeling in the country. During the autumn session, the *Daily News* published a weekly list of Liberal MPs absent from Education Bill divisions, a list which was headed during the week ending 18 October by Campbell-Bannerman himself. On 31 October, eleven Nonconformist MPs complained to Campbell-Bannerman of the slack Liberal attendance at divisions. It was the Free Church Council rather than the National Liberal Federation (NLF) which took the initiative in organizing meetings and demonstrations of protest in the country.[7]

The major Nonconformist campaign against the Bill came after it had passed into law. As early as May 1902 the *Examiner* had called on Nonconformists to refuse to pay the education rate if the Bill was enacted. By November, militant Nonconformists accepted that 'passive resistance' offered their most effective means of protesting against the new policy. The leader of the passive resisters was Dr John Clifford, the foremost English Baptist and a lifelong political radical and admirer of Gladstone. Clifford possessed the fanaticism of the seventeenth-century Puritans. An impassioned speaker, he had the ability to arouse his flock of martyrs in the centuries-old struggle of Nonconformity to resist oppression by the established Church. Their cause commanded the sympathy of most Liberals and Nonconformists, including those who could not accept their methods. Only the *Methodist Recorder* maintained a steadfast opposition to passive resistance. The Wesleyan Methodist Conference of 1903, however, passed a resolution expressing sympathy with those who refused to pay the education rate.[8]

Most Liberals and Nonconformists were not passive resisters. Instead, they tried to thwart the intensions of the Act by political means. By securing the election of Liberal Nonconformists to county, city, or town councils, they could assure the appointment of education committees which were sympathetic to their views. In Wales, where Liberal Nonconformists dominated local government, the county councils refused to aid denominational schools unless the schools agreed to appoint two of their four managers and all their teachers from names submitted by the councils. Everywhere, the thrust of Liberal policies was to make existence as difficult as possible for the denominational schools and to delay and mitigate by every possible means the implementation of the obnoxious provisions of the Act.

Resistance to the Education Act, however, remained a grass-roots movement. The official leaders, having no wish to associate themselves with illegal actions, limited themselves to general statements of opposition. By 1903 they had agreed upon a policy which was satisfactory to all opponents of the Act and which embodied the principles of religious and civil liberty for which they were fighting: where public money was spent, there must be full public control, and there could be no religious tests for teachers in state-aided schools. They remained divorced, however, from the intense ferment, with its concurrent divisions, which continued to stimulate the opposition to the Act in the country. Indeed, their attention was soon diverted by an issue of far greater interest and concern to them than education.

On 15 May 1903, Joseph Chamberlain spoke out for an imperial customs union to strengthen the bonds between Britain and her colonies, as well as to strengthen the British Empire in the economic struggle with Germany and the United States. In succeeding months, Chamberlain constructed from this foundation a comprehensive programme for imperial unity, economic regeneration and social reform. Free trade, he argued, had ruined British agriculture, while industry had never regained the prosperity of the early 1870s. Protection from foreign competitors, who used tariffs to keep out British goods, was necessary for the recovery of both sectors. At the same time, Chamberlain proposed a system of imperial preference whereby members of the empire would reduce their tariffs on each other's goods. This not only would strengthen the ties between the colonies and the mother country; it would also give British industry access to a market comparable in size to those of her greatest economic rivals. The combination of protection and preference would make possible an expansion of the economy which would relieve unemployment, while the additional revenues resulting from a broadened tax base could be used to pay for social reforms such as old-age pensions. In Chamberlain's hands, protection had become a national programme, designed to strengthen Britain by strengthening her imperial ties, and to benefit the business and agricultural communities as well as the working class.[9]

In attacking free trade, Chamberlain chose as his target a policy which had been accepted by all Liberals as the basis of British prosperity for the previous fifty years. Liberal replies to Chamberlain therefore claimed first that a protective tariff would undermine the nation's prosperity. Liberals pointed out that tariffs on raw materials and semi-finished goods would increase the prices of British finished goods. They added that tariffs on food would either increase the cost of living of the workers or, if wages were increased as compensation, add to the cost of exports. There was no way, they argued, that a tariff could succeed in its goal of reducing imports without adversely affecting exports and thus the wealth of the nation. A second line of attack by Liberals was to point out the inconsistencies in Chamberlain's proposals. They challenged imperial preference on the grounds that the economic interests of the colonies differed from each other and from those of the mother country. Attempts to overcome these differences would lead to friction rather than harmony within the empire. Balfour's more limited proposal, to place tariffs only on manufactured goods from countries whose own tariffs kept out British products, was equally impossible. Britain could not avoid taxing food or raw materials, for she did not import from her competitors the same products which she wished to export to them. Most aggravating of all to Liberals was what they viewed as the spirit of Chamberlain's proposals. They believed that the effect of tariff reform would be to create new special interests and privileged groups. As William Robson pointed out,

> the principles which lay at the basis of Liberalism in fiscal as in other matters, [were] that we should always distrust and oppose that evil instinct which led particular sections to make Government the instrument of their own rapacity at the cost of the community as a whole.[10]

Tariff reform thus challenged the fundamental principles of liberalism. The man who was a Judas to all Liberals threatened the well-being of the nation on behalf of vested interests. Here was a formula ideally suited to arouse the fighting spirit of the Liberal Party. In the eyes of the Liberal leaders, the defence of free trade immediately became the over-riding issue of politics. For a year following Chamberlain's opening salvo, every speech of every Liberal leader was devoted to combating tariff reform. This revived interest was reflected in the constituencies as well. In April 1902 an officer of the Home Counties Liberal Federation had written to Gladstone bemoaning 'the present dearth of eligible candidates'; by July 1903 Gladstone could write to a Liberal MP that the 'majority of candidatures are now filled up, & of those wh. are still open very few can be said to offer a good chance'.[11] In order to mobilize the anti-protectionist forces more effectively, the Free Trade Union was established in the summer of 1903. Although in theory it was a non-party organization, its officers were all well-known Liberals. Initially it functioned primarily as a propaganda organization; Gladstone, however, also wanted it to get involved in electoral activities. His goal was a free-trade organization in every constituency which would assist the local party organization with registration and canvassing in support of free-trade candidates. Gladstone hoped that the Free Trade Union and its local associations, like the Liberal League, would be a vehicle through which conscientious Unionists could more easily support Liberal candidates with their money, political work and votes.[12]

Another part of the Liberal leaders' effort to consolidate the opposition to Chamberlain was their search for a means of accommodating the fifty or so Unionist MPs and the handful of Unionist peers who were opposed to all tariffs on food. Although their numbers were small, the prestige of these Free Fooders was enormous, for they included several Cabinet members and two former chancellors of the Exchequer. The need to work with them seemed more imperative in October 1903 after Chamberlain and the Free Fooders had resigned from the Cabinet.

Chamberlain immediately launched a nationwide speaking campaign on behalf of tariff reform. At the same time, Balfour came out in favour of retaliatory tariffs while opposing duties on food. The Liberal leaders feared that the public would be tempted by such a compromise, which appeared to give the government a weapon against industrial rivals without taxing food. The prospect seemed to be for a difficult struggle in which the assistance of the Free Fooders would be valuable.

Some of the Free Fooders were easily provided for. Sir John Dickson Poynder, MP for North-West Wiltshire, eventually crossed the floor and was adopted as the Liberal candidate for his constituency. Only five other Free Fooders, however, sat for constituencies which they might hope to win against Unionist opposition, and which still had no Liberal or Labour candidate in the field. New constituencies might be found for some. The advantages of having a Free Fooder contest a seat which a Liberal would have little chance of winning were obvious. The problem was whether the Nonconformists would give such a candidate a free run if he were unsafe on education.

The Nonconformists were troubled by Chamberlain's tariff reform proposals. They assumed, with some justification, that he was trying to divert attention from the Education Act and assure that the next general election would not be fought on the education issue.[13] The response of the Liberal Party to Chamberlain's proposals seemed to justify their forebodings. The speeches of Liberal leaders and the editorial columns of Liberal newspapers concentrated on the evils of protection, seemingly to the exclusion of all other issues. Nonconformists feared the Liberals could betray them again as in 1870.

To prevent this, they sought to demonstrate their power to the Liberals. The Free Church Council abandoned its non-political position and used its nationwide organization, which included some 800 local Free Church Councils and 40 district federations, to work for amendment of the Act. It distributed an election manual which provided all necessary information for organizing a campaign – how to raise money, select candidates, arrange meetings, distribute literature, canvass voters and get them to the polls. Included were suggested test questions to be put to all candidates. The effect was to render the Free Church Council an independent auxiliary of the Liberal Party. At the same time, the Free Church leaders – especially Clifford – tirelessly stumped the country, speaking at demonstrations against the Act. Finally, the Council made a concerted effort to get more Free Church candidates. It was even willing to sponsor candidates for hopeless seats, and it started a campaign fund for this purpose.[14] With the Nonconformists organizing to fight in every constituency, they were in no mood to compromise.

Compromise was rendered more difficult by the question of religious education. At issue was what, if any, religious instruction elementary school children should receive. While some Baptists and Congregationalists preferred that the state be responsible only for secular education, most Nonconformists objected to what they considered to be 'Godless schools'. They believed that the elementary schools should continue to provide Bible instruction, while the sects would be free to supplement that instruction as they chose. Most Nonconformists, however, were not prepared to allow priests into the schools (especially the council schools already subject to full public control) during school hours to provide such denominational instruction, nor would they accept its being given by the regular teachers. On many of these issues, however, a minority of Nonconformists were prepared to be more generous to the sects, while many Liberals also took a less rigid approach to the religious education question. Campbell-Bannerman, for example, preferred a secular system, while even Perks was willing to consider sectarian instruction in former denominational schools during school hours.[15]

This subterranean divergence between an uncompromising Nonconformist position and a more generous Liberal position also occurred on the subject of Roman Catholic schools. Catholics insisted that their children be educated in Church schools under clerical control. Since their schools usually were in urban areas where alternative schools were available, the Liberal leaders, who were concerned about saving the Irish Catholic vote in the English boroughs, wanted to treat them as a special case. Among Nonconformists, however, there remained an acute dislike and distrust of Roman Catholics. They were most suspicious of any hint of a bargain with the Catholics on education, and Liberal candidates who wanted to woo Irish voters by favouring special treatment for Catholic schools risked losing Nonconformist support.[16] Rather than alienate the Nonconformists, the Liberal leaders never raised the issue. This preference for burying differences over religious education made good electoral sense; however, it stored up many problems for Liberal education policy from 1906–14.

Clearly the Liberal leaders would risk nothing that might arouse the suspicions and dampen the ardour of their Nonconformist supporters. This limited the possibilities of an arrangement on behalf of those Free Fooders who could contest seats which Liberals might not win. In a letter to Clifford, James Bryce tried to impress upon him that the Nonconformist cause could not possibly benefit by letting in protectionists who were less sound on education than the Free Fooders and who would always oppose a Liberal government. The response of the Nonconformist leaders, however, was uncompromising. In addition to opposing sectarian tests for teachers and supporting popular control of the schools, a candidate must oppose clerical right of entry in school hours if he expected full Nonconformist support.[17]

Gladstone continued to do what he could to help individual Free Fooders. Only six were left unopposed in their old constituencies. Three of these crossed the floor and ran as Liberals, two of them holding their seats in 1906. Of the remaining three, only one was victorious, and he proved so unsatisfactory that the Liberals successfully opposed him in January 1910. Even a man like A. Cameron Corbett of Glasgow (Tradeston), who was an active temperance reformer as well as a free trader, continued to be opposed (unsuccessfully) until he crossed the floor and ran as a Liberal in December 1910. New seats were found for three other Unionist MPs who had crossed the floor. Winston Churchill at North-West Manchester, Ivor Guest at Cardiff and J. B. Seely at Liverpool (Abercromby) all were placed in business constituencies with large middle-class populations in the hope of winning the votes of Unionist free traders. In the end, however, little could be done for the Unionist Free Traders because most of them would not promise to support a Liberal government.

Incorporating New Issues

By 1904 the Liberals were confident that they would win the general election. With Chamberlain's campaign for tariff reform finally falling flat, they could see opportunities for making heavy gains in the Unionist strongholds of Lancashire and Western Scotland. In an assessment of Liberal prospects in 442 English constituencies drawn up in February 1904, Gladstone estimated that the Liberals had some chance of winning 298 seats, while only 123 were deemed certain losses.[18] Given the party's traditional strength in Wales and Scotland, victory seemed assured. As a result, the Liberal leaders could cease to harp on protection in their speeches and begin to deal with a broad range of issues in a massive indictment of the record of the government.

The Liberal leaders were especially intent upon demonstrating that they had positive alternatives to tariff reform. First and foremost, Chamberlain was arguing that a prosperous British economy required protection for British industry. Liberals believed that many of the problems of British industry would be solved if the wasteful use of economic resources was ended. In a speech at Cambridge on 21 November 1904, Asquith argued that

> the most serious burden upon the industry of Great Britain ... [was] the enormous and progressive increase in what the State took, and was taking, by taxation and by borrowing out of the pockets of the people of this country ... if a Liberal Government came into power, the first duty they set before themselves would be a reduction in the country's expenditures ... it would mean a great lightening of the burden lying upon every productive industry in this country.[19]

Retrenchment appealed to the party's rank and file, who had been raised in the Gladstonian political tradition. It did not, however, match Chamberlain's appeal to the working class with promises of greater employment and more money to finance social reforms.

The keystone to Liberal social policy was land reform. The landlord had been a Liberal enemy for generations. All Liberals believed that 'the land question is at the bottom of all social questions and social wrongs' in the country.[20] The first step in the Liberal land programme was to stop the decline of rural England. Liberals believed that security of tenure and compensation for improvements for the farmer would encourage a more efficient and entrepreneurial agriculture which could offer more employment. Furthermore, by giving local authorities greater power to purchase land for small holdings and workers' cottages, they hoped to improve the condition of the rural labourer and stop the drift of the population to the cities. Only by cutting off the supply of excess labour at its source could urban overcrowding be relieved. A second Liberal prerequisite for ending overcrowding was to rate land rather than buildings. The present policy, they argued, encouraged landlords to leave lots vacant and to allow existing housing to become delapidated. To compound the inequity, the market value of urban land had increased enormously during the past thirty years of urban growth. Since the tenant paid the rate on buildings, the landlord had profited from the enterprise of the community while contributing nothing in return.

The Liberal solution to these urban problems was the rating of land values. Once improvements were no longer taxed, there would be no advantage in leaving land vacant or allowing houses to run down. If, in addition, municipal authorities had greater powers to acquire land for housing and rapid transit systems, the working-class housing market could expand to the point where rents would be reduced and congestion would be relieved. The rating of land would also shift the tax burden from the 'hard-working' labourer and entrepreneur to the landlord, who Liberals believed did nothing for his income. Finally, it would provide local government with a new source of revenue. Similarly, the taxation of land values would give the national Exchequer new money with which to finance social reform. Land reform thus offered an ideal alternative to tariff reform. It embodied a comprehensive programme to improve conditions among the rural and urban working classes, provide money for social reform, and relieve the burden on entrepreneurship, all at the expense of the privileged landlord.[21]

The Liberal leaders did not give land reform the prominence which its advocates desired. When the Unionist government further alienated important segments of the electorate in 1904, the Liberals did not wish to divert attention to their own policies. One of the most egregious electoral blunders of Balfour's government was to authorize the use of indentured Chinese labour in the Rand mines. The Chinese were to be bound to remain in the Transvaal for a fixed number of years and then to return home. While in South Africa, they were to be segregated in their own compounds, and their movement was to be severely restricted. The government hoped to revitalize the Transvaal economy with cheap labour, while avoiding a permanent Chinese migration to South Africa and minimizing contact between the Chinese and other races while they were there.

The Chinese Labour Ordinance seemed to confirm the worst charges of the pro-Boers. Liberals saw an alien race being imported into South Africa in near servitude at the behest of greedy Rand capitalists. Worse still, the Chinese were being forced to live in conditions which Liberals feared would inevitably lead to 'moral degradation' (which meant homosexual activity). The Nonconformist conscience, which had been divided over farm-burning and concentration camps, now came down with full force in condemnation of 'Chinese slavery'.[22] Even more dangerous to the government, the working class was outraged by this challenge to free white labour in South Africa. Opponents of the government did not hesitate to imply that the same means might be used to combat trade unionism and high wages in Great Britain.[23] The Liberal leaders also argued that the Chinese would replace white labour in South Africa, limiting the opportunities for white immigrants and hindering its development as a white man's country. This argument echoed what was being said by the most articulate spokesmen of the working class.[24] The Chinese labour issue thus gave fresh impetus to the Liberal revival by offending both the party's Nonconformist and its working-class constituencies.

Temperance reform stood with land reform at the foundation of Liberal social policy. Nonconformists in particular saw the traffic in alcohol as the source of much of the social evil in the country. As the *Examiner* argued in a 21 January 1904 leader,

> No careful observer can doubt that drink is the curse of this country and a most serious menace to our national prosperity. Every judge can tell us that it is the one fruitful cause of immorality and crime, and every social observer knows that nine-tenths of the distress and poverty that we see around us may be put down to its door.

The promoter of all this evil was 'the trade', which, the *Methodist Recorder* suggested on 21 November 1901, 'has secured a place of influence, amounting as many think to the balance of power, side by side with the King, the House of Lords, the House of Commons, the Church, and the Press'. Innocent women and children were not the only victims of the trade. Liberals also believed that the economy suffered, for money was wasted on drink which could have been used to buy the goods of productive industries. Thus, the trade was merely the most outrageous example of a vested interest, protected by the Conservative Party, retaining a privileged position which was antipathetic to the welfare of the community at large. The Liberals' solution to the problem was as characteristic as their analysis: give each community the power to determine if it wanted to support this evil. Local option would put control of the trade where it belonged – in the hands of the people. By a two-thirds majority, they should be able to vote to suppress all licenses in their district. Few Liberals appear to have doubted that the people would exercise this option responsibly and choose to suppress the evil within their midst.

Temperance reform, like education and land reform, was a venerable article of the Liberal faith. A generation spent converting the Liberal Party reached fruition when local option, as part of the Newcastle Programme, received the blessing of William Gladstone in 1891. Sir William Harcourt even placed it at the forefront of his campaign in the 1895 general election. Following his humiliating defeat, however, local option came to be regarded as an election liability equalled only by Home Rule. In 1898 Herbert Gladstone, in a speech to his constituents in West Leeds, repudiated it as unattainable and unfair. He urged instead a more moderate temperance policy based on reducing the number of public houses (with compensation to those dispossessed) and the more severe punishment of offences of drunkenness.[25] A year later, Sir John Austin, the Liberal member for the Osgoldcross division of Yorkshire, having been censured by his

Liberal association for voting against a Scottish Local Option Bill, resigned his seat and ran for reelection. He defeated his Liberal opponent, a temperance enthusiast, by a vote of 5,818 to 2,893. The party clearly was ripe for a modification of its temperance policy.

In 1899 a Royal Commission on liquor licenses confirmed the enormity of the evils caused by drink. The Minority Report, which was signed by the chairman of the commission, Viscount Peel, recommended a statutory reduction of licenses. The reductions would be carried out over a period of seven years, with compensation being paid to the holders of suppressed licenses as a matter of grace rather than of right. The funds for compensation would come from a levy on remaining license-holders, whose licenses would have increased in value as a result of the reduction. The local licensing authority, which would be partially elected, would have complete control over all licenses, as well as the power to shorten hours of sale and enforce Sunday closing. Following the seven-year period, local option would automatically be introduced in Scotland and Wales. England, however, was not considered ripe for local option, so its introduction would be left to the discretion of the local licensing authorities. No compensation would be paid for licenses suppressed after the seven-year period.

The Peel Report provided a basis for practical temperance legislation which all but the most extreme Liberals and Nonconformists could support and work for. In two speeches in November 1899 Campbell-Bannerman urged its acceptance on all temperance reformers. On 7 December, a statement signed by nearly every leading temperance reformer was published in the press. The signatories assumed that Campbell-Bannerman was committing the next Liberal government to legislation along the lines of the Peel Report, and on that basis they commended 'to Temperance electors the policy it embodies as worthy of their support at the next General Election'.[26] Sir Wilfred Lawson and the most extreme members of the United Kingdom Alliance, however, could not support any policy which did not include local option for England. In a 21 December reply to a letter from Lawson, Campbell-Bannerman expressed what was undoubtedly the consensus opinion among Liberals: 'From my point of view it appears wiser to put all our strength into carrying what can be accomplished at once ... I must honestly say I am weary of doing nothing in order to attain perfection.'[27]

For the next four years, peace reigned in the temperance movement. The calculations of Liberals and temperance reformers were upset, however, by the Unionist government's Licensing Bill of 1904. While there was no legal obligation to pay compensation for a suppressed license, all but temperance enthusiasts felt that the licensee should be compensated as a matter of equity. The Bill introduced by Balfour in 1904 provided for the payment of compensation for licenses not renewed from a fund levied on remaining license-holders. Balfour's Bill, however, included no time limit, thus establishing an indefinite legal right to compensation. Liberals viewed this as the creation of a new vested interest of license-holders and, since most licenses were held by tied houses, a fresh endowment of the trade by the Conservative Party. At the same time, the Bill's proposal to transfer discretion on licensing from the local magistrates to the Quarter Sessions further removed regulation of licenses from public control.

Once again Liberals saw the interest of the community being sacrificed to serve a privileged group. The full force of Liberal and Nonconformist opinion, however, already had been mobilized against the government. A significant exception was the Wesleyan Methodists, who had been divided in their response to the Education Bill. The Wesleyans had a long-standing commitment to temperance reform, and their opposition to the Licensing Bill appears to have been unqualified.[28] Thus, after 1904 official Wesleyanism could join the opposition to the government with a unanimity which hitherto had not been possible.

With the right to compensation legally recognized, future temperance legislation first would have to amend the Licensing Act of 1904. This strengthened the position of the moderates, for an immediate local option bill was now impossible. The Peel Report also disappeared from official Liberal thinking about temperance reform. Instead, the Liberal leaders formulated a more general temperance policy based on a time limit for compensation and restoration of control over licenses to the local licensing authorities.[29] Thus, the Liberal leaders followed the same line on licensing which they had already adopted towards education – limiting their policy statements to general principles upon which most reformers were agreed, while saying as little as possible about legislative details.

By 1905 the Liberal programme for the next general election was before the public. It was grounded in a comprehensive indictment of the Unionist government. The principal features of the Liberal attack were familiar – the defence of free trade; reform of the Education and Licensing Acts, of the systems of land tenure and taxation, and of Irish government; an end to Chinese labour; and the need for retrenchment. Enthusiasm in the country remained high. When Balfour resigned in December, Campbell-Bannerman decided to accept office rather than risk damping this fighting spirit of the rank and file. He launched the general election campaign on 21 December before an enthusiastic audience at the Albert Hall. The speech contained no surprises, being a restatement of the themes the Liberal leaders had been dwelling upon for the past year. On 4 January 1906, the Free Church Council issued a manifesto adopting a position on education, temperance and Chinese labour which could only be taken as an endorsement of the Liberals. Liberal candidates focused their campaign on these same issues in order to maximize the support of the Nonconformist and Liberal activists. The issues most frequently mentioned in Liberal election addresses were the defence of free trade (in 98 per cent of the addresses), amendment of the Education Act (86 per cent), reform of Irish government (78 per cent), amendment of the Licensing Act (78 per cent), Chinese labour (75 per cent), and general criticism of the performance of the Tory government (70 per cent).[30]

Free trade was clearly the issue with most universal appeal. In conjunction with the assurance that there would be no Home Rule Bill, the threat of protection allowed large numbers of Unionists to vote Liberal or to abstain. This helped give the Liberals unexpected victories in traditional Tory strongholds such as Lancashire and Southeast England. At the same time, the Education Act of 1902, with the 1904 Licensing Act and the Chinese Labour Ordinance, mobilized militant Nonconformity in the constituencies on a scale unknown since the Bulgarian agitation of the 1870s. Local Free Church Councils canvassed on behalf of Liberal candidates, Nonconformist ministers chaired Liberal meetings, and intensive speaking tours were carried out in every region of the country by the Free Church leaders. Their reward for all this work was the new House of Commons. Approximately 185 Nonconformists were returned (compared with the 109 who were elected in 1900), including 30 passive resisters.[31]

The Nonconformist political revival[32] was crucial in assuring that intensity of commitment by the Liberal rank and file which was necessary to win elections. Even it would not have been sufficient, however, if the Liberal Party had not been able to garner the working-class vote. The formation of the Labour Representation Committee in 1900 threatened to divide the labour vote from liberalism. It was this division, rather than the one between little-Englanders and Liberal Imperialists, which posed a fundamental threat to the survival of the Liberal Party.

4

The Progressive Alliance

Liberals had long thought of themselves as the party of the working class. According to their analysis, the Conservative Party stood for the interests of the landlords, the Church, the trade and other vested interests, while theirs represented the interest of the community as a whole – including the working class. One of Chamberlain's goals in promoting the new radicalism had been to strengthen the ties of the working class to the Liberal Party. Liberals believed their concern for the working class was reflected in the Newcastle Programme, which they perceived to embody a policy of social reform. This judgement of the Newcastle Programme was later revised by some of the Liberal Imperialist leaders. They feared their party was no longer attracting the working-class voter, and one of their objectives in trying to 'modernize' liberalism was to reestablish the party's commitment to social reform.

As further evidence of their party's concern for the interests of labour, Liberals pointed to the presence since 1874 of working-class MPs in the parliamentary party. There were from nine to eleven of these so-called Lib-Labs in the House of Commons between 1885 and 1895, mostly from mining constituencies. By 1895, however, there seemed to be little prospect of this number increasing significantly. Most working men could not afford either the cost of a parliamentary election or the lost income if they were successful. The miners' MPs were supported by their union. Without such external support, a working-class candidate was not likely to be nominated by local Liberal associations. With money problems of their own, the constituency organizations were looking for candidates who would contribute to their treasuries, not make further demands upon them. Furthermore, the middle-class Nonconformists who dominated the local parties were not very sympathetic to working-class candidates. They thought business or legal experience was more relevant to the management of the affairs of a commercial nation. As a result, in the English Liberal heartland of the East Midlands, West Riding of Yorkshire and North-East, only óne Lib-Lab had a safe seat outside of the mining areas – Henry Broadhurst in Leicester. There were no Lib-Labs at all in Scotland, and only one miner in Wales.

Given the Liberal Party's heavy dependence on the working-class vote, it could face a serious crisis should workers cease to be content to be represented by men of the middle class. Signs of dissatisfaction began to emerge in the 1890s, and in 1900 the Labour Representation Committee (LRC) was formed to secure the election of labour MPs who would be independent of the Liberal Party. A concerted challenge by the LRC could be a disaster for the Liberals. By splitting the working-class vote, it could allow normally safe seats to fall to the Unionists, as the second Leicester seat did in 1900. The alternative seemed to be to turn over some seats to LRC candidates. Local Liberal parties, however, would not easily yield seats which they held or had a good chance of winning. They would be all the more reluctant to yield seats to a party which stood for class representation and which included socialists who proclaimed their hostility to the Liberal Party. Thus, two problems confronted Campbell-Bannerman and Herbert Gladstone as they faced the challenge of the LRC. The first was to try to prevent a confrontation between the new organization and the Liberal Party in parliamentary elections. The second was to assure that the Liberals remained a party of social reform which could appeal to working-class voters.

THE CHALLENGE OF INDEPENDENT LABOUR

In 1893 the Independent Labour Party (ILP) was founded to promote working-class candidates independent of the Liberal Party. The ILP was socialist, but its socialism was not revolutionary. Instead, it was based on a belief in the solidarity of a working class whose interest was distinct from the interests of other classes. Rooted in Nonconformist humanitarianism, it sought to promote legislation to relieve the poor and improve the conditions of life and work for labourers. The founder of the ILP was James Keir Hardie, a Scottish miner who had served as an independent Labour MP for South West Ham from 1892–5. Hardie recognized that no independent political labour movement could thrive without the financial support of the trade unions. Years of effort were rewarded when the LRC was formed in 1900. The LRC was an alliance of affiliated trade unions and socialist organizations like the ILP and the Fabian Society. The LRC was not socialist; it had no programme. Its job was to secure the election of MPs who would promote the interests of labour. These MPs would organize, like the Irish Nationalists, as an independent party prepared to work with whichever of the major parties would support legislation of concern to the working class.[1]

The formation of the LRC focused Liberal attention on the question of working-class representation. Liberals disliked a party based on class. The view that labour had definable interests which were opposed to those of capital, and thus needed promotion in Parliament, challenged the Liberal belief that Parliament should promote the interests of society as a whole rather than those of any section. Although Liberals conceded that it was desirable that more working men should be elected to Parliament, they would not admit that class alone was a justifiable criterion for selecting a candidate. They especially feared that working-class MPs paid by their trade unions would act as delegates for particular interest groups rather than as independent representatives of the constituencies which they had been elected to serve.

Liberals also could see no need for a working-class party. The Liberal Party was a proven instrument of social reform; therefore, any step which weakened it would retard the cause of progress. The proper course for working people, Liberals argued, was to work through the representative organizations of the Liberal Party in the constituencies. There they could put forward their claims for labour representation and their views on policy, to be weighed in accordance with what would best promote the progressive reforms which they all desired. Even socialists should work with Liberals to secure agreed measures of practical reform rather than promote unattainable policies which were far in advance of public opinion. The tone of the leading articles which urged these views was not hostile; rather, it implied that those with long political experience needed to explain political realities to novices.[2]

This attitude of patient instruction was severely tested, however, whenever independent Labour candidates opposed Liberals in parliamentary elections. Whenever a Unionist won a three-cornered contest on a minority vote, Liberals were convinced that the seat would have been theirs had it not been for Labour intervention. For this reason, Liberals wanted the two sides to consult to determine which had a better chance of winning a given seat. Often, however, the LRC candidate was first in the field, thus leaving local Liberals with the choice of giving him a free run or risking losing the seat to the Tories. As a result of such tactics, although the Liberals of South-West Manchester did not run a candidate in the 1900 general election, the local Liberal association refused to endorse the LRC candidate. Similarly, when Philip Snowden of the ILP contested a by-election at Wakefield in March 1902, the *Leeds and Yorkshire Mercury* supported the Wakefield Liberals' refusal to endorse a candidate who was thrust upon the constituency by an outside organization rather than put forward by the local electors. The *Mercury* argued that, until the ILP showed 'a disposition to give and take in the matter of Labour representation, Mr. Keir Hardie is entitled neither to claim nor to have

Liberal support for the candidates of the party of which he is the political boss'.[3]

While local Liberals resisted the claims of independent labour, the official leadership adopted a more conciliatory attitude. Herbert Gladstone had done what he could to avoid three-cornered contests in the general election of 1900. His greatest success had been to persuade Derby Liberals to adopt only one candidate, giving a free run to Richard Bell, the secretary of the Amalgamated Society of Railway Servants. Bell and the Liberal Sir Thomas Roe had finished at the top of the poll, and the Derby arrangement became a model for other two-member constituencies. Gladstone also began the difficult task of convincing Liberals in the constituencies to be more receptive to the claims of independent labour. In speeches at Leeds in October 1901 and at Bristol in May 1902 he expressed his desire to make an arrangement with the LRC. This conciliatory attitude was supported by the two most influential organs of advanced liberalism – the *Daily News* and the *Manchester Guardian*.

The difference between the party's leadership and the rank and file concerning working-class representation became acute when, in June 1902, Sir Ughtred Kay-Shuttleworth was given a peerage, thus vacating his seat in the Clitheroe division of Lancashire. The Clitheroe division was dominated by cotton weaving towns. The cotton unions recently had affiliated to the LRC. The Clitheroe vacancy provided the traditionally Conservative spinners of the Manchester region and the traditionally Liberal weavers of northern Lancashire with their first opportunity to join forces to secure the election of one of their leaders as an independent Labour MP. The man they selected was David Shackleton, vice-president of the United Textile Factory Workers Association. Shackleton, a Nonconformist, had in the 1880s been active in the Accrington Liberal Association. In 1900 he had been invited by the Darwen division Liberals to contest the seat, but he had declined.

On 3 July, the Clitheroe Liberal Council unanimously invited Philip Stanhope, the former MP for Burnley, to contest the seat. Stanhope would not run without trade union support; therefore, when Shackleton was officially adopted, Stanhope declined the Council's invitation. Although both Gladstone and Campbell-Bannerman urged that it was in the interest of the party for Clitheroe Liberals to unite behind Shackleton, the local executive was determined to fight. Only when no candidate could be found who would risk alienating labour did it recommend that Shackleton be allowed a free run. The Association, however, opposed the recommendation, with only six members voting for it, and it asked its president to run. With his refusal, there was no one left to carry the Liberal standard. Once it was determined that there would be no Liberal candidate, the Conservative also decided to stand aside, and Shackleton was returned unopposed.[4]

Liberal opinion was not satisfied with the Clitheroe result. The local press was furious with Shuttleworth and the national leadership for preventing a fight. Elsewhere, there was a feeling of annoyance with the LRC. The *Leicester Daily Mercury*, in a leader on 19 July 1902, regretted that Shackleton had not been adopted by a conference of all sections of the 'Progressive party':

> Mr. Shackleton's friends take up a dictatorial attitude . . . Some of them, at any rate, appear to think that the Liberal organization should just stand aside, although it was under its auspices that previous victories for the Progressive cause were gained . . . Such an attitude is neither reasonable nor sagacious. It is tantamount to saying that at the bidding of a section, Liberals should throw over their organization, if not their principles, and enrol themselves under another in which they will have no voice. There is no democracy in that kind of thing.

Throughout the summer of 1902 the *Daily Mercury* attacked the undemocratic principles upon which the LRC was organized and the sectional nature of independent working-class representation. It argued that an MP should be elected as the representative of a community, not an interest, and that he should be chosen on the basis of character and ability, not class. As far as Liberal opinion was concerned, the LRC remained contrary to the principles of liberalism.

The Clitheroe by-election merely served to reinforce Gladstone's conviction that some sort of accommodation should be reached with the LRC. There was no discernible reason why a trade unionist like Shackleton, whose sympathies were Liberal and who represented the dominant trade of the region, should not receive unreserved Liberal support. Gladstone agreed with the Liberals in the constituencies that the LRC merely represented an advanced section of the Liberal Party. His conclusion, however, was different from theirs: they should accept independent Labour, for it represented no threat to liberalism.[5] Gladstone also believed that the Liberals could not afford the luxury of standing aloof from Labour. By early 1903, LRC membership had grown to nearly 850,000, more than double what it had been in June 1901. More important still, at its annual conference at Newcastle in February, the LRC created a parliamentary fund to help pay election expenses of candidates and provide salaries for those members who were elected. The fund gave the executive of the LRC a means of preventing local alliances with Liberal associations and thus assuring its independence of the Liberal Party. The LRC seemed to be preparing for a limited electoral assault which could only hurt the Liberals by splitting the working-class vote.

On 6 March Jesse Herbert, the man responsible for candidatures at the LCA, and Ramsay MacDonald, secretary of the LRC, met to discuss an arrangement. Both Keir Hardie and Campbell-Bannerman knew that their lieutenants were working for an agreement, but otherwise it was a well-kept secret. The LRC demanded absolute independence for its candidates; it did not desire Liberal Party approval of them nor of their principles. It asked that the LCA work to assure that LRC candidates were not opposed by official Liberals. If the Liberals insisted upon confrontation, the LRC threatened to oppose Liberal candidates whether or not there was a Labour candidate in the field. Liberals could not dismiss such a threat. They knew they could no longer take the working-class vote for granted. Herbert feared that, if LRC influence were used against them, the Liberals could lose most borough seats as well as many of the county divisions of Lancashire and Yorkshire.[6]

There were positive arguments for accommodation as well. MacDonald shrewdly emphasized both the strong liberal sympathies of most LRC candidates and the probability that, once in Parliament, they would usually support a Liberal government. Herbert believed (incorrectly) that the LRC had an election fund of £100,000 and that the Liberal Party fund would be saved about £15,000 if an agreement were reached. He believed that the LRC could win ten seats from the government and use its influence in other constituencies on behalf of Liberal candidates. Most important of all, Herbert believed, would be 'the effect upon the public mind of a conviction that the Liberal Party will win the Election, a conviction which will prevail everywhere when it is seen that the Labour Party and the Liberal Party are no longer fighting each other'.[7]

A week later, Gladstone embodied in a memorandum his understanding of what an agreement would involve. The key would be to secure for some thirty Labour candidates and twelve miners' candidates an open field against the Unionist opposition. To make such an agreement effective, the LCA would use all its influence on the constituencies involved to assure the Labour candidates a free run. If, however, a local Liberal association insisted upon running a candidate, the LCA would have to support that candidate. Thus, in theory, the autonomy of the constituencies was to be maintained.[8]

The discussions of 6 March did not result in a formal understanding. Gladstone recognized that local Liberals must be persuaded to accept independent Labour candidates if any such arrangements were to work. In May he made new efforts to encourage co-operation in the constituencies. In a letter to a correspondent published on 2 May 1903 he argued.

> I do not see why a candidate of character and capacity, who is ready to support all the leading proposals in which Liberals are interested, should

be objected to on the ground that he calls himself a Labour, and not a Liberal candidate ... If a candidate can stand the reasonable tests which Liberal electors may apply to them in respect to their views, I sincerely hope that our party will be sufficiently large-minded to secure the substance of what they want, and refrain from looking too much to adjectives and names.[9]

Two weeks later, Gladstone repeated the case for co-operation in a speech to Liberal secretaries and agents at the annual meeting of the NLF.

Gladstone's problems in the constituencies were well illustrated by the effort to secure MacDonald a free run in Leicester – an obvious prerequisite before any agreement could be concluded. Leicester had an active ILP which had secured as many as four seats on the town council by 1899. After MacDonald's intervention in 1900 cost the Liberals one of the parliamentary seats, those in favour of progressive co-operation captured the party. Negotiations with the ILP reached an impasse, however, when the Liberals insisted that the sitting Lib-Lab Henry Broadhurst should be the Labour candidate. The ILP proceeded to adopt MacDonald. If the Liberals wanted an agreement, they would have to nominate the working-class Broadhurst or dump him for a businessman replacement. The Liberals' initial preference was to run two candidates. No prominent outsider, however, would touch the nomination with a Labour candidate in the field. When left with the alternative of accepting MacDonald or supporting Sir Israel Hart, a local clothier and staunch opponent of progressive co-operation, the Leicester Liberals accepted the inevitable and nominated only Broadhurst.[10] Two days later, on 6 September, Herbert and Mac-Donald formalized an agreement based upon the terms discussed the previous March. The Liberals would try to secure a free run for LRC candidates in designated constituencies, while the LRC would encourage working-class support of Liberals elsewhere.[11]

THE PROBLEMS OF PROGRESSIVE CO-OPERATION

The Liberal leaders were not alone in having to persuade their rank and file to abide by an agreement. Hardie and MacDonald were faced with two problems. The first was to retain the allegiance of their socialist left-wing. These activists were anti-Liberal in their rhetoric and acutely suspicious of the least hint of an alliance between Liberal and Labour. Secondly, the Labour leaders wanted to gain as much support as possible among Conservative working men. For both of these reasons, it was absolutely essential that the LRC insist upon its complete independence of the Liberal Party.

Liberals resented both socialist hostility and Labour's insistence on independence. Their idea of a proper arrangement was that arrived at for the industrial regions of North Staffordshire. Enoch Edwards, the leader of the Staffordshire miners, was adopted as a Lib-Lab candidate for Hanley, which he had unsuccessfully contested in 1900. At the same time, when John Ward, the founder and secretary of the Navvies Union, agreed to place his name before the executive committee of the Stoke Liberal Association and abide by its decision, he was also adopted as a Lib-Lab candidate. By May 1903, both Ward and Edwards were supporting Liberal candidates in the region, as well as efforts to organize a Shropshire Liberal federation.[12]

If an acceptable Labour candidate insisted upon running independently of the Liberal Party, then Liberals believed there should at least be complete co-operation between the two wings of progressivism to secure his return. The Woolwich by-election of March 1903 was taken as a model for what such co-operation could achieve. Woolwich had been a solidly Tory seat, since many of the workers at the arsenal voted Conservative. By 1903, however, co-operation between the radical clubs and progressives on the one hand and the trade unionists and socialists on the other was commonplace in local elections. As a result, when Will Crooks was nominated as the Labour candidate for the by-election, he received the support of the London Liberal Federation. Several Liberal MPs spoke for him, members of the local radical clubs worked for his return and the *Daily News* collected £844 towards his election expenses. The result was an astounding victory for Crooks, converting a Tory majority of 2,800 in 1895 to a Labour majority of 3,200. Liberals insisted that the victory demonstrated the power of Liberals and Labour working together as a united progressive force.[13] They continued to believe that the only way for the working class to increase its parliamentary representation was with the help of the Liberal Party.

The by-election for the Barnard Castle division of Durham in July 1903 was crucial in forcing Liberals to come to terms with labour independence. Arthur Henderson, the Labour candidate, had been a Liberal in politics for most of his adult life. Not only had he been the sitting Liberal's election agent for seven years, but he had been active in local politics as well. Henderson had the support of the traditionally Liberal Barnard Castle miners; however, when he declined to allow his name to be submitted to the Barnard Castle Liberal Association, the majority decided to oppose him. Their candidate was Hubert Beaumont, a son of Lord Allendale, a former MP for Northumberland and an important landowner of the region. Beaumont had the support of Samuel Storey, the president of the Northern Liberal Federation, who was an opponent of independent working-class representation.

A three-cornered fight in Barnard Castle was considered a disaster by official liberalism. J. M. Paulton, the member for the neighbouring Bishop Auckland division and an honorary secretary of the Liberal League, had written to Gladstone as early as 14 April that Beaumont's candidature must be resisted: 'It would have the worst possible effect on the working-class electorate and lay the Liberal Association and the Party open to the charge of active hostility to Labour interests in the case of a Labour candidate already in the field.'[14] When the incumbent Sir Joseph Pease died on 23 June, precipitating a by-election, influential Northern Liberals, like J. A. Pease and Arnold Rowntree, increased the pressure on Beaumont to withdraw.[15] The Barnard Castle Liberals, however, were determined to contest the seat, and they were getting plenty of outside encouragment. The Liberal election agent at Clitheroe, for example, wrote the chairman of Beaumont's election committee urging him to fight. He claimed that the Clitheroe organization was falling apart as a result of their failure to contest the 1902 by-election. Furthermore, while some of his staunchest activists were talking about supporting the Tories, Labour was more arrogant than ever in its refusal to consider co-operation. Similarly, the presidents of nineteen Liberal associations in the Northern Counties wrote to Storey in support of his refusal to abandon Beaumont.[16] There was clearly a strong feeling among the rank and file that the time had come to stand up to the pretensions of Labour.

Barnard Castle, however, was not the right place for resistance. Henderson's local standing and liberal credentials were too strong. His popularity with the miners increased when he promised to support all miners' candidates at the next general election. Even worse, in the first by-election since Chamberlain had made his proposals for tariff reform, both Beaumont and Storey were weak in their commitment to free trade. Henderson was supported by much of the influential Liberal and Nonconformist press, while neither Gladstone nor Campbell-Bannerman endorsed Beaumont. The result was that Henderson defeated his Conservative opponent by 47 votes, with Beaumont finishing a further 561 votes behind.[17]

Many Liberals were chastened by the Barnard Castle result. The *Leicester Daily Post*, which had blamed Henderson for the division of the progressive forces, concluded after the election:

> It is useless to ignore the fact that the Labour party has got to be reckoned with. Its claims to representation are admitted, and they must be conceded. For reasons of their own, they are determined to act independently of either political party – Liberal or Tory. At the same time they recognise that they are more likely to be in agreement with Liberal ideals than with those of the other party ... Some sort of understanding in order to prevent a waste of forces ought not, therefore, to be difficult of attainment.[18]

Such a conclusion, however, was by no means unanimous. The *Leeds and Yorkshire Mercury*, which for some time had been waging a vigorous campaign against the ILP, represented a different current of Liberal opinion. As early as 19 June the *Mercury* had supported the Liberal decision to contest the seat. While recognizing Henderson's liberal credentials, it argued that to support him 'would simply be unconditional surrender to the Keir Hardie extremists, who have captured the Labour Representation Committee, and are directing its policy of absolute independence'. Thereafter, it never wavered in its support of Beaumont. On the eve of the election, the writer of its 'London Letter' attacked the 'pusillanimous individuals who preside at the Liberal head-quarters' and those 'chicken-hearted Members who, desperately scared lest the I.L.P. bogey should appear in their own constituencies, have been afraid to come to his [Beaumont's] assistance'. After the returns, the *Mercury* concluded that the example of the Barnard Castle Liberals would have to be followed,

> unless Liberal Associations and Liberal electors are to be content to surrender their cause to those who, whilst professing their readiness to support Liberal measures, are bound by a pledge to have nothing to do with the Liberal party or with Liberal candidates.

On 28 July it noted that others were using the Barnard Castle result as an argument for closer Liberal–Labour co-operation. The *Mercury* argued, however,

> that if the advice as to an understanding between Liberals and Labour is to have any effect, it can only be when Liberals have succeeded in showing the Labour Representation Committee that they cannot be hustled out of the way and treated as of no account.

The extent of such anti-Labour sentiment in the Liberal Party became manifest after the Norwich by-election in January 1904. The borough had been represented since 1895 by two popular local Conservatives, and in 1900 the Liberals had not even bothered to contest the seats. By 1903 the Liberal Party and the LRC each had nominated one man to run at the next general election. Louis Tillett was a solicitor and the leader of the Norwich Liberals; George Roberts was a member of the Typographers' Union and the ILP and president of the Norwich Trades Council. When Sir Harry Bullard died in December 1903, both men announced their candidature for the vacancy. Not only were local Liberals solid in their support for Tillett, but this time they were supported by the national leadership and the *Daily News*. Labour, on the other hand, was divided. As a result, Tillett won the three-cornered contest handily, polling more than 6,000 above Roberts's paltry total of 2,440.

Liberals were elated by the Norwich results. At last they had demonstrated conclusively that Labour candidates must have Liberal votes to win. More importantly, as Gladstone told Walter Runciman, Norwich would put the ILP in its place.[19] The hostility of Norwich Liberals to the ILP, with its policy of 'smashing the Liberal Party', came to the surface following the by-election. The ILP, the *Eastern Daily Press* claimed on 18 January 1904, 'has no more right to describe itself as the Labour [Party] than any other score or so of irresponsible and unrepresentative persons, coming together as an association, would have'. The executive of the Norwich Liberal Association followed by affirming its willingness to support a Labour candidate for the second seat – if he were nominated by a representative meeting of Norwich trade unions (including those not associated with the LRC) and approved by the Liberal executive. In response, Roberts gradually became more conciliatory. His speeches were friendlier as he made clear his desire for Liberal support. More important still, he indicated that his own followers would be free to vote for Tillett. Finally, on 3 March 1905, the Norwich Liberals confirmed their decision not to contest the second seat.[20]

The political reality revealed by the Norwich by-election was not the only force for moderation influencing ILP candidates. The Trades Union Congress (TUC) insisted on endorsing all candidates favourable to a reversal of the Taff Vale decision of 1901 which had found that trade unions could be sued for damages resulting from strikes. Most such candidates were Liberals. On 15 February 1905 representatives of the TUC and the LRC reached an agreement. The TUC promised to support all LRC candidates (which it had failed to do at the Norwich by-election), while the LRC would support all TUC candidates (including Lib-Labs) in so far as its constitution permitted. Furthermore, when there was no Labour candidate in the field, the LRC would make it clear to its supporters that independence did not mean abstention, thus encouraging them to vote for the more progressive candidate.[21]

The Liberals in turn finally began to accept Labour independence. As they admitted, they had been arguing all along that there was little difference on questions of policy between Liberals and Labour. Since both represented sections of one progressive force which would necessarily act together in the House of Commons, what did it matter if the labour men preferred to organize as an independent party? The behaviour of the new Labour MPs – Henderson, Crooks and Shackleton – reassured Liberals on this score. Although there continued to be suspicion of socialists who insisted upon attacking the Liberal Party as reactionary, the Liberals were becoming convinced that it was the moderate trade unionists rather than the ILP which dominated the LRC and the labour movement.[22] Thus, at last, the arguments which

Herbert Gladstone had been preaching since 1901 were being accepted by some among the rank and file in the constituencies.

If the progressive alliance was to be effective, however, it was not sufficient to have a working arrangement between the Liberal Party and the LRC. The Miners' Federation of Great Britain, the largest trade union in the country, had refused to affiliate with the LRC. The leaders of the miners in Northumberland, Durham, Yorkshire and South Wales all had sat in the House of Commons since 1885 or before, and they remained loyal to the Liberal alliance. On the other hand, the ILP had made some headway among the younger generation of miners. As a result, the pressure increased for more seats so that the miners' representation would more closely reflect their voting strength.[23] The North-East, the West Riding of Yorkshire and South Wales, however, all were Liberal strongholds, and the local Liberal associations were reluctant to turn safe Liberal seats over to the miners.

In Durham and Yorkshire, the union leaders joined with the Liberals to resist the claims of radical sections of the unions. In Yorkshire they were successful. The miners got only one new seat which, like the one they already had, would be contested by a Liberal official of the Yorkshire Miners' Association. In Durham, however, two members of the ILP were chosen to run with John Wilson, the Liberal leader of the Durham miners, while J. W. Taylor, the miners' candidate for the Chester-le-Street division, faced Liberal opposition. In South Wales, relations between the Liberals and the miners were even worse. Gladstone had great difficulty persuading local Liberals to adopt working-class candidates. West Monmouthshire Liberals adopted a miners' candidate by a vote of only sixty-two to fifty-one, while South Glamorganshire Liberals protested an LCA arbitration decision in favour of a miner. At Brecknockshire and Gower, moreover, Liberals insisted upon running their own candidates, in the latter case reversing an earlier decision to support the miner.[24] Thus, despite the theoretical alliance between the miners and the Liberal Party, relations in the constituencies were strained as the two vied for seats which the Liberals previously had controlled with miners' votes.

The problems of the miners reflected a continued reluctance by Liberals in areas where the party was strong to hand seats over to Labour candidates. The difficulties in Durham, for example, resulted from the persistent objection of North-East Liberals to independent Labour. Their resistance was unchecked by the failure at Barnard Castle and required enormous pressure by the LCA to overcome. Even so, two of the six LRC candidates in the region faced Liberal opposition in 1906, as did the LRC miner in Chester-le-Street. The West Riding of Yorkshire proved even more difficult. This area was the home of the ILP. As a result, local Liberals had never shown much sympathy for a progressive alliance. Hostility in Leeds intensified when Labour launched a concerted attack on Liberal as well as Conservative seats on the city council, increasing its representation from one in 1903 to seven in 1905. For their part, Leeds Liberals did everything possible to find a candidate to oppose Labour's James O'Grady in East Leeds, and Gladstone, himself a Leeds MP, did little to discourage them. Labour was equally militant, desiring to oppose Gladstone in West Leeds and J. Lawson Walton in South Leeds. In the end, pressure from MacDonald saved Gladstone from opposition, while Gladstone refused to come up with any money to assist a local Liberal who was prepared to run against O'Grady.[25] Even so, of the eight West Riding seats contested by the LRC in 1906, five also had Liberal candidates.

While Gladstone often had difficulty with local Liberal associations that had no interest in co-operating with Labour, his influence over prospective candidates was greater. They were most reluctant to act contrary to the wishes of the Chief Whip, who, if they were defeated, could recommend them to promising or hopeless constituencies on the basis of past co-operation. Liberal candidates also feared that if they opposed an official Labour candidate, the LRC would work against them in any future election they might contest. Similarly, Liberal candidates and MPs alike refused to speak for colleagues who opposed Labour candidates for fear of alienating the working-class voters in their own constituencies. For example, the Liberals of the Gorton division of Lancashire were prepared to support E. F. G. Hatch, the Unionist Free Trader who had represented the constituency since 1895, against John Hodge of the Steel Smelters. When, however, Hatch discovered that none of the candidates for the adjoining constituencies would support him, he chose instead to give up the seat.[26]

The regions where the Liberals traditionally had been weak presented Gladstone with fewer problems, for the advantages of co-operation were more obvious. In London, which contained sixty-one seats (including West Ham), the LRC was allotted only three. Liberals or Lib-Labs won thirty-nine of these seats in 1906, sixteen of which had not been won in any of the three previous general elections, and another fifteen of which had last been won in 1892. Labour fared better from the allocation in Lancashire–Cheshire, where it won thirteen seats in 1906. The Liberals also did well, winning forty-one of the region's total of seventy seats. Twenty-one of these had been lost in the three previous elections, while another seven were last won in 1892.[27] Overall, the progressive alliance clearly enabled the Liberals to make enormous gains in regions previously dominated by the Unionists. There was a second benefit for the Liberals from the progressive alliance. Liberals faced LRC opponents in twenty-five contests and independent socialists in thirteen others. Unionists won seven of the former and two of the latter on a minority vote. There probably would have been more such losses without the co-operation of the two parties of the left.

The labour movement also did well as a result of progressive co-operation. The LRC won thirty seats of the fifty-six which it contested. In addition, sixteen miners were returned, thirteen of whom were not connected with the LRC. Finally, twelve Lib-Labs who were not miners were returned. Thus, the working class was represented by fifty-five MPs in the new Parliament. The LCA considered the result a complete vindication of its deal with Labour. Only six of the new LRC members had been opposed by Liberals. All Lib-Lab candidates won, and none faced LRC opposition. Only one miners' candidate was defeated – by a Liberal. On the other hand, only seven of the twenty-six unsuccessful LRC candidates were given a free run, while all thirteen independent socialist candidates were defeated in three-cornered contests. Liberal support clearly was crucial to the impressive labour returns.

The general election of 1906 resulted in one of the most devastating landslides in British history. The Liberals won 400 seats – a gain of 216 over their total in 1900. They had a majority of 130 over all other parties combined. If, as usually would be the case, the 83 Irish Nationalist and 30 Labour MPs voted with the Liberals, they would have a majority of 356 over the 157 Unionists. Such a victory was possible because all of the party's forces were united and enthusiastically behind the liberal cause. The myth of a fundamental schism over external affairs had been buried. Nonconformity was united and organized to work for the return of Liberal (and Labour) candidates. Both of these factors helped to galvanize the party activists and secure for the party the quantity and quality of constituency work which was the prerequisite for electoral success. At the same time, the leaders undertook the necessary work of negotiation and compromise to assure the allegiance of the other components of the liberal alliance. They found a means to shelve Home Rule while securing an unambiguous endorsement from the Irish Nationalist leaders. Finally, the progressive alliance mobilized the working-class vote behind the parties of the left more effectively than ever before.

To keep this coalition together, the new Liberal government would have to satisfy the different interests. The Nonconformists would require legislation on education and temperance. The Irish would require the end of coercion and an administrative measure leading towards Home Rule. The working class would require social reform.

LIBERALISM AND SOCIAL REFORM

For Liberals, the progressive alliance was more than a convenient electoral arrangement over paliamentary seats. It was also an expression of a common commitment to social reform. Beginning in the 1880s, Liberals, like everyone else, had become increasingly aware of the social problems in the nation's cities. In response, Liberals at all levels were coming to accept, as Augustine Birrell told an Edinburgh audience in 1905, state intervention 'on a large and national scale for the benefit of the unsuccessful and for those who started life at grievous disadvantage'.[28] Liberals saw nothing in this more flexible attitude towards the role of the state which was inconsistent with their traditional principles. They believed that the history of liberalism was evidence of the party's ability to absorb new progressive viewpoints as the problems facing government changed. Because liberalism had proved its ability to evolve with the times, Liberals urged the political labour movement to join with them now to enact practical measures of social reform. It made no difference, the *Eastern Weekly Press* argued on 10 June 1905, if Labour and Liberals had a different vision for society in the future.

> The notion that there are certain ultimate things about which Liberalism and Labour will sooner or later disagree in action because they do not at present altogether agree in theory about them, leaves out of account that Liberalism is not a stagnant opinion, but a flowing stream – the expression of the Progressive idea ... It will cease to be Liberalism when it ceases to be progressive and becomes fixed.

Despite such Liberal claims, there *was* a gulf which divided them from Labour which, although difficult to document, was real. It was identifiable in the patronizing tone which Liberals often adopted when they told workers where their best interest lay, or when they praised the character and quality of the working-class MPs. It was revealed in the indifference of most of the English working class to all organized religion. The Nonconformists were acutely aware of the predominantly middle-class atmosphere of their churches. Yet they were never able either to mobilize the Nonconformist conscience in support of issues of social reform or to bring the working class within the fold of the Free Churches.[29] In short there was a communication problem between Liberals and workers resulting from a sense of superiority which made Liberals certain that they knew what was best for the working class as well as for society as a whole.

Even the Liberals recognized that there was a gap dividing them from the socialists. The ILP programme included a legal eight-hour day for all workers; the abolition of overtime and piecework; state provision for the sick, disabled and aged as well as for widows and orphans; the collective ownership of the land and of all the means of production, distribution and exchange; the provision of properly remunerated work for the unemployed; the abolition of indirect taxation; a graduated income tax and the taxation to extinction of all unearned income (interest as well as land values). No Liberal could endorse such a programme. Even among Liberal and Labour candidates during the 1906 general election, however, there was a clear difference of priorities. The four issues most frequently mentioned in Liberal election addresses were free trade and the reform of education, Irish government and licensing. The four issues most frequently mentioned in LRC election addresses were working-class representation, the reversal of Taff Vale, unemployment and old-age pensions. In addition, 67 per cent of LRC election addresses called for the socialization of property, 58 per cent for shorter working hours and 42 per cent for graduated taxation. None of these issues was mentioned by Liberal candidates.[30]

This difference of emphasis represented a genuine difference in the way most Liberals and Labour representatives thought about working-class problems. For years, for example, Liberals had resisted working-class representation as a matter of principle. They denied that class was a legitimate criterion for selecting a candidate and that class interests should be promoted in Parliament. This difference in approach was equally evident in Liberal thinking about the other three issues which were given priority by LRC candidates. Take first the legal position of trade unions. Liberals believed that trade unions, like other institutions which benefited from the protection of society, should be subject to legal penalties for actions contrary to the interests of society. No one wanted trade union funds collected for benevolent purposes to be liable; nor did anyone believe that unions should be responsible for unauthorized actions by individual members. Liberals proposed to separate the unions' benevolent funds from their strike funds. Then the laws of conspiracy and agency could be amended so as to punish the unions only when illegal actions resulted from authorized union policy. Although many Liberal candidates in the 1906 general election went further and favoured the reversal of Taff Vale, the Liberal press of Norwich, Leeds and Leicester did not adopt such a position. The consensus Liberal opinion remained that trade unions were necessary to assure orderly industrial relations, that the law should be amended to allow the trade unions to exercise their functions effectively and with discretion, but that it would be irresponsible to free the unions from all liability for their actions.

The Liberal attitude towards old-age pensions was considerably more ambiguous. Most Liberals were prepared to accept the aged poor as a class of people unable to help themselves and therefore meriting assistance from the state. Few worried any more about the effect pensions would have on the individual workman's diligence at his job or his incentives to thrift. Joseph Chamberlain's espousal of old-age pensions during the general election of 1895 had thrust the issue into the arena of partisan politics. Liberals emphasized the difficulty of providing a workable pension scheme. After the outbreak of the Boer War, they argued that it would be irresponsible to introduce pensions until the national finances had been straightened out so that the money could be assured.[31] Once Chamberlain tied the provision of old-age pensions to tariff revenues, however, it became impossible for a Liberal government to avoid grappling with the problem. As a result, by November 1905, the moderate and apolitical *Methodist Recorder* had joined the radical *Examiner* in calling for them. In the general election of 1906, 59 per cent of Liberal election addresses supported old-age pensions.[32] The Liberal Party, however, had done little to place itself in the vanguard of the movement prior to 1906. On the contrary, its dominant theme had been the difficulty of dealing with the problem.

The most important issue to the working class during the years following the Boer War was unemployment. With the recession of 1903–5, both of the major parties were forced to formulate an unemployment policy. Most Liberals no longer believed that all unemployment was due to defective character. They now recognized that, particularly in times of slack trade, large numbers of people could be thrown out of work through no fault of their own. At the same time, most Liberals agreed with the *Examiner* that there were 'plenty of people always ready to live on charity, and in consequence their right to live at all is questionable. We need sharply to apply the maxim, "He that will not work neither shall he eat. "'.[33] In formulating an unemployment policy, it always remained a primary concern of Liberals to separate these people from those who were legitimately unemployed. A second criterion of Liberal unemployment policy was that it could not interfere with the free working of the market economy. These two constraints helped to determine the kinds of proposals which would be acceptable to Liberals.

Leicester was a city in which unemployment was especially severe during these years. The *Leicester Daily Mercury* identified two problems – providing work for those temporarily unemployed and increasing the productive capacity of the nation to generate more permanent jobs. The first was the more difficult to deal with, for it involved recognition that the municipalities might have to supply jobs for those temporarily out of work. Any such programme, however, had to be carefully regulated if it were to achieve its purpose. Those employed by the municipality could not be paid more than a living wage, for this might serve to attract the lazy away from private industry. Also, it would be useless to supply jobs which competed with private industry, for that would merely throw other people out of work. By November 1904 the *Daily Mercury* was prepared to admit that public works need not be remunerative to be preferable to charity. None the less, most Liberals did not believe in making work which was not needed. The most common proposal before the country during these years was for farm colonies which would eventually prepare the workers to return to the land. This belief in the land also dominated Liberal thinking about the problem of increasing national productivity. Whether embodied in proposals to increase small holdings or in large programmes of public works, it was to the development of the land that they turned when searching for the means of generating new and permanent employment. The only alternative suggested was that a drastic reduction in expenditure on drink would divert consumption into other more productive industries, thus creating more jobs.[34] The ties to traditional liberalism could hardly be more evident.

Chamberlain's promise that protective tariffs would reduce unemployment forced the Liberal leaders to think about an unemployment policy. In December 1904 Herbert Gladstone sent a memorandum on the subject to Campbell-Bannerman, the main proposals of which he summarized in a speech to his West Leeds constituents on 5 December. Gladstone argued that, because the scale of unemployment during trade depressions was so severe, the localities were unable to deal with the problem unaided. He suggested that the government undertake large public works which eventually would prove remunerative to the national economy. These projects required such large outlays of capital, and the return was so long delayed, that private enterprise would not undertake them. Examples of such works included harbour, canal and road improvements; land reclamation; and afforestation. Work on such projects could be accelerated in periods of slack employment and slowed down or even halted when the economy had recovered.

Gladstone's memorandum was circulated to others among the leaders. Their response was a qualified endorsement. Campbell-Bannerman emphasized in a speech at Limehouse on 20 December that works undertaken merely for the purpose of giving employment could not be justified. If, however, they could be proved to be 'reproductive', then he believed such a scheme should be considered. James Bryce stressed that there could be no implication that the Liberals recognized an obligation on the part of the state to provide work. Sir Henry Fowler was fearful that the logical implication of Gladstone's proposals was national workshops, and the Chief Whip had to reassure him that he opposed involving the state in any projects which would compete with private industry. All agreed that the

81

difficulty and complexity of the problem meant it would have to be approached cautiously. Lord Spencer, Bryce and Campbell-Bannerman were inclined to turn to land reform, rating reform and an attack on vested interests and monopolies as the best means of dealing with unemployment on a permanent basis. Asquith asserted that the 'vast and profligate expenditure' of the government was the major cause of unemployment. The problem, he argued, could only be dealt with by ending economic extravagance and returning the nation to a system of sound and efficient finance.[35]

Clearly, the Liberal leaders, like the provincial press, were unwilling to do anything which might damage the private sector or involve the state in projects which could not be justified on economic grounds. This severely circumscribed their thinking about unemployment. In the end they could do little more than assert a general commitment to public works and traditional Liberal policies as the best means of attacking the problem.

Liberal thinking about unemployment was typical of the Liberal approach to social reform before 1906. It tended to be limited to the policies of the traditional Liberal programme. When Liberals approached new problems, possible solutions were subject to liberal tests concerning individual responsibility, financial economy, and not interfering with the free market system. The working class, however, was less and less receptive to the kinds of limitations which liberalism sought to impose. The LRC was one example of this, and Liberals did not altogether like it. They saw in the LRC much that was anti-liberal. It shunned co-operation with other progressives in the selection of candidates and the discussion of policy. This 'undemocratic' behaviour was all the worse because the LRC stood for class representation and class legislation. Indeed, the implicit basis of a working-class party was that, because the Liberal as well as the Conservative Party represented a class interest, the former could not protect the interests of labour. Liberalism vehemently repudiated any such suggestion, claiming to represent the interest of the community as a whole rather than any sectional interest. Worst of all, the LRC encompassed socialists who seemed to Liberals to threaten everything they valued. For the moment, the leaders were able to impose a progressive alliance because it was in their electoral interest to do so. Its long-run stability, however, would depend on two things. The Liberals would have to show greater imagination than they had thus far in developing policies which dealt with the matters of greatest concern to the working class. The leaders also still had much work to do to reconcile the party activists to co-operation with Labour.

5

Domestic Policies:
The Years of Disappointment
1906–1908

The first priorities of the new Liberal government were to pass education and temperance bills acceptable to the Nonconformists, and to make some attempt to satisfy the Irish Nationalists while Home Rule was in abeyance. In each case, however, the House of Lords blocked any legislation which would be satisfactory to these constituencies. At the same time, the government was reluctant to confront the House of Lords on these issues, although they had been central to the mandate which it had received in 1906. The government could not risk a showdown with the Lords because it could not be certain of the ardour of the Nonconformists, which had been crucial to the vitality of the constituency organizations in the triumph of 1906.

Many Nonconformists were disappointed with the government's efforts between 1906 and 1908 to redress their education grievances. In attempting to draft education legislation which would prove acceptable to the general public, ministers compromised on issues which their more extreme Nonconformist supporters considered matters of principle. Although the activists grudgingly accepted these compromises, their enthusiasm for the final bills was restrained. At the same time, the government's failure to challenge the Lords appeared weak, thus further discouraging the rank and file. The government's successful start towards implementing a social reform programme did little to revive their spirits. While the activists welcomed action to relieve poverty and satisfy the party's working-class constituency, these were not their primary concerns. As a result, by the end of 1908 the party was thoroughly demoralized and appeared headed for a debacle at the next general election.

THE CONFRONTATION OVER EDUCATION

In August 1903 the Liberal leaders had promised that the first obligation of a new Liberal government would be to introduce a new education bill. The man chosen by Campbell-Bannerman to head the

Board of Education was Augustine Birrell. Despite his Baptist upbring-ing, Birrell had little in common with the leaders of militant Noncon-formity. A man of ironic and detached good humour, he was incap-able of the fanatical devotion which drove the Nonconformist activists. Birrell was not unsympathetic to the Nonconformists' griev-ances over education. None the less, his more restrained temperament dictated that he devise a solution which was acceptable to their opponents as well.

The principal barrier to any education settlement continued to be religious education. Most of the Nonconformist rank and file opposed any concessions to either the Anglicans or the Catholics. Not only did they insist that any denominational instruction in former sectarian schools must be given outside school hours, but they also were determined that no exceptions should be allowed for Catholic schools. Birrell, on the other hand, believed that a final settlement would have to make a fair provision for denominational education. Initially, he proposed two concessions in return for bringing the denominational schools under public control. First, facilities for denominational instruction would be given not only in the former sectarian schools, but in the council schools as well. Second, the conditions pertaining to Bible teaching and denominational teaching would be the same. Both would be given either in or outside school hours. Birrell also proposed to give special treatment to Catholics. If four-fifths of the parents at a school in an urban area requested denominational teaching in a particular faith, such teaching might be given daily, at the discretion of the local education authority. Birrell expected that the local authorities would in fact grant the request and appoint only teachers of that faith to such a school.[1]

The risk involved in such a sweeping compromise was greater than the Cabinet was prepared to take. Most of Birrell's concessions to the Anglicans were eliminated for fear of provoking a Nonconformist rebellion comparable to that of 1870.[2] Under the Education Bill which was introduced in the House of Commons on 9 April, all sectarian schools in receipt of state aid were to be rented by local authorities during school hours. Twice a week the sects would be allowed to provide denominational instruction. This instruction, however, had to be given at the expense of the sect, and it could not be given by the regular teachers. Both denominational and Bible teaching were to be given outside school hours. The council schools continued to offer only non-denominational instruction, which was given at the expense of the state by regular teachers. Thus, Bible teaching continued to receive preferential treatment.

The reception of the Bill by Liberals and Nonconformists was generally friendly. It embodied the four major principles which they considered crucial to a settlement of the education question: a national system including all schools receiving state aid; complete popular control of public elementary schools; no religious tests for teachers; Bible teaching to be given at all schools. Inevitably there were reservations, but only one was of major importance – that concerning the special provisions for Roman Catholic schools. Whereas the Cabinet had eliminated Birrell's proposals for conciliating the Anglicans, those for conciliating the Catholics had been left untouched and were embodied in Clause 4 of the Bill. The Liberal and Nonconformist press reluctantly accepted Clause 4 as a generous concession to assure fair treatment for Catholics. The Catholic hierarchy, however, would accept the Bill only if Clause 4 were made mandatory upon the local education authorities. The removal of this last vestige of popular control was intolerable to Nonconformists. If the Catholics were not satisfied with Clause 4, they said, let it be eliminated so that the Bill could be made consistent with democratic principles. Dr Clifford threatened 'that if Clause 4 was allowed to remain in the Bill, the Government could not rely upon the continued support of the large Nonconformist section of the Liberal party.'[3] Thus, while the Education Bill continued to be viewed by many Liberals and Nonconformists as fair and statesmanlike, parts of it were opposed by those militant Nonconformists who had been at the forefront of the education agitation of 1902–5. Their hostility to all government attempts to conciliate clericalism was merely increased when the House of Lords transformed the Bill into a comprehensive endowment of denominationalism.

Birrell, on the other hand, argued that 'a great, almost an heroic, effort should be made to save this Bill'.[4] By 12 December an agreement was reached with the Catholics. Its effect would be to make it easier for schools to qualify for special treatment – a provision which would benefit the Anglicans as well. All teachers appointed to such schools by the local authority had to be approved by a parents' committee. The government also sought to effect a compromise with the Anglicans over religious instruction in Church schools that did not qualify for special treatment. Negotiations finally foundered over the question of whether regular teachers should be allowed to volunteer to give denominational instruction in those schools. Campbell-Bannerman rightly believed that his followers would not accept concessions on the issue.[5] As a result, on 17 December the House of Lords insisted on its amendments, thus killing the Bill.

As the institutional embodiment of the privileges which Liberals were sworn to destroy, the House of Lords long had been a target of Liberal invective. Liberal dislike was accentuated by the partisan nature of the Upper House. Of the 602 peers who were eligible to sit there in 1906, only 88 were even nominally Liberals.[6] This imbalance had made a mockery of the Lords' supposed function as a revising chamber. At least since 1892 it had acted on purely party lines, and a call for 'mending or ending' it had been included in the Newcastle Programme of 1891. The issue had remained dormant during ten years of Unionist government, but the Lords' actions in 1906 gave it new immediacy. Besides blocking the Education Bill, they vetoed a Plural Voting Bill and significantly altered several lesser bills. Clearly the constitutional position of the House of Lords had to be modified if two-party government was to be a reality. Yet, according to Lloyd George, when the Cabinet met to consider the question after the withdrawal of the Education Bill, only he and Grey favoured an immediate dissolution.[7]

With their enormous majority, the Liberals surely would have won such an election. The by-elections indicated that the government's popularity was holding up quite well. The Cabinet, however, had no policy for dealing with the House of Lords. This meant that any election would have to be fought solely on the Education Bill. The problem facing the government was that its most enthusiastic supporters hated the Bill. The concessions which had been wrung from the Cabinet by its opponents had left both Nonconformists and Liberals disillusioned. Thus, the news that the Education Bill had been withdrawn was unanimously welcomed. Typical was the response of the *Leicester Daily Mercury* on 20 December 1906:

> We confess to no regret at the death of the Education Bill . . . Their Bill as originally drafted did not satisfy those who regard education from the educational standpoint, as distinct from the merely sectarian; by their concessions they so whittled away the best part of the scheme that it had become a poor, attenuated thing, whose demise we can regard with composure.

Yet even as they proclaimed their dissatisfaction with the Education Bill, these same Liberals and Nonconformists welcomed its death as a prelude to a confrontation with the House of Lords. They could not see that their indifference or hostility to the Bill rendered such a confrontation impossible. At the same time, the government's procrastination in proceeding against the Lords merely served to accentuate further the disillusionment created by its education policy. The Liberal rank and file were ready for a fight, and they wanted a clear lead from the government for immediate action.

The government was, in fact, soon engaged in formulating a plan for dealing with the House of Lords. In March 1907 a Cabinet committee proposed that when the two Houses could not agree on a measure, the deadlock should be resolved by a joint sitting of the House of Commons and 100 representatives of the House of Lords.

Campbell-Bannerman, however, persuaded his doubtful colleagues to adopt the 'suspensory veto' instead. This embodied the principle that a measure passed in three successive sessions by the House of Commons should become law despite amendment or veto by the House of Lords.[8] It is likely that Campbell-Bannerman feared the party would not accept a proposal which did not assure the ultimate supremacy of the Commons when the two Houses came into conflict, whatever the size of the Liberal majority. On 24 June, Campbell-Bannerman explained the details of the government's proposals to the House of Commons. Liberals considered them fair and even moderate, but they expected immediate action against the Lords. There is no evidence, however, that the government ever intended further action, and with fresh delays, discontent again set in.

The session of 1907 contributed to the growing impatience with the government. The principal measures of the session – the Irish Council Bill and the territorial army scheme – were of no great interest to the Nonconformists, and the licensing bill which had been promised was postponed until the next year. Most of all, Nonconformists lost patience with the government's halting education policy. They dismissed as wholly inadequate a bill intended to end passive resistance by taking sectarian teaching off the rates. The bill required sectarian schools to return to the local education authorities one-fifteenth of the salaries of all teachers who had given denominational instruction. Nonconformists wanted no such partial measures. They wanted an education bill which did not compromise liberal principles. Then, if it were rejected by the House of Lords, they would be ready for a showdown with the Upper Chamber.[9]

The government dropped the Passive Resisters Bill in favour of a comprehensive education bill to be introduced in 1908. Still, it had to do something to demonstrate that it was prepared to satisfy Nonconformist demands. What they wanted, said Rev. Silvester Horne, the foremost spokesman for progressive Congregationalism, was 'a repudiation of the Balfourian principle that it is the business of the State to teach denominationalism at the public expense'.[10] This was the purpose of the new regulations to deal with Exchequer grants to teacher training colleges which were proposed by Reginald McKenna, who had replaced Birrell in early 1907. Most of these colleges were Anglican or Catholic, and 95 per cent of their funds came from the Exchequer. To continue to receive this money, the colleges now would have to make a conscience clause available to all students, freeing them from requirements to attend religious services or classes in religious instruction. No applicant, moreover, could be rejected solely on the grounds of his religion, and a procedure was defined to assure compliance. Liberals and Nonconformists were elated. Here, at last, was an affirmation of the principle that schools dependent upon public money must be accessible to students of all sects without imposing upon their consciences. The importance of these regulations for holding Nonconformist support was enormous, and McKenna was adamant in refusing to compromise with the Anglican Church.[11] Still, with both education and temperance bills due in 1908, the burden would be on the government to produce acceptable measures if it were to prevent the Nonconformist activists from retiring from the political arena in disgust.

SATISFYING THE IRISH

There was no more thankless task in British government than that of the Chief Secretary for Ireland. Campbell-Bannerman's choice of Chief Secretary was James Bryce. Although he was a man of great intellect and good political sense, Bryce lacked humour, imagination and a strong will. At least some of these qualities were essential if an Irish Secretary were to have any chance of success governing a people who wanted to govern themselves.

A dominating influence in the Irish Office was the permanent Under-Secretary, Sir Antony MacDonnell. MacDonnell's views had been shaped by his experience in the Indian civil service. He believed that efficient government in Ireland was impossible as long as the Irish parliamentary party retained its stranglehold on internal political affairs. He wanted to encourage a moderate party in Ireland, which meant breaking this Nationalist monopoly. The Nationalists, on the other hand, believed that the government should, as John Dillon wrote to Bryce, 'govern the country, so far as the present system allows, in accordance with Irish ideas – ascertaining those ideas from the representatives of the Majority of the Irish people'.[12] The debate within the Cabinet over the reform of Irish government in large part involved a struggle between the views of Dillon and MacDonnell, with Bryce initially taking the part of the latter and Birrell later siding with the former.

MacDonnell believed that the Irish Council which the Liberal government planned to create would enable the Irish to prove they could govern themselves. At the same time, as moderates rose to power in Irish administration, Unionists would have no more cause to fear Irish self-government. The immediate problem, then, was to frame a proposal which would be accepted by the Unionists and passed by the House of Lords. This meant that it had to be so moderate that it could in no way be mistaken for a form of Home Rule.

Bryce's initial proposals reflected these views. He recommended the

creation of a small Council which would be delegated limited administrative responsibilities. Bryce's preference was that one-third of the
Council should be appointed, while the remaining two-thirds would
be chosen by indirect elections. The Council would be granted an
annual sum fixed at five-year intervals with which to manage its
affairs, but any action on its part had to be approved by the Lord
Lieutenant. John Redmond and John Dillon, the leaders of the
Nationalists, could not accept these proposals. They were well aware
that MacDonnell wanted to break the power of their party. As Bryce
wrote Campbell-Bannerman on 8 October, Redmond 'conceives that
the creation of a new body in Ireland created irrespective of the
existing Irish members, would fatally reduce the importance of the
latter and practically deprive them of the power of criticizing most
branches of Irish administration'.[13] This fear determined the counter-
proposal which the Irish leaders submitted on 14 December:

> That the new Council should be formed of the Irish Members of the
> House of Commons, together with such a number of additional Members
> nominated by the Lord Lieutenant as will give the minority in Ireland a
> strong representation, while leaving a working majority to the repre-
> sentatives of the great majority of the Irish people ... [14]

The Nationalists apparently wanted a body which had the appearance
of a Home Rule parliament, and all their actions during the next six
months were directed towards approximating this ideal. When their
initial proposal was rejected, they pressed for direct elections to a large
Council using the parliamentary constituencies. These proposals were
supported by Birrell, who had replaced Bryce in January 1907. Mac-
Donnell, however, opposed them because he wanted to break up the
old spheres of influence which had been established in the existing
constituencies. The Cabinet went as far as it could in conciliating the
Nationalists. Although it altered some of the electoral districts, the
Council was drastically enlarged, and 82 of its 107 members would be
elected directly.[15]

  The Irish Council Bill was a fair attempt to reconcile Irish desires for
self-government with English suspicions of Home Rule. The Council
would be given administrative control of eight departments, including
local government, agriculture and education. It would be financed by
block grants from the Exchequer, and it would have complete freedom
in spending that money. It would have, however, neither legislative
nor taxing powers. At best, the Bill provided for Irish administration
more nearly according to Irish ideas, and on that basis it was supported by Liberals. This improvement was not sufficient for the
Nationalist leaders, who rejected it once they realized the extent of the
hostility of their followers. Liberal opinion was generous to the
Nationalists – endorsing Campbell-Bannerman's decision to withdraw

a Bill which was unacceptable to Irish opinion. The abortive Bill, however, contributed to the declining standing of the government with its own supporters. It stood as yet another example of the futility of timorous measures which attempted to satisfy their opponents rather than their friends.[16]

It is difficult to imagine that the Liberals could have produced any measure of Irish devolution short of Home Rule which the Nationalists could have accepted. The Irish leaders wanted a measure which had some of the trappings of Home Rule and which, because of its obviously temporary nature, would make Home Rule inevitable. Administrative devolution, however, had often been put forward by opponents of Irish nationalism as a substitute for Home Rule. The Nationalist leaders therefore proposed that the Irish MPs be constituted as the Council. Such a reform would give the Irish legislators constitutional recognition as the administration of Ireland. When this proposal was rejected as politically unacceptable for the Liberals, they could not accept a lesser Bill which might prove to be a barrier to Home Rule.

The failure of the Irish Council Bill weakened Redmond's position in Ireland. Recognizing the importance of strengthening Redmond's hand, Birrell turned to other measures desired by the Irish.[17] An immediate problem was land. In the congested districts in the West, the Land Act of 1903, providing for purchase by tenants, was ineffective because much of the land was pasture and thus untenanted. In 1907 a new agrarian agitation broke out, and enormous pressure was brought upon Birrell to introduce a coercion bill. The Chief Secretary refused. Instead, he introduced a bill, which was passed in 1909, giving the Congested Districts Board both the power and the money to purchase compulsorily most land – including grazing land – in the West for settlement by peasant proprietors.

Birrell's energies were also directed to resolving the problem of creating an Irish university. With their long-standing opposition to state endowment of sectarian education, neither Nonconformists nor Liberals could support the endowment of a university in Ireland unless it was 'subject to no religious tests, open to all, providing no endowment for theological chairs out of State funds, and under the control of a representative Senate'.[18] Birrell decided to resurrect a scheme first proposed by Haldane in 1899 which would create two new universities. One would consist of Queen's College Belfast, and the other would include the Queen's Colleges of Cork and Galway and a new teaching college in Dublin. While all colleges would be nonsectarian, their locations assured that the student body of Belfast would be predominantly Presbyterian, and that of the others would be predominantly Catholic. This would assure the Catholic atmosphere demanded by the Irish hierarchy. At the same time, although the university senates and the governing bodies of the constituent colleges were to be elected, all but Belfast would be dominated by Catholics and the Church if that was what the electors wanted. The Catholic hierarchy was satisfied with the measure and it passed in 1908 with little difficulty.[19]

Liberal opinion was enthusiastic in its support of a scheme which allowed the party to satisfy a major Irish demand without violating liberal principles. The Nonconformists were more doubtful. Many were less concerned with the *de jure* triumph of their nonsectarian principles than with the *de facto* triumph of the Catholic hierarchy in securing the endowment by the state of a university in which the Church would have a predominant voice. Undoubtedly, they were further disillusioned by the government's willingness to meet the demands of Irish Catholics on Irish education, while at the same time it refused to satisfy their own demands as to English education.[20]

Despite the triumph of the Irish University Bill, the Irish leaders faced an increasingly unruly party in 1908. With progress towards Home Rule impossible during the present Parliament, Redmond was subjected to pressure to take the Nationalists into opposition. By early 1909 he in turn was pressing Asquith to give a Home Rule pledge for the next general election if the Nationalists were to continue to support the government.[21] Thus, once more the Liberals were faced with the distinct possibility that Home Rule would have to be the priority item in their programme if they wanted Irish support. No other application of liberal principles to the government of Ireland could satisfy the demands of Irish nationalism.

Moving Towards a Crisis

Militant Liberals and Nonconformists had every reason to be impatient with the government as it entered upon its third year. After two years, virtually nothing had been done to resolve the education question along lines satisfactory to them. The licensing bill promised in 1907 had been postponed, and the Prime Minister had refused to commit himself to a timetable for Welsh disestablishment. Finally, the government had shown a want of decision in its policy towards the House of Lords. With the opening of the new year, the reaction began to set in – a reaction which was intensified by a severe trade depression. In January 1908, the previously solid Liberal seat at Mid-Devon was lost to the Conservatives. Two weeks later the opposition regained the seat at South Hereford which it had lost in 1906. These two elections began a trend of Liberal reversals which was to persist throughout the remainder of the year.

The beginning of 1908 also brought a change in the party's leadership. Campbell-Bannerman had proved to be a successful leader of a Liberal majority which included over 200 new members. His willingness to give extremists ample opportunity to express their views had proved an appropriate means of maintaining the loyalty of his heterogeneous body of supporters. The Prime Minister's health, however, had been declining since the death of his wife in the summer of 1906. A severe heart attack at Bristol in November 1907 began the precipitous decline that was to end in his resignation on 5 April 1908 and his death some two weeks later.

At the time of his resignation, Campbell-Bannerman was undoubtedly the most popular man in his party. His strength as a leader was that he was a radical by conviction. As a result, he was trusted by the rank and file, who, like the *Eastern Daily Press*, recognized that 'Sir Henry Campbell-Bannerman is the best possible representative of the views and the policy of Mr. Gladstone.' Rev. Silvester Horne, following Campbell-Bannerman's death, expressed the same thought: 'He quickened old and noble convictions that had suffered loss. He saved from ignominy great watchwords of progress. Peace, retrenchment and reform became once again triumphant assets in political warfare.'[22] By contrast, Asquith, Campbell-Bannerman's successor, was suspect to radicals. This was due in part to his record during the Boer War and his association with Rosebery. More importantly, Asquith was a political pragmatist. The moderation and gift for statesmanlike compromise, which were his greatest assets among ordinary voters, made him an object of distrust for the radical and Nonconformist enthusiasts who viewed all compromise as a sacrifice of principle. Thus, during his first years as Prime Minister, Asquith had to win the confidence of his party activists.

The first order of business for the new Prime Minister was to redeem the promise to reverse the consequences of the Licensing Act of 1904. Most Liberals and Nonconformists were united in demanding a moderate bill which would restore local control of drinking establishments without attempting any form of prohibition. Even a moderate measure, however, created exceptional difficulties for a government which desired to be fair without overly straining the loyalties of temperance advocates. All agreed that, after a specified number of years, the rights of license-holders to compensation when their licenses were suppressed should cease, and all but the most extreme temperance reformers believed that the time limit should be generous. It was also agreed that, during the specified time period, there should be a reduction in the number of public houses by about one-third.

Discretion on licensing matters should be returned to the local licensing authorities. Finally, special provision should be made for local option in Wales. The purpose of these proposals was to end the vested interest of the license-holders in their licenses, to give to the local authorities a large amount of discretion in licensing matters, and to reduce the number of public houses in a way that would be fair to license-holders.

The issues that were most troublesome to the Cabinet committee drafting the bill were those which divided temperance reformers themselves. The principal questions were whether, at the expiration of the time period, any provision should be made either for the recovery of the monopoly value of licenses or for local option. The monopoly value was represented by the difference between the value of a public house and the value of the property when used for another purpose. A school of temperance reformers, led by Sir Thomas Whittaker, wanted all licenses to be granted annually at the end of the time period upon payment of the monopoly value. Representatives of the liquor trade objected that this amounted to the expropriation of their profits by the state. The supporters of local option also opposed the transfer of the monopoly value. They feared that, if localities were given a financial interest in the preservation of licenses, this would decrease the likelihood of their exercising the veto. Whittaker, on the other hand, believed that local option would be useless after the statutory reduction. He argued that the remaining public houses in a district would be sufficiently few in number and sufficiently high in quality that there would be little need to exercise the veto.[23]

Every tradition of liberal government dictated that the final bill should have included neither of these contentious policies. Both offered the enemies of temperance reform opportunities to portray the bill as vindictive, unfair and prohibitionist. Yet the Licensing Bill which Asquith introduced on 27 February 1908 provided for both the transfer of the monopoly value and local option at the end of the fourteen-year period. Most probably, Asquith did not expect the Bill to be passed by the House of Lords, however moderate its provisions. The best policy, therefore, was to deliver a bill which would be popular among the activists. In this he succeeded. Especially among the Nonconformists, the apathy and dissatisfaction which had been so evident in 1907 seem to have been checked.[24] A bill which even the United Kingdom Alliance could support with minor reservations, however, was not likely to be popular in the country. The by-election swing against the Liberals accelerated. Five more seats were lost in 1908, while Liberal candidates barely managed to hold such safe seats as South Leeds, Dewsbury and East Wolverhampton. Only in Scotland and Wales did the majorities of 1906 hold up.

The Cabinet was under no illusions as to the reception of the Bill in the country. Asquith repeatedly emphasized that no government courting popularity would have introduced it. At the same time, by introducing the Licensing Bill himself, taking charge of its management in the House of Commons, and using the language of traditional liberalism to defend it in the country, Asquith went a long way towards restoring his credit among the militants who had distrusted him.[25] Asquith needed all the leverage he could muster, for even as he was guiding the Licensing Bill through the House of Commons, he was preparing an education compromise which Campbell-Bannerman had refused to consider two years earlier.

With the prospect of a new education bill in 1908, Nonconformists and Liberals expected the government to forgo compromise and establish a national system of education with complete popular control and no religious tests, and with no exceptions. The Cabinet, however, was no more prepared to impose a bill which was unfair to the sectarian schools than it had been in 1906. The bill which McKenna introduced on 24 February required any school receiving rate aid to come under complete popular control and to impose no religious tests on teachers. All sectarian schools in single-school areas had to become part of the national system, in return for which they would be allowed facilities for denominational instruction three times a week. Such teaching would be paid for by the sects, would be outside school hours, and could not be given by the regular teachers. All other sectarian schools could contract out of the national system and receive Exchequer grants (but no rate aid).

The contracting-out clause in McKenna's Bill was nearly as controversial as Clause 4 of Birrell's Bill. Liberals accepted the Bill as a necessary compromise to resolve the education question. Nonconformists, however, accepted the contracting-out clause only with the greatest reluctance. They hated any scheme which allowed the denominational schools to continue to receive public money, and they insisted that no further financial aid should be given to schools which contracted out. They obviously hoped to use financial pressure to force Church schools to close down or enter the national system.[26]

Throughout the spring, the Cabinet received evidence that Liberals (and even Nonconformists) wanted the education issue settled.[27] As a result, when Walter Runciman replaced McKenna, he made a concerted effort to reach a compromise with the Archbishop of Canterbury. The settlement which they agreed upon in November gave enormous benefits to the Church. Denominational instruction in school hours could be given in all council schools as well as in transferred sectarian schools. All assistant teachers could volunteer to give denominational instruction, as could existing head teachers. Given these concessions, most Anglican schools were expected to come under public control. Nonconformist gains from the proposed compromise were also substantial. All schools in single-school districts were to be transferred, thus placing a public elementary school within reach of every child. Bible teaching was to be given in all public elementary schools at public expense, while all denominational instruction was to be given at the expense of the sects. All teachers were to be appointed by the local authorities free of religious tests.

Runciman had begun consulting some of the Nonconformist leaders in May. By July he had secured their agreement to substantial concessions. On 9 November a meeting of some 100 Nonconformist MPs voted in favour of proceeding with the negotiations along the lines Runciman outlined. When, however, Runciman had to demand further concessions – the end of all local control over sectarian entry into council schools and over the right of teachers to volunteer to give denominational instruction – the effect was to place an almost intolerable strain on Nonconformist loyalty. Those, like Silvester Horne, who were most eager for a settlement, went back on earlier statements and supported Runciman's Bill embodying the compromise, although without enthusiasm. Others, like John Clifford, reluctantly agreed to mute their opposition. Still, Runciman and J. A. Pease (the Liberal Chief Whip) believed that the Bill had to be rushed through Parliament as quickly as possible before the militants on *both* sides were able to mobilize their opposition.[28] They could not move quickly enough. First the Archbishop and then the Church Council undermined the settlement by demanding new concessions. Furthermore, all indications were that the militant Anglicans would block the Bill's passage through the House of Lords. So once again, the government was forced to withdraw its measure.

The failure of the education compromise further increased the tension between the government and its Nonconformist followers. As had been the case in 1906, the hostility of the latter to the concessions which had been extracted from them surfaced quickly once the prospects for a settlement collapsed. Once again, the futility of a policy of conciliation seemed to have been confirmed, and they were increasingly impatient with the government's insistence on pursuing such a course. The rejection of the Licensing Bill by the House of Lords just added to their sense of frustration. Their dissatisfaction was in no way mitigated by the government's progress in enacting a programme of social reform.

In Search of a Social Reform Policy

The Liberal government's social reform policy in December 1905 was the traditional Liberal programme of retrenchment and free trade, housing and land reform, and temperance reform. By 1906, however, Liberal intellectuals like J. A. Hobson and L. T. Hobhouse had gone a long way towards expanding upon the new liberalism of the 1880s so that it provided the basis for more radical social policies. Their views were being publicized among the rank and file by C. P. Scott of the *Manchester Guardian*, A. G. Gardiner of the *Daily News*, and (from 1907) H. W. Massingham of the *Nation*.

The ties between the new liberals and traditional radicals were strong, and their views of liberalism had much in common. New liberals, like traditional radicals, were committed to the promotion of individual liberty and equality of opportunity. For both, privilege, monopoly and class politics were the barriers to these goals, while liberalism represented the common good against such sectional and class interests. Both were also committed to free trade and the preservation of a capitalist system which rewarded effort and thus offered incentives to individual improvement. Both believed that reform was central to the purpose of liberalism, that reform should be gradual and practicable, and that reform policies should be designed so as to preserve character and encourage moral improvement. Furthermore, both accepted that reform policies might involve state interference with the rights of private property. Finally, both took the Gladstonian view that external policies should be guided by moral criteria.

The new liberalism offered an intellectual framework which justified government in going beyond the traditional liberal policies to achieve social reform. In place of an individualistic society, new liberals posited an organic society. Individual development, as it had been defined by the new liberals in the 1880s, remained the goal. This could not be achieved, however, merely by a selfish pursuit of one's own interest. Man could develop fully only if the society in which he lived developed fully. Thus, each member of society had an interest in the moral and material development of all other members. This meant that society had a responsibility to take whatever steps were necessary to assure each member the opportunity to develop to his full potential. Society especially could no longer accept the less desirable effects of a competitive economy – such as poverty, slums and unemployment – because these left many people unable to compete and thus unable to contribute fully to society. In taking steps to remove these blights, government would merely be promoting genuine equality of opportunity. It had a right to call on others to share the cost since all would benefit from a more prosperous society. In particular, it had the right to use wealth which was unearned or created by society to promote social goals.

To what degree was such thinking perceived to be socialism? New liberalism and socialism had emerged at the same time in the 1880s. Both embodied a humanitarian revulsion against poverty, a denial that poverty was the result of flaws in character rather than flaws in the economic and social systems, and a belief that the state must intervene to reduce and prevent poverty. There had been considerable interaction between some of the new liberals and Fabian socialists in the 1890s. The Boer War, however, had led these new liberals to reevaluate a socialism which could support imperialist aggression and to reject the anti-democratic Fabian vision of a bureaucratic state run by experts. They rejected even more firmly a Marxian analysis based upon class conflict and the goal of nationalizing the means of production, distribution and exchange. To them, the root of socialism was ethical and humanitarian, and its central message was that society had a responsibility for its members. They found such a socialism perfectly compatible with liberal principles of individual liberty, equality of opportunity, and reward for initiative.[29]

It is not clear to what extent the new liberalism influenced the Liberal Party's social policies. For the most part, the intellectuals who helped define the new liberalism were not in the vanguard in defining new policies.[30] None the less, they helped create a climate which insisted that the role of the Liberal Party was to legislate on behalf of the poor and that new policies needed to be developed for this purpose. Furthermore, they influenced a group of 'social radical' MPs who sought to put pressure on the government to introduce a programme of radical social reforms. These radicals, however, were never able to organize so as to mobilize their influence effectively. Thus, while they might muster fifty or sixty votes on a particular issue, their core of support in the Parliaments of 1906–14 was only twenty-five to thirty MPs.[31]

The 'social radicals' were obviously in the vanguard of the Liberal Party. The party's viability as an effective vehicle for protecting the interests of the poor and the working class, however, depended upon its ability to carry the rank and file with it in the pursuit of a new programme of social reform. The governments of 1906–8 were successful in achieving this. The rank and file generally were able to support the new social policies because government legislation was moderate in scope and justifiable in terms which were consistent with traditional liberalism.

Two major measures of social reform were passed in 1906. The Workmen's Compensation Act extended the Act of 1897 to new classes of workers, while enabling workers to claim compensation for industrial diseases. It was easily accepted, for it built on an existing measure which had proven itself. The provision of meals for school children was a more difficult matter. For several years, ILP leaders in the cities had been urging the local provision of meals. Liberals initially were hostile to this socialist campaign. During the 1900 School Board elections, the *Leicester Daily Mercury* of 1 December called the ILP proposals for free meals 'of very doubtful value'. It argued that 'children should not be pauperised in the schools', believing the parents 'to desire that they should fulfill their own responsibilities towards their off-spring.' The economic recession following the Boer War, however, gave Liberals cause to rethink the issue. Since many Liberals were prepared to admit that a worker could be unemployed through no fault of his own, they also had to concede that, without any implication of dereliction in performing his duty, he might be unable to feed his children adequately. Thus, subject always to the condition 'that adequate steps are taken to compel parents to do their duty by their offspring so long as they have the power', many Liberals by the end of 1904 had accepted the case for some municipal intervention in this area.[32] They did not, however, accept that such intervention should involve rate aid, which they believed would demoralize the self-respecting parents while encouraging the lazy and shiftless to shirk their responsibilities. For this reason, the *Leeds and Yorkshire Mercury* censured eleven Liberals on the Bradford City Council in December 1904 when they voted for a socialist motion to meet the cost of feeding underfed school children from the rates. The *Mercury* believed that these Liberals had failed to stand by their convictions on a 'vital principle'. Four days later the Bradford Liberal Association met and voted to ask Liberal councillors to press for a reversal of the vote. Following a twelve-hour debate at the next meeting of the Council, reversal was secured.[33]

When the new Parliament met in 1906, it remained the objective of the Labour and Lib-Lab MPs to remove all responsibility for the provision of meals from the Poor Law guardians. While many Liberals now admitted the need for legislation, they were not prepared to make the full resources of the community available, and they were determined that those parents who neglected their children should be 'called to account'.[34] Thus, the Act of 1906 was considerably more moderate than the bill introduced by the Labour Party. For example, whereas the Labour bill *required* local authorities to provide meals where a need was found to exist, the government measure was permissive. Also, whereas the Labour bill *allowed* the local authorities to recover the cost of the meals from the parents, the government required that they do so whenever possible. Finally, if a local authority chose to spend money from public sources to supply meals, the government limited the amount which it could spend in any year to the equivalent of a half-penny in the pound rate. The result of such changes was to assure that, despite the socialist and labour initiative in pressing for state action, the final measure was thoroughly liberal in conception and scope.[35]

The principal measure of social reform for the 1907 session was to have been the Licensing Bill. When this was postponed, the government was left with nothing. For social radicals, such inaction merely added to the disillusionment resulting from the government's unwillingness to confront the House of Lords. None the less, the government required neither the prodding of its more radical supporters nor the shock of two by-election losses to socialists in July to force it to proceed with a policy of social reform. With no programme to hand upon taking office, the Cabinet inevitably proceeded deliberately. Yet it *was* moving forward. In 1906 Herbert Gladstone, the Home Secretary, appointed a committee to inquire into the economic effects of an eight-hour day in the coal mines – the last step prior to the introduction of a government bill in 1908. Similarly, in 1907 Gladstone appointed a select committee to consider the best means of dealing with sweated industries – which would result in the government's bill of 1909. Most important of all, in his 1907 budget speech, Asquith, the Chancellor of the Exchequer, announced that he was providing the funds for old-age pensions, which would be introduced the following year.

By 1907 the momentum behind old-age pensions was enormous. Only unemployment was an issue of greater concern to working-class leaders, while over half the Liberal MPs elected in 1906 were pledged to support a pension scheme. Asquith, however, would make no promises as to when a measure would be introduced. As he told a TUC deputation in 1906, he did not have the funds, and he had 'no reasonable expectation' of possessing them. 'The only way', he concluded, 'by which this money can be obtained for this and other social reforms depends in the long run on our keeping down extravagance, by reducing the Debt, and by bringing the finances of the country into a sounder and healthier condition'. It was increasingly clear to the Treasury, however, that retrenchment alone could not supply all of the funds Asquith needed. Additional sources of revenue had to be found.[36]

The new government immediately appointed a select committee to investigate graduation of the income tax and the practicability of differentiation between earned and unearned income. The principle that taxes should be borne in proportion to the ability to pay had been applied to the death duties in Sir William Harcourt's 1894 Budget;

moreover, it was implicit in the abatements from incomes under £700 allowed under the income tax system. New liberals justified the taxation of unearned income at a higher rate than earned income because the former was produced by the growth of society rather than the effort of the individual; hence, the community had a right to claim for itself some portion of the return. In November 1906, the committee recommended the extension of abatements, the introduction of a super-tax on incomes over £5,000, and a differential rate for earned and unearned incomes. In his 1907 Budget, Asquith introduced only a reduction in the tax rate on earned income for those whose income was below £2,000. In addition, he increased the rate of graduation on death duties, and he introduced a super-tax on all estates worth over £1 million. This allowed him to set aside funds to help finance old-age pensions the next year.

Asquith's Budget created little excitement in the Liberal press. It welcomed the reduced rate on earned income as providing much needed tax relief to the middle class. Most of all, Liberals were pleased because Asquith was restoring order to the nation's finances by retrenchment. By March 1909 the government had reduced the debt by £41 million, taxation by £7.75 million, and expenditure on the army and navy by £5.6 million.[37] Liberals therefore could accept that the way had been prepared for a responsible scheme of old-age pensions.

There was no consensus among the supporters of pensions as to the most appropriate scheme. The Cabinet committee which drafted the government's proposals was principally concerned with cost, administrative simplicity and the incorporation of tests for character and thrift. A universal scheme was the simplest but would be prohibitively expensive. A contributory scheme would be the most economical and would assure thrift on the part of the recipient. It would, however, be extremely difficult to administer, and the poorest men and most women would be unable to participate. The government therefore settled on a limited, non-contributory scheme which would include some tests for thrift and character. Any man or woman seventy years of age or older who was not in receipt of an income exceeding 10s a week was to be entitled to a weekly pension of 5s (7s 6d for married couples). Everyone who received poor relief after 31 December 1907 was excluded. In addition, to assure industry on the part of the recipient, no person who 'has habitually failed to work according to his ability, opportunity, and need, for the maintenance of himself and those legally dependent upon him' would be eligible for a pension.[38] After amendment in committee, contribution for the ten years preceding the age of sixty to a provident fund sponsored by a friendly society or trade union was accepted as sufficient evidence of thrift and character. Other amendments in committee introduced a sliding scale, gave full pensions to married couples and limited the poor relief disability to 1908 and 1909.

In a speech at Nottingham on 11 December 1907 Asquith had impressed upon his audience

how necessary it was to proceed in this matter [of old-age pensions] step by step. The great thing was to start their plan on lines which were capable of development as time went on and experience increased, and when they were able to obtain a deeper insight into the necessities of the case than they could now when they were experimenting.

The Liberal press fully approved of this approach. Indeed, the press claimed that part of the greatness of the scheme was the ease with which it could be extended when money and understanding allowed. Nor were Liberals troubled by its non-contributory nature. They accepted that workers had earned their pensions by a lifetime of service to the community, and argued that the pensions would encourage rather than discourage thrift by supplementing the small savings which were the most that workers could accumulate.[39]

The Old-Age Pensions Act was a revolutionary piece of legislation. For the first time, the central government provided relief for the poor as a matter of right, with no taint of pauperism attached and no disabilities for those who received it. This dramatic change was initiated with a caution worthy of the oldest traditions of liberalism. Every reasonable precaution was taken to assure that the new measure would not place an undue burden on the nation's finances. Furthermore, while liberalism recognized the right of those who had served society by their years of labour to receive assistance from the state, that assistance was contingent upon a fairly stringent test of need and a less severe test of worthiness. Finally, the experimental nature of the measure was used as the principal justification for its modest extent.

Liberals had greater difficulty accepting a legal limitation on the hours of adult men who worked in the coal mines. To regulate hours was to intervene directly in the market economy, with results which seemed all too predictable. It was feared that the output of coal would be reduced, leading to an increase in its price. This in turn would increase the costs of all industries which used coal, rendering them less competitive on the international market. The cost of living of households also would be increased. Thus, a strong case could be made that the interest of the community would be sacrificed to the claims of one section for special treatment.

None the less, the Liberal Party had shown itself sympathetic to the case of the miners. For example, an Eight Hours Bill in 1893 was given a second reading, with 184 Liberals voting for it and only 36 voting against. How were Liberals able to justify supporting such a policy? Mining had long been subject to government regulation because it was an unusually dangerous, arduous and unhealthy trade. For the most part, however, Liberals who supported the measure responded to the economic arguments against it. They conceded that a restriction of hours could have an adverse effect on output, price and safety, but claimed that whatever dislocations occurred would be temporary, and that the increase in prices would be much smaller than their opponents predicted.[40] Yet they remained troubled by these considerations, and their concerns were reflected in the Act which was finally passed in 1908.

It was perhaps inevitable that the new Liberal government would take up the miners' cause. The Parliament of 1906 contained 119 Liberal or Labour members who at some time had voted for an eight hours bill, including most of the members of the government. Furthermore, the miners were Lib-Labs; the party needed to demonstrate that it could protect their interests. The minister responsible for the measure was the Home Secretary, Herbert Gladstone. Gladstone had proved himself politically as the architect of the landslide of 1906. He was a diffident person, and as a Cabinet minister he was more likely to see the political problems rather than possible solutions when considering legislation which affected powerful economic interests. Even though Gladstone's instincts were moderate, however, the Home Office achieved an impressive record of reform under his leadership – including the Workmen's Compensation Act, the Coal Mines (Eight Hours) Act, an extension of the Factory and Workshop Acts, and measures to reform the penal system, the system of juvenile detention, and the law relating to children.

The committee (chaired by the Liberal shipowner Russell Rea) which Gladstone appointed to assess the economic effects of an eight hours bill issued its report in 1907. It concluded that an eight-hour day 'cannot but result in a temporary contraction of output, and a consequent period of embarrassment and loss to the country at large'.[41] The Bill which Gladstone introduced into the House of Commons early in 1908 was intended to minimize that loss. Instead of the bank-to-bank bill favoured by the Miners' Federation of Great Britain (MFGB), it followed the Rea Committee by excluding one winding.[42] To give added flexibility to the mineowners, each miner could be asked to work up to sixty hours of overtime in a year. Finally, certain classes of workmen responsible for overseeing the safety of the mines were excluded from the Bill.

Even with these qualifications, Gladstone was not satisfied that the Bill adequately minimized the dangers either to the economy or to the men. He wanted to exclude the second winding, thus giving the average miner another half-hour underground. Gladstone therefore took the extraordinary step of inducing opposition to his own measure by industrial consumers of coal. In a 10 March Cabinet memorandum, he explained the reason for this action: 'This will go far to reassure the consumer that the Government have not imposed on the industry an arbitrary arrangement without proper regard to the conditions of the trade, and the general economic result of legislation.'[43] In effect, he wanted to reassure the public that both sides were being treated fairly and that its own interests were being protected.

As a result of Gladstone's action, the Coal Consumers' Defence League was formed. It immediately attacked the Bill in a manner which was likely to impress ordinary Liberals. At a 17 March protest demonstration, speakers stressed the damage that the Bill would do to the nation by increasing the price of coal and thus limiting trade. They criticized the government for risking the national welfare to satisfy a section of the community which was well able to take care of itself. With the additional leverage provided by the League, Gladstone was able to persuade Enoch Edwards, president of the MFGB, of the need to exclude the second winding. The result was an Act which the mineowners and leading Liberal industrialists could tolerate. Both groups thanked Gladstone for his firm action in resisting attempts to rush a bank-to-bank bill through the House of Commons without full consideration of its economic impact.[44]

The Coal Mines (Eight Hours) Act was difficult for many Liberals to accept. Some leading Liberal industrialists and businessmen remained opposed to the measure. During the report stage in December, ten Liberal MPs voted for a wrecking amendment. The measure also was given an ambiguous reception by the provincial press. While generally accepting the humanitarian argument that no one should have to spend more than eight hours underground, the editors were clearly troubled about the effects on the price of coal. Their support was hesitant, and, as in the case of the *Eastern Daily Press*, contradictory positions were adopted at different times.[45]

This uncertainty illustrates the constraints on Liberal thinking about social legislation. Such legislation was rooted in a humanitarian response to offensive conditions. The humanitarian argument, however, needed reinforcement from traditional liberal ideology. When, on the contrary, there appeared to be clear evidence that state interference would lead to economic dislocation, it was difficult for Liberals in good conscience to defend the legislation. Yet, a Liberal government with pretensions to promoting the well-being of the working class could hardly resist a measure which long had been supported by the TUC and the MFGB. It could only try to minimize the adverse effects on the economy in general and on the coal industry in particular. By keeping such experimental legislation cautious and carefully safeguarded, ministers hoped to reassure the public of their commitment to the general welfare of the community.

In any case, these social reform measures were not the primary concern of most Liberals at the end of 1908. They were delighted by the Old-Age Pensions Act, which quickly became the principal evidence of the party's commitment to the poor worker. Far more pervasive, however, was their frustration at the government's inability to implement its education and temperance policies. Worse still, a trade depression and the party's pitiable by-election performance presaged a revival of tariff reform as the Unionist solution to the nation's economic and social problems. If the Cabinet was to rekindle rank-and-file enthusiasm, it had to resolve the two issues which now were of principal concern: the defence of free trade and the power of the House of Lords to block measures which Liberals cared about the most.

6

Domestic Policies:
The Years of Achievement,
1909–1911

At the end of 1908, Liberals were discouraged, and the party appeared headed for electoral defeat. By the end of 1911 they were exhilarated, having won two general elections the year before. The Budget of 1909 was responsible for this transformation. First, it gave the government the resources to pay for a comprehensive programme of social reform: old-age pensions, trade boards, labour exchanges, a development fund, and health and unemployment insurance. This programme confirmed the expectations of most Liberals that their party could develop policies consistent with liberal principles which would meet the needs of poor and working men and women.

The Liberal rank and file recognized the importance of social reform to the electoral strength of their party, and they endorsed the government's policies as justification for continued working-class support. None the less, it was far more important to the party activists that the Budget offered a policy which dealt with traditional Liberal concerns. Most importantly, it appeared to provide a means for implementing Liberal land and licensing policies without the approval of the House of Lords. Even better, when the Lords rejected the Budget, the Liberals were able to end the absolute veto. Just as importantly, the Budget was the Liberals' answer to tariff reform. By proving that free-trade finance was sufficiently elastic to raise the funds needed for national defence and social reform, it was a decisive riposte to one argument for protection. These were the reasons the Budget revived the enthusiasm of the rank and file and enabled the Liberals and their allies to win both general elections in 1910. The new social reforms were an important, even a necessary corollary. They were not, however, what motivated the party activists who made the Liberal Party an effective fighting machine.

The People's Budget

The rejection of the Licensing Bill of 1908 merely increased rank-and-file impatience with the government's passivity before the provocations of the House of Lords. Yet the unpopularity of the Licensing Bill rendered an immediate dissolution impossible. Because all other legislative routes were obstructed by the Lords, the budget offered the only credible means for the government to fight back. It long had been accepted constitutional practice that the Lords could not amend a finance bill. Furthermore, some of the traditional Liberal policies which had been blocked by the Lords could be partially realized by taxation. A drastic increase in duties on licenses to sell liquor, for example, offered a means for the state to recover some of the monopoly value of the license. At the same time, it probably would drive many of the poorer public houses out of business.

More important still, the budget offered the means for the Liberals to launch their land programme. Some progress had been made already in enacting the Liberal land policy. A Land Tenure Act in 1906 had given English farmers greater compensation for improvements and for damage to crops by game, and greater freedom in determining how the land would be used. In 1907 a Small Holdings and Allotments Act had provided a means for encouraging, and even compelling, county councils to satisfy local demand for small holdings. On the other hand, in 1907 and 1908 the House of Lords had forced the government to drop two Scottish land bills.

A land valuation was the crucial first step for most Liberal land reformers. It was the prerequisite for the separate taxation of land values (the value of the site exclusive of improvements). Only then, they believed, could the monopoly of the landlords be broken and land be freed at fair prices for the benefit of the community. In the new parliament, 280 Liberal and Labour MPs joined the Land Values Group supporting the rating of land values. No English valuation bill was produced, however, because John Burns, who as President of the Local Government Board was the responsible minister, blocked separate site valuation. As a result, land reformers began to urge the inclusion of land taxes in the budget as a means of circumventing both Burns and a veto by the House of Lords.[1]

By the end of 1908 many Liberals were expecting the next budget to embody a strong challenge to the House of Lords. Asquith, who was well aware of the restlessness of his rank and file, announced the government's intention to launch such a challenge in a speech to some 200 Liberal MPs at the National Liberal Club on 11 December. It was not, however, the government's intention to frame a budget which the Lords would reject, thus provoking a crisis. While Asquith was fully cognizant of the possibility of a Lords veto, and warned J. A. Pease (the Chief Whip) that there could be a general election in July, no one expected them to use it. The budget was a means of circumventing a veto, not inducing one.[2]

The man responsible for framing the budget was David Lloyd George, whom Asquith had made Chancellor of the Exchequer upon his own succession to the premiership in April 1908. During the Boer War and the campaign against Balfour's Education Act, Lloyd George had proved himself a superb controversialist and *provocateur*. He understood the importance of the Liberal rank and file, and he used his gifts as a public speaker to rouse them as no one else could. None the less, his primary concern was to get things done. He was a staunch liberal in his desire to limit privilege (especially landed privilege), assist the poor, encourage industry and commerce, and satisfy Welsh grievances; however, he would consider any means of furthering those goals. Means were never matters of principle for Lloyd George. This willingness to compromise had enabled him to be a pragmatic, tactful and constructive President of the Board of Trade from 1906 to 1908. On the other hand, it might some day evoke the distrust of Liberal activists for whom means often were the embodiment of their principles.

Lloyd George was not going to accept defeat at the next general election as inevitable. Furthermore, he recognized that if the party's electoral fortunes were to be reversed, it must appeal to both the general public and the Liberal rank and file. The budget was the perfect instrument. It offered the basis for a broad appeal to the working class because more money was needed to pay for old-age pensions, as well as for the schemes of disability and unemployment insurance which he and Winston Churchill envisioned. At the same time, taxes on liquor licenses and land values would appeal to the party activists. Lloyd George's task was complicated in early 1909 by the need to find still more money to finance an accelerated naval building programme.[3] Such a programme would alienate some of the Liberal activists, although its probable effect on the general voter was less certain. In the end, Lloyd George sought to convert the naval estimates into an electoral asset with both constituencies by using them to justify the substantial increase in direct taxation and in graduation which were incorporated into the 1909 Budget.

There was considerable hostility in the Cabinet when Lloyd George presented his Budget proposals in March 1909. In part, his colleagues thought him ignorant and lazy because of his casual work habits, his indifference to detail and his unwillingness to read memoranda. Furthermore, Lloyd George jettisoned orthodox liberal finance by looking for ways to spend money so as to magnify the prospective deficit and justify all of his taxes. As a result, his colleagues distrusted him.[4] Asquith, however, was firm in his support. He agreed with the Budget proposals, which implemented reforms for which he had prepared the way as Chancellor of the Exchequer. His principal concern was to ensure that it was perceived to be fair. Thus, Lloyd George was forced to modify his land taxes, as Asquith told the King, 'with the object of minimising cases of possible hardship and safe-guarding existing contracts'. Similarly, Asquith assured Lewis Harcourt that he had told Lloyd George that there should be 'some toning down of the middle steps of the scale' for the death duties. On the other hand, Asquith supported Lloyd George in resisting efforts to have the land taxes dropped altogether.[5] Overall, the Prime Minister and political necessity assured that the Cabinet imposed no fundamental changes.

Lloyd George introduced the Budget in the House of Commons on 29 April. Most of the provisions he announced for meeting an anticipated deficit of £16 million involved adjustments in existing taxes. The most radical were his changes in direct taxation. Child allowances were introduced for incomes below £500; the tax rate on earned incomes below £5,000 was graduated; the tax rate on unearned incomes was raised; and a super-tax of 6d was introduced for all incomes over £5,000, charged on the amount over £3,000. The rate of graduation of the estate duty was steepened sharply, while the other death duties were increased. Finally, selected stamp duties were increased. The estimated increase in revenue from these changes was £7 million. The major change in indirect taxes was increases in the duties on beer, spirits and tobacco worth £3.5 million. The most controversial parts of the Budget were those designed to appeal to the Liberal rank and file. Lloyd George proposed a comprehensive revision of the rates for licenses to sell beer and spirits, as well as new duties on licenses for brewers and distillers. Licenses for public houses were fixed at 50 per cent of their annual value, subject to a minimum. Finally, four new land taxes were proposed: a 20 per cent tax on the increased value of land (the unearned increment) each time it changed hands; taxes of ½d in the £ on undeveloped land and on ungotten minerals (the latter was changed in committee to a tax on mining royalties); and a 10 per cent reversion duty on the increased value of leased property each time the lease was terminated. The license duties were expected to yield an additional £2.6 million, the land taxes £500,000. Finally, the contribution to the Sinking Fund was reduced by £3 million.

The effect of the Budget was to increase the proportion of revenue raised by direct taxation at the expense of the very rich but not of the middle class. Only 12,000 people would be affected by the super-tax, while those with earned incomes under £2,000 would benefit from the new graduated rates and the child allowances. The stamp duties, land taxes and new estate tax rates similarly would be borne primarily by the rich. The poor would bear a disproportionate burden of the increase in indirect taxes; however, they were expected to be the beneficiaries of the social reforms which the Budget was to help finance.[6]

Liberals defended the Budget as the embodiment of liberal principles. It was, they claimed, a fair and prudent means of raising the money required to pay for social reform and national defence. It was not revolutionary. Most of it, Asquith pointed out, was merely an adjustment of existing taxes or a new application of existing fiscal principles. These changes, moreover, placed the burden primarily on those best able to bear it – the superfluities of the rich were taxed rather than the necessities of the poor. Most Liberals could accept the principle of progressive taxation by which this was implemented. The *Leicester Daily Mercury* argued that 'wealth exists, and is protected, not that it may be accumulated more and more until it becomes a menace to the general interest, but that it may contribute to the general welfare . . . It has its rights . . . But wealth has its duties also'. By contrast, the Unionists would raise the money by placing tariffs on the working man's food. Tariff reform, claimed Horace Mansfield, the Liberal MP for the Spalding division of Lincolnshire, was inherently unfair. By putting 'private interest before the true interests of the state', it transformed 'the legislature into a number of men all seeking to represent their own interests, and all conspiring to advance those interests'.[7] The success of the drink trade over the years was sufficient evidence for Liberals of how real this danger was. These were the evils which the Budget protected the nation against.

Liberals saw one final proof of the Budget's fairness. It forced the two great monopolies – the liquor trade and the landlords – to contribute something to the nation in return for the privileges it had conferred on them. The monopoly value of the liquor license and the increased value of urban land were both the result of action by the community. Thus, Liberals argued, there was nothing unfair in singling out either for special taxation. On the contrary, the injustice heretofore was being suffered by the community, which was paying higher prices for values which it had created. Such taxes were not confiscation of private property. Indeed, the *Eastern Daily Press* claimed that the land taxes were 'an assertion of the fundamental principle which alone makes private property valid – the principle that the ownership of wealth should be with those whose energy and thought creates it'. Once again, Liberals saw a striking contrast with tariff reform. While the Budget, Asquith told the Yorkshire Liberal Association, taxed unearned increments for the benefit of the community, tariff reform involved 'the creation at the cost of the community of an unearned increment which is to go into the private pockets of protected industries'.[8] Furthermore, while tariff reform would place new burdens on commerce by raising prices, the land taxes would lower the costs of industry by bringing more land on to the market.

Liberals did not ignore the implications of the Budget for social reform. Lloyd George and Winston Churchill regularly emphasized the policies it would help to finance. Most Liberals, however, concentrated on refuting charges that the Budget was socialism. The greatest danger to the present system, they claimed, was poverty and the discontent which it bred. The Budget affirmed that 'poverty can be dealt with within the existing social order'. Thus, 'in its tendency to encourage individual effort and to afford wider scope for every citizen to develop his talent and energy the Budget is really a barrier to the spread of Socialism'.[9]

Some Liberals could not accept this view and were deeply troubled by the Budget. Men like T. P. Whittaker, the temperance advocate, J. E. Ellis, the pacifist and former pro-Boer, Sir Robert Perks, the Nonconformist activist and Liberal Imperialist leader, and Sir Walter Runciman, the shipowner and chairman of the Northern Liberal Federation, had dominated the party's rank and file since 1886. It could not afford to lose their money or their sense of commitment. All told, some thirty MPs expressed reservations concerning the land taxes to Asquith and Lloyd George on 17 June. In response, the Chancellor made some judicious concessions, and only two Liberals voted against the third reading, though several others abstained.

Irish opposition was another danger. The Irish parliamentary party received financial support from the publicans and distillers, who opposed the license duties and taxes on spirits. Furthermore, the Budget was unpopular in Ireland. When Lloyd George refused to modify these taxes, there was enormous pressure on Redmond and Dillon to oppose the Budget. Only the crisis with the House of Lords saved them by making Home Rule a live issue once again.[10]

Despite these elements of discontent, the Budget was popular with most of the Liberal rank and file. In June, the Budget League was organized to carry the campaign for the Budget to the constituencies. By July, the effects of the Budget were becoming evident, as the Liberals held four seats in by-elections, including the vulnerable High Peak division of Derbyshire. Lloyd George had no doubt that the key to this revival was the land taxes. These, he told J. A. Spender, had roused 'the fighting spirit of our forces'; without them, 'our followers would have been indifferent'.[11] This conviction shaped Lloyd George's first major defence of the Budget at Limehouse on 30 July. In a rousing speech, he justified each of the land taxes, giving examples of specific peers who had reaped enormous profits by selling land at inflated values created by the enterprise of others. It was designed to incite the rank and file against their traditional enemies, the landlords and the House of Lords. Asquith was troubled by the speech. He believed, as he told Lloyd George on 3 August, that the need was for 'reasoned appeal to moderate and reasonable men'. Many among the rank and file, however, welcomed the fighting speeches of Lloyd George and Churchill. As a result, by August, the revived state of party morale was evident to all. Fred Horne drew the inevitable lesson: 'the political barometer has varied according to the boldness or timidity of the Government's proposals'.[12] Success came when it stood firmly by its principles rather than compromising them to placate its enemies.

Central to the Liberal revival was the conviction that the Budget had provided an effective retort to the House of Lords. The role of the House of Lords in the political system violated the liberal commitment to fair and democratic government. The House of Lords had the power to thwart the will of the people as expressed through their elected representatives in the House of Commons. Yet, because peerages were hereditary, the Upper Chamber could not be held accountable for how it used that power. Worse still, the Lords acted in a purely partisan fashion as the instrument of the Unionist Party whenever a Liberal government was in power. In this way, Liberals believed, the Lords protected the privileges of class, wealth, land and liquor, which were all they really represented. The national interest was sacrificed and progressive legislation was blocked by selfish vested interests concerned only about themselves.

By the summer of 1909, Liberals began to see the Budget as the first step in a campaign against the Lords. Eager for a fight, they hoped the Upper House would reject the Budget. These were the sentiments of Churchill and Lloyd George as well, and each in his public speeches became increasingly provocative towards the peers, both to keep the spirits of the Liberal activists high and to encourage a veto. Lloyd George's speech at Newcastle on 9 October was a masterpiece of the sort of ridicule they engaged in. Despite Tory predictions to the contrary, he pointed out, the economy had done just fine since the introduction of the Budget.

> Only one stock has gone down badly; there has been a great slump in dukes. (Laughter and cheers.) . . . One especially expensive duke made a speech, and all the Tory Press said: – Well now, really, is that the sort of thing we are spending £250,000 a year on? – because a fully-equipped duke costs as much to keep up as two Dreadnoughts; and dukes are just as great a terror and they last longer. (Laughter.)

The party of the constitution, he warned, was in fact threatening it.

> They are forcing revolution . . . The question will be asked, 'Should 500 men, ordinary men (laughter), chosen accidentally from among the unemployed (laughter), override the judgement – the deliberate judge-

111

ment – of millions of people who are engaged in the industry which makes the wealth of the country?'[13]

In fact, by October the Lords needed no further prodding from Lloyd George. The Unionists viewed the Budget as a socialist measure which threatened the security of property. With the country in the midst of a depression, conditions seemed ideal for a showdown on the issue of tariff reform versus socialism. As a result, there was near unanimity among Unionists when the Lords finally rejected the Budget on 30 November.[14]

Liberals already had been building a constitutional case against the Lords. Rejection of the Budget, they argued, would be a revolutionary act which challenged the fundamental principles of parliamentary government. First, the Lords would be challenging the principle of no taxation without representation by usurping the financial prerogatives of the House of Commons. Second, by denying supplies, they would be claiming the power to make and unmake governments, thus challenging the principle that the confidence of the Commons was sufficient to justify a government's remaining in office. Third, by claiming the right to force a dissolution, they would be usurping the prerogative of the Crown. The issues therefore seemed simple to Liberals: How was Britain to be governed – by popular democracy or by irresponsible privilege, by the people or by the peers? Such issues were the essence of liberalism, and the rank and file were delighted to be able to go to the country on them.

THE GENERAL ELECTIONS OF 1910 AND THE END OF THE VETO

If the Liberals were to succeed in the general elections which followed, it was crucial that they mobilize the same forces which had made possible the landslide of 1906 – the Irish, the Nonconformists and the working class. Given Redmond's increasing difficulties managing his party, nothing short of an unambiguous statement by Asquith committing the Liberals to Home Rule would be sufficient to justify Irish support. At the Albert Hall on 10 December, amidst cries of Home Rule and cheers from his audience, Asquith reaffirmed that the only solution to the Irish problem was a system of Irish self-government subject to the ultimate authority of the Imperial Parliament. Furthermore, he insisted that future Liberal governments would be free to enact that policy. This was more than sufficient for the Nationalist leaders, who did everything in their power to assure Irish support for Liberal candidates in Britain in both 1910 general elections.[15]

The Nonconformists were crucial to Liberal prospects for success.

112

Yet, as Rev. James Pickett warned Runciman, because of the government's continued inability to resolve the education question, 'the enthusiasm and support of thousands of its most ardent supporters are being immensely jeopardised, if not entirely forfeited'.[16] The confrontation with the House of Lords was critical in reviving the enthusiasm of such Nonconformist activists. In September, the National Passive Resistance League called on its supporters to concentrate on the destruction of the Lords' veto as the only means of redressing their grievances. Clifford carried the same message to the Baptist Union the following month. On 27 October, Asquith assured the Free Church Council that Nonconformist education grievances would not be allowed to continue should the government win the coming election. As a result, on 6 December the Council published a manifesto urging support for candidates who would satisfy Nonconformist demands on education and temperance. Local councils organized (Clifford alone spoke in some thirty constituencies) and 1.5 million leaflets were distributed. Some 125 Free Churchmen were elected in January 1910, including Silvester Horne as MP for Ipswich.[17]

None the less, the Free Churches could not mobilize their forces with the same unanimity as in 1906. Since the failure of the Licensing Bill in 1908, the *Methodist Recorder* had become resolutely apolitical, a position endorsed by most of its correspondents. Furthermore, while many Nonconformist trade unionists in the North were associated with the Labour Party, others among the middle class had founded the Nonconformist Anti-Socialist Union. In such circumstances, official association with the Liberals was increasingly divisive, and there was growing pressure from the laity for the Churches to stay out of politics. Although the Free Church Council issued a manifesto sympathetic to the Liberals prior to the December general election, F. B. Meyer, the secretary, urged local councils not to engage in political activity if they had a significant minority who were opposed to it. Thus, although Nonconformity remained an important political force in areas of traditional Liberal strength like Wales and the West Riding of Yorkshire, there were signs of future trouble. With the Wesleyans leading the way, the Free Church Council was retreating from political activity. At the same time, the politically divided laity was less willing to follow the Liberal lead which the more militant clergy continued to provide.[18]

The progressive alliance was as important to the Liberals as Nonconformist militancy, for any significant division of the working-class vote could mean disaster at the polls. The years 1906–9 had revealed continued rank-and-file dislike for an agreement which included socialists who attacked the Liberal Party. In Scotland, where there never had been an alliance, Liberals still opposed any arrangement. At its 1906 meeting, the Scottish Liberal Association voted by fifty-five to thirty-four in favour of a resolution asserting

> that it is a primary duty of the Liberal party to present strenuous opposition to all candidates who are not prepared to dissociate themselves from the Socialist party, the avowed object of which is the complete destruction of those principles of individual liberty for which Liberalism has always contended.

A February 1908 report from the Association's secretaries, however, confirmed the continued progress of socialism within both the trade unions and the Labour Party in Scotland. There was no question in their minds that the 'Socialists are really the driving force behind the Labour movement, and their main policy and aim is to form a distinct political party' hostile to the Liberals.[19]

Concerns about the increasing influence of socialism were not limited to Scotland. The *Leeds and Yorkshire Mercury* engaged in a campaign against the socialists in the early autumn of 1906. It concluded with an endorsement of the Scottish Liberals' resolution: 'Labour interests may suffer in consequence, but as long as bona fide Labour Members . . . allow themselves to be led by the nose by the Socialist group, they have only themselves to blame.' Liberal fears were accentuated in July 1907 when socialist candidates won by-elections in Jarrow and Colne Valley, both northern constituencies long represented by Liberal industrialists. Worse news followed in 1908. The Labour Party Conference in January adopted by a vote of 514,000 to 469,000 a resolution stating that 'the time has arrived when the Labour Party should have as a definite object the socialization of the means of production, distribution, and exchange.' The delegates also voted overwhelmingly not to incorporate the commitment to socialism into the party's constitution, where it might drive away non-socialists. Four months later, the Miners' Federation voted by 213,000 to 168,000 to affiliate with the Labour Party. The growth of the socialist ILP in the mining areas was primarily responsible for ending the miners' long-standing ties to the Liberals.[20]

The threat of socialism seemed all the more real because local Liberal parties were being challenged by an aggressive political labour movement which was led by socialists. Labour did not always get very far. In London, for example, the meagre successes of the ILP in the 1907 and 1910 elections for the London County Council came when the Liberals gave the candidates a free run against Conservatives. At Sheffield, Labour representation on the City Council peaked at three in 1908. Efforts at Norwich to consolidate a local progressive alliance broke down in 1906. None the less, Labour never was able to win more than six of the forty-eight elected seats on the Town Council between 1906 and 1913.[21]

By contrast, in other cities there was already evidence by 1910 that the Liberals had reason to fear a socialist-led Labour challenge. The Bradford Labour Party polled 35 per cent of the vote in the 1910 municipal elections, an increase from 22 per cent in 1905. At Leeds, the Labour Party was contesting nine to eleven of the sixteen wards at each municipal election. The Liberals offered no coherent response to such a challenge. As a result, in 1907 and 1908 the party's elected representation fell from twenty-six to fifteen (of forty-eight). The Liberals professed to be untroubled by such losses because, as a result of a split, the Labour Party's elected representation in 1908 also had fallen from eight to three. At Leicester, the opponents of progressive co-operation finally seized control of the party in 1907. At an April meeting of the Leicester Liberal Association, Councillor Kemp charged that the policy of conciliating Labour had led to apathy in the wards. Let there be 'no more talk about "two wings of a Progressive party"', he urged. They must fight the socialists 'or they would be wiped out'.[22] Yet their more aggressive electoral strategy achieved little. Between 1906 and 1910, the elected Liberal representation on the Town Council fell from thirty to eighteen, while Labour's increased from ten to thirteen. The principal beneficiary of the Labour challenge was the Conservatives, whose elected representation jumped from eight to seventeen. The phenomenon of a Conservative revival between 1907 and 1910 was a common one. Often, as at Norwich and London, they succeeded by directing their campaign against socialism and high rates.[23] Thus, rank-and-file Liberals thought they saw evidence that socialism was driving moderate voters towards the Conservatives.

The foundations of the progressive alliance therefore remained tenuous. In 1908 Arthur Henderson told J. A. Pease, the Liberal Chief Whip, that the only constraints on Labour activity at the next general election would be financial, and Labour was already preparing to attack Liberal seats. While the Liberal press and MPs continued to urge progressive unity, local Liberals were increasingly unwilling to stand aside, to the detriment of their organizations, while having to vote for a socialist or a tory. The confrontation with the House of Lords, however, forced the leaders on both sides to rein in their activists and combine against the common enemy. Pease was prepared to give Labour candidates a free run in seats they or the miners had won in 1906; he was not prepared to concede new constituencies, and he threatened retaliation if Labour attacked Liberal or Lib-Lab seats.[24] Because of the suddenness of the election, Labour could not take up such a challenge and had to give way.

The general elections of 1910 seemed to justify Pease's uncompromising attitude. In January, there were twenty-seven seats where

Liberal and Labour candidates faced each other. Labour lost all of them, finishing last in twenty-three. The Liberals, on the other hand, lost only four seats due to Labour intervention, while they regained three seats from Labour. Finally, Labour candidates won forty of the fifty-one seats in which they were given a free run against Unionists. The lesson seemed clear to Liberals: while Labour was dependent upon Liberal support to win, Liberals could win even in opposition to Labour. Thus, in December the Labour Party cut back its activities even further. It contested only fifty-six seats, with a free run against the Unionists in forty-five. Labour won West Fife from the Liberals and held Gower in the face of a Liberal challenge; it won forty of the seats in which it was given a free run.[25] The Liberals had not merely kept the progressive alliance alive, with the many working-class votes that secured, but they also had limited Labour Party representation to about forty, and proved that an aggressive policy against Labour could be successful.

Some Liberals were not convinced that the party had succeeded in containing either Labour or socialism. On the contrary, they found the government's policies too socialistic. Rosebery and Perks were merely the most prominent of these disillusioned Liberals. Julius Bertram, MP for North Hertfordshire, told Pease as early as 1907 that he would not stand for re-election: 'There are far too many Socialists among the Lib'l rank and file in the H. of C. for me.' Pease's brother Alfred, who had represented the Cleveland division from 1897–1902, protested that the Liberals 'continue to bid for the Socialist vote and go on buying support out of the taxes'. All together, perhaps one-third of the Liberal MPs who retired in January did so because they did not like the government's legislation.[26]

While such defections by prominent and wealthy Liberals could never be lightly dismissed, they were not so numerous as to hamper the party's efforts in the January general election. Nor did the government's 'socialistic' legislation emerge as a major issue during the campaign. On the contrary, both parties were eager to turn the election into a referendum on free trade versus tariff reform, and that issue dominated the debate. The actions of the House of Lords were nearly as important for Liberals, who also devoted a considerable amount of attention to defending the Budget. Social reform, apart from the mention of old-age pensions, was not prominent in the Liberal campaign.[27] The Liberals won 275 seats to 273 for the Unionists, 82 for the Nationalists, and 40 for Labour. The sweeping victory of the Liberals in the North and the Unionists in the Midlands and the South gave the appearance that Britain was divided along class lines. None the less, many exceptions mitigate against a class interpretation. The Liverpool and Birmingham working class continued to vote

Unionist, as did many rural labourers in the South. The Nonconform-ist middle class of Wales, Scotland and the North of England con-tinued to vote Liberal. Furthermore, the campaign was not fought on class issues but on the old issues of free trade, the House of Lords, the navy, and the power of the liquor trade and the landlords. In areas of Unionist strength, like the Home Counties, government policies probably drove the middle class back to its traditional allegiance after the aberration of 1906. For the moment, however, middle-class Liberals in cities like Norwich, Leeds and Leicester could continue to support Liberal (and Labour) parliamentary candidates just because the traditional Liberal issues were still paramount.

The general election gave the Liberals and their allies a majority of 124, which was more than sufficient for the government to proceed with a policy to limit the powers of the House of Lords. The Cabinet, however, was divided over what to do. Grey, Haldane, Churchill, McKenna, Runciman, Lord Crewe and Herbert Samuel all believed that the government should formulate a plan for reforming the House of Lords. They argued that the Liberals had been persistently attacking the hereditary principle and would look ridiculous if they now left it untouched. They asserted that Campbell-Bannerman's plan for a suspensory veto, which had been agreed upon in 1907, created single-chamber government, which most moderate electors opposed. The reforms they envisioned would continue to assure the Commons' supremacy on financial matters, but other deadlocks between the Houses would be resolved by a system of joint sittings. They believed that such a plan was more consistent with Liberal commitments to representative and two-chamber government and would force the opposition to defend privilege and hereditary government.[28]

Despite this formidable array of ministers and arguments in support of reform, the Cabinet remained undecided. The parliamentary party and the constituency activists were nearly unanimous in opposing reform as a substitute for limiting the veto. They were stunned to learn on 21 February that, contrary to what they had been led to believe, Asquith had not secured a promise that the King would create enough peers, if necessary, to assure that the Lords would pass a bill limiting the powers of the Upper Chamber. When the King's Speech also hinted that the Cabinet was undecided between limiting the veto and reforming the Lords, party morale collapsed. The cry went up from the constituencies that the rank and file had no interest in reform, and the word went back to the Cabinet of demoralized meetings and dangers of rebellion.[29]

With such a gulf between so many ministers and the rank and file, there can be little wonder that the Cabinet was dispirited. Twice there was talk of resignation.[30] Only slowly did members regain their confidence and see their way towards a resolution of their problems. First, they decided to proceed with the Campbell-Bannerman plan, modified to allow the three successive passages of a bill through the House of Commons to be in different Parliaments. In a preamble to the bill, they would affirm their ultimate intention to reform the House of Lords. Then, they decided to pass the Budget as quickly as possible without altering it to woo Irish support. Finally, they accepted that they would have to seek guarantees from the King concerning the creation of peers prior to a second general election, and they would have to announce that policy immediately to reassure the activists. The response of the rank and file was as enthusiastic as the Cabinet could have wished. The Irish, too, were satisfied that their primary objective would be achieved, and were ready to give the government the support it needed.

The way seemed prepared for a July general election when Edward VII died on 7 May. Very quickly the Cabinet recognized that it could be disastrous electorally to appear to be placing undue pressure on the new King.[31] On 6 June it therefore decided to propose a conference with the Unionists to try to achieve a settlement by consent. The rank .and file were fearful about a further postponement of a showdown with the House of Lords.[32] While affirming that Liberals would welcome an agreed settlement, the press constantly warned that there could be no compromise on ending the Lords' veto. The conference of four leaders from each side met twelve times between 17 June and the end of July, and several more times in October and early November. It finally broke down over the Unionists' insistence that bills dealing with 'constitutional' issues should be submitted to a referendum if they were rejected twice by the Lords. Asquith knew not only that his rank and file were unalterably opposed to the referendum, but also that they would not accept the exclusion of matters like Home Rule and Welsh disestablishment from the normal mechanism of resolving differences between the Houses.[33]

By the end of the first round of meetings in July, it probably was clear to Lloyd George, one of the Liberal participants, that agreement on the House of Lords was unlikely. He therefore sought to broaden the basis for discussion in an attempt to facilitate compromise. On 17 August he dictated a memorandum proposing a coalition government. Lloyd George argued that the threat to the national prosperity posed by expanding foreign competition justified an extraordinary British response. Such a response needed to be outside the framework of party government because partisanship and the pressure of party activists prevented both parties from exploring unconventional solutions. Lloyd George then discussed a wide range of issues in the most general terms, asserting the importance of each to the national well-being and that it could be dealt with more effectively by a coalition.

In early October, Lloyd George approached Balfour with his proposals. Balfour consulted other Unionist leaders, several of whom appeared to be interested. Lloyd George lured them on with concessions on issues which were of concern to them – the possibility of conscription, a large grant for the navy, an inquiry without prejudice into tariff reform. Once it was clear that Balfour was interested, Lloyd George showed his memorandum to Asquith, and at his suggestion Crewe and Grey were consulted. In talking with his colleagues, Lloyd George began to identify the concessions that the Liberals would require: Welsh disestablishment, education reform along the lines of Birrell's Bill, a general scheme of devolution as a resolution to the Irish question.[34] Throughout the discussions, the mode of procedure was typical of Lloyd George. He conducted the negotiations himself, keeping the parties apart, emphasizing to each the possible areas of benefit while minimizing differences. Slowly, he identified a series of concessions that could provide the basis for a comprehensive solution which in turn would justify compromise on each specific issue. At this point, Lloyd George's negotiations foundered on the issue which also ended the constitutional conference – Irish Home Rule. Balfour feared that any settlement which admitted Home Rule, even in the attenuated form of a general scheme of devolution, would destroy his party.

Balfour's was not the only party which could have been destroyed by such a coalition. Lloyd George's August memorandum repeatedly repudiated policies which the Liberal rank and file believed embodied fundamental liberal principles: licensing reform (described as 'a rigid and sterile plan'), small holdings ('of very doubtful utility'), voluntary recruitment, free trade. It is little wonder that C. F. G. Masterman, Under-Secretary at the Home Office and one of Lloyd George's closest confidants, was amazed and appalled when he saw the memorandum. As he told Lloyd George, 'the mere idea of Tory-Liberal coalescence in the constituencies would seem like blasphemy to the rank and file'. He himself would not be able to join such a coalition – 'a rather scandalous proceeding . . . it is a frank juggle with the principle of representative government'. On 28 October, J. A. Spender sent out the same message in the *Westminster Gazette*. Perhaps Asquith had consulted with him about Lloyd George's proposals; perhaps Asquith was using him to help kill them. Whatever the explanation for Spender's leader, there can be no doubt that he spoke for the bulk of his party:

> There are people who talk glibly of the existing parties having done their work and seen their day, and dream of a great 'national party' . . . In our

opinion, there never was a time when a strong Liberal party was more important to the well-being of the country, and we look confidently to the Liberal leaders to bring their party out of the Conference as they took it in – a Liberal Party standing on a Liberal foundation, and not a coalition or a group of opportunists.[35]

For the moment, the danger had passed. On 16 November Asquith secured the necessary guarantees from a reluctant King concerning the creation of peers, and Parliament was dissolved. Far more than in January, the December election was fought on the issue of the House of Lords. The argument between free trade and tariff reform was much less important this time, although it became more so after Balfour agreed to submit tariff reform to a referendum. The Unionists tried to make Home Rule an issue, but only with modest success. Social reform was even less important as an issue than in January.[36] The result was much the same as January's. With 272 Liberals, 84 Irish Nationalists, and 42 Labour MPs, the government's supporters had a majority of 126 over the 272 Unionists.

As far as Liberals were concerned, the issue was now settled. The remaining suspense was provided by the Unionists, for there was a danger that the Lords would reject the Parliament Bill, thus forcing a mass creation of peers. Many radicals found such a prospect attractive, but it appalled the King. It required the votes of thirty-seven Unionist peers and thirteen Anglican bishops, as well as the abstention of hundreds of other Unionists, for the Parliament Bill to pass the Lords on 10 August.

Thus, after years of Liberal frustration, the veto of the House of Lords had been curtailed. The Parliament Act ended the Lords' veto of money bills, provided that any other measure passed in three successive sessions over at least two years by the House of Commons would become law, and reduced the maximum length of a Parliament from seven years to five. It also promised in its preamble a measure to reform the Lords. In 1913 a Cabinet committee considered the question of reform; however, after it proposed two alternative schemes, the matter was allowed to drop. There remained some Cabinet interest in pursuing reform. The Parliament Act, however, had given the rank and file all they wanted, so they were indifferent.

LIBERALS AND THE NEW LIBERALISM

While the Liberal government was achieving the party's most important traditional goal by limiting the powers of the House of Lords, it was also enacting a comprehensive programme of social reforms. For the rank and file, the traditional ideals retained their primacy: peace, retrenchment and reform; the extension of democracy; the limitation of privilege; and the promotion of individual liberty. All of these values, however, could be reconciled with a philosophy of social reform which incorporated the language of the new liberalism. Most Liberals now spoke in terms of creating the conditions for individual development within an organic society where each depended on the development of all. They therefore accepted that it was the responsibility of a Liberal government to assist those who were poor due to circumstances over which they had no control. Government action would enable such people to compete effectively within a capitalist system, thus promoting genuine individual liberty and equality of opportunity. At the same time, leading Nonconformists were also urging a more active role for the Churches in promoting social improvement. Some, like the Wesleyan S. E. Keble, had concluded that the Free Churches must 'insist that all social evil, preventable or curable by Act of Parliament, shall be prevented or cured'.[37]

Liberals and Nonconformists saw incalculable benefits to society from positive steps to help the poor. Industry would have a more productive and contented work-force. This, in turn, would encourage social harmony, reducing the hostility between capital and labour, rich and poor. There would also be a reduction in other social costs: crime, drunkenness, pauperism, immorality. To succeed, however, policies must not weaken the character of the beneficiary. They must preserve independence by encouraging individual initiative and personal responsibility. Liberals did not doubt that this was possible. With the dread removed of an unforeseen catastrophe which could wipe out all savings, they hoped that workers would see a real prospect for self-improvement which would encourage work and thrift.

Liberals and Nonconformists were always careful to distinguish their approach to social reform from socialism. They commended the spirit of humanitarianism, justice and brotherhood which motivated socialists. None the less, they argued, socialism embodied a dangerous utopianism which posed a threat to national prosperity and individual liberty. It would kill trade by destroying the motivation which came from competition and profit. It would stifle individual initiative and weaken personal responsibility by its failure to reward both effort and the inherent differences in men. Liberalism, by contrast, mitigated the evils of the capitalist system without destroying its economic and moral benefits. At the same time, Liberals claimed, unlike conservatism, it offered a barrier to a socialist revolution by recognizing the necessity of social reform to remove the causes of popular discontent. Thus, the *Eastern Daily Press* concluded, the Liberal Party provided 'the true political rendezvous of all moderate minded men who would neither inflate the rights of property on the one hand nor throw them into the Socialist melting pot on the other. It is at once the party of conservation and social reform.'[38]

By 1909 Liberals of every sort – intellectuals, Cabinet members, back-benchers, Nonconformist ministers, provincial newspaper editors and municipal politicians – were employing the language of a constructive liberal ideology, between the extremes of socialism and toryism, to justify their party's social reform policies. None the less, there was a fundamental constraint which limited the rank and file's commitment to the new liberalism: they did not see social reform as involving matters of principle. It was the old issues, not the new ones, which embodied their liberalism, and were worth fighting for. For example, in June 1911 Silvester Horne expressed his frustration as bills providing health and unemployment insurance, limiting the hours of shop assistants, and permitting political activities by trade unions all were hung up in the House of Commons. 'We are just a little tired', he wrote, 'of Bills which are supposed to make equal appeal to all parties. We think we might have one downright Liberal measure. We are spoiling for something to fight for'. He suggested a plural voting bill replace one of the others.[39]

Such a restricted view of liberal principles inevitably affected the priorities of the Nonconformists. In April 1911, Horne laid out his priorities once the Parliament Bill was passed: popular control of education, licensing reform, devolution (Irish Home Rule), electoral reform, disestablishment, land reform and the limitation of arms. Similarly, John Clifford, who for many years had been using the language of the new liberalism, told a reporter in February 1911 that, if he were prime minister, his programme would include the end of plural voting, registration reform, Home Rule for Ireland, licensing reform, education reform and disestablishment of the Anglican Church in Wales. Horne and Clifford were in the forefront of the movement to involve the Nonconformist Churches more directly in promoting social reform. If they were unable to reorient their priorities, it was even more difficult for those Wesleyans who sought to keep their Church out of party politics. Rev. Walter J. Bull, who claimed advanced views on social questions, concluded that it was better for the Methodist Church to risk alienating the working class further rather than see its assemblies turned into 'political cock-pits' by taking a position on social issues.[40] Yet the Churches – even the Wesleyans – did take a position on temperance and education. They could do so, while maintaining their claim that they were not political, because these issues were perceived to be religious. Because social questions (apart from temperance, gambling and sexual purity) were placed firmly on the political rather than the religious side of the divide, it was impossible for the Nonconformist activists to generate great enthusiasm for social reform policies.

Nonconformist ministers were not alone in defining their liberalism primarily in terms of the traditional issues. Every Annual Report of the NLF from 1909–13 had a section devoted to the fiscal question and the fallacies of tariff reform; every annual meeting except 1910 had a free trade resolution. No other issue received such attention. Walter Runciman, whose Dewsbury constituency was in the industrial West Riding, devoted relatively little attention in his speeches to the social issues which he, as a member of the government, was seeking to deal with. Instead, he focused on the traditional issues which divided Liberals from Unionists: free trade versus tariff reform, the House of Lords, aliens, education, land and licensing. The Liberal rank and file were similarly limited in their concerns. Welsh Liberals (Lloyd George notwithstanding) showed little interest in either social reform or the new liberalism. On 22 February 1909, as the government was launching its social reform programme, the *Leicester Daily Mercury* cited the issues which demanded immediate political action by the forces of progressivism: 'monopolies in land, in liquor, in ecclesiasticism, in electoral machinery, and in the House of Lords, which is the very holy of holies of monopoly'. More than three years later, with the government's programme virtually complete, E. G. Hemmerde, one of the leaders of the land taxers, was adopted as Liberal candidate for North-West Norfolk. His adoption speech dealt with Welsh disestablishment, Irish Home Rule, franchise reform, education, licensing, land taxation, the government's social reforms, labour unrest, the navy, peace and conscription. He concluded by describing himself as 'one of the advance guard of Liberalism'.[41] Thus, although Liberals adopted the language of the new liberalism with little difficulty, for most this represented no redefinition of their priorities. Their primary concerns remained what they always had been: the traditional issues for which the Newcastle Programme had defined policies in 1891.

The issue which was of paramount concern to organized labour between 1906 and 1910 was unemployment. Any Liberal government with pretensions of representing the interests of the working class had to develop a policy to deal with this problem. Most Liberals had little difficulty in accepting the need for state intervention on behalf of the unemployed. They recognized that many of the unemployed were not at fault. The cost of preventing or relieving unemployment would be more than recovered if the policies protected the worthy poor from sinking into a state of lethargy and demoralization which would make them a permanent burden on the poor rates. If state action were to be consistent with liberal principles, however, it must not interfere with the free market in labour, and it had to provide some mechanism for discriminating between the respectable poor who wanted to work and the loafers and wastrels who were unemployable.

In 1905 the Unionist government had passed the Unemployed Workmen Act, which empowered local authorities to form distress committees to assist the unemployed. The distress committees could provide work if they chose to do so, but they could not pay wages out of public funds. The Act failed as a measure for assisting those temporarily out of work. Most of those resorting to the distress committees were casual labourers and 'unemployables'. Furthermore, the measure confirmed Liberal doubts about relief works which either paid men to do unnecessary work or paid the unskilled to do useful work less efficiently and at greater cost than if the community had hired trained labourers. At the same time, the Act also demonstrated the limited value of farm colonies to retrain the urban unemployed for resettlement on the land or for emigration. John Burns, the new President of the Local Government Board (LGB), concluded that farm colonies were just like relief works.

> [They] were costly and ineffective. They displaced agricultural labourers who supported themselves by useful work, and introduced men who could not, at least for a long time, be profitably employed on the land. The agricultural labourer, deprived of his livelihood, was demoralised by knowing that men were receiving the equivalent of more than double his old pay for doing work that was practically valueless.[42]

The King's Speech of 1906 promised that the Liberal government would amend the Act. Burns, the man responsible for developing a liberal alternative, was a former socialist agitator among the unemployed and the first working-class cabinet minister. By 1906, he had repudiated his former socialism and adopted a strict liberalism which rejected any measure which might weaken character or which could not be justified on strict grounds of economy. Burns hated the 1905 Act and blocked all attempts to modify it. By 1907 Liberal and Labour MPs alike were growing impatient with his inaction. Sydney Buxton told Lord Ripon that Burns 'will lose us all our seats in London if he's not careful'. Some seventy Liberal MPs supported a Labour amendment to the 1908 King's Speech protesting the failure to promise any measure for the unemployed.[43]

In 1908 the Labour Party introduced its own unemployment policy in the form of the 'Right-to-Work' Bill. It required that every unemployed man or woman be provided with either suitable work or maintenance by the local authority for as long as the registrant was unemployed. All work provided would be compensated at the rate of wage prevalent in the locality. Liberals were unrestrained in their condemnation. The principle seemed to embody socialism in its most

124

dangerous form. As the Lib-Lab Fred Maddison told the House of Commons, 'If the right to work were admitted, it must be followed up by giving the State – upon whom the burden of providing the work would be placed – a control over the lives of the workers, to which no self-respecting people would submit.' If trade union rates were paid, the *Leicester Daily Post* feared that all casual and rural labourers who received a lower wage would 'prefer to remain on the staff of the local authority year after year rather than trouble to look for work themselves'. It is little wonder that Liberals opposed the Bill. As the Lib-Lab Henry Vivian concluded,

> To the degree to which they inculcated the idea that an individual's salvation could come from anything apart from his own energy, forethought, and sense of duty, and self-sacrifice, they weakened national life. By this Bill they were not making work, but they would destroy the character, the self-reliance, and the moral fibre of the men of the country.[44]

With a trade depression setting in, however, Liberal MPs from working-class constituencies were insisting that the government do something. The man who took up the challenge was the new President of the Board of Trade, Winston Churchill. Churchill was a recent convert to liberalism, having broken with the Unionists in 1904 on the free trade issue. The conversion was timely for Churchill's career, exposing him to suspicions of opportunism. Further doubts concerning his commitment to any fixed principles occurred when he embraced the liberal faith in its most radical form with the gusto and enthusiasm which characterized all his actions. Social reform offered an irresistible attraction to Churchill. It was sufficiently fashionable and controversial to allow him both to display his dramatic flair and to achieve substantial results quickly. As an unconventional liberal, he was attracted to the Fabian socialism of Beatrice and Sidney Webb. Their outlook embodied a combination of humanitarianism and authoritarianism, which suited Churchill's temperament. At the same time, his obvious love of the limelight and his provocative oratory rendered him an object of distrust among his colleagues.

Because the Board of Trade was responsible for labour statistics and industrial relations, there was an arguable case for its taking responsibility for employment-related policies. This was all the opening Churchill needed. With William Beveridge, whom he brought to the Board of Trade over the summer, he set to work to develop a Liberal unemployment policy. By December he was able to present the Cabinet with an outline of his proposals for labour exchanges and unemployment insurance. A system of labour exchanges would serve as a clearing house where the needs of the employers and the unemployed from all over the country could be correlated. Far from interfering with the free enterprise system, they would help it to work more smoothly by improving information and the mobility of labour. Furthermore, by providing a common reserve from which all employers of casual labour could draw, they would enable more people to be employed regularly. Thus, labour exchanges were a means of reducing the waste which resulted from under-utilized labour resources and inefficiencies in the labour market. Labour exchanges also provided the means for administering unemployment insurance. A worker who was unemployed and who had contributed to the scheme would be entitled to a weekly payment for a limited period of time. He would have to register at a labour exchange in order to collect his benefits. Since the labour exchanges would have information about employment, this would give the state a means of testing his willingness to work as well as of assuring that he was legitimately unemployed. The insurance principle guaranteed thrift. All contributors to the insurance fund benefited from the system. The worker got assured relief without the demoralizing effects of pauperization. The employer got a better worker who could maintain his efficiency when out of work. The community got a more productive work force and a more effective system for relieving unemployment.[45]

Churchill introduced legislation for labour exchanges in 1909. He did everything possible to assuage trade union fears that the exchanges might be a source of blackleg labour during a strike. He consulted with the TUC in preparing the bill, and trade unionists were involved in implementing it. Overall, the bill generated little excitement. The Unionists never divided the Commons at any stage. The provincial Liberal press, while welcoming labour exchanges as a useful piece of administrative machinery, gave the measure little attention.[46] Unemployment insurance was equally non-controversial. The National Insurance Bill of 1911 proposed a compulsory scheme to be applied to a few selected trades – construction, shipbuilding and engineering – which were especially susceptible to cyclical or seasonal unemployment. Workers, employers and the state all would contribute to the fund. The unemployed worker, following a week's waiting period, would be entitled to a weekly payment of 7s for fifteen weeks in any twelve-month period. Liberals welcomed these proposals as a practical experiment in relieving workers from the fear of unemployment. Since it offered substantial benefits to trade unions, the scheme was also supported by the representatives of labour. The policy was so successful that by 1914 the government was preparing to extend it to some other trades.[47]

In commenting on these measures, Liberals admitted that they would do nothing to create work and thus reduce unemployment. Once again, it was Churchill who took the initiative in confronting the problem. He had a clear conception that government spending programmes could be regulated according to the dictates of the trade cycle. He envisioned an inter-departmental committee which each year would adjust the schedule of government projects in the light of unemployment forecasts.[48] Lloyd George went some way towards implementing this kind of thinking when the 1909 Budget provided for a Road Fund and a Development Fund. The former would be used to improve existing roads and build new ones. The latter would be used to support a wide range of development projects which Liberals had been promoting for years as part of their campaign to revive rural Britain: experimental farming, canals and rural transport, afforestation, land reclamation, coast erosion, harbours, fisheries. A Development Commission was charged with determining priorities and using the fund to encourage worthy projects. The development proposals were received enthusiastically by the Liberal rank and file. 'We have here', the NLF claimed in its Annual Report, 'a far-sighted and far-reaching attempt to stimulate, by scientific and co-operative means, the energies and inventive resources of the community, and to enlarge the volume•of employment by utilising and developing hitherto unused and undeveloped national resources'.[49]

By the end of 1911, the Liberal government had implemented an unemployment policy which satisfied the criteria Asquith had set out to a deputation of Labour MPs in December 1908:

> humanitarian in spirit, but businesslike in methods which would ... enable them to say that every man and woman honestly desiring to work, be the conditions of the market what they were – he would not say work was to be found for them; that, perhaps, would be too strong a phrase, but that conditions and machinery should exist for, as far as possible, mitigating the hours of misfortune and providing an avenue to a better state of things.[50]

Nevertheless, there were problems. First, the Development Commission did not become a source of seed money for major new employment-generating programmes. Increasingly, Liberals turned to the old stand-bys – temperance reform and land reform – to provide long-run solutions to the unemployment problem. Secondly, labour exchanges did not reduce the pool of casual labour. Finally, the Liberals never figured out what to do with the 'unemployables'. Some were willing to consider compulsory detention in labour colonies. There, the *Leicester Daily Post* said, the lazy 'will sooner or later be compelled to realise that industry, like honesty, is, after all, "the best policy"'.[51] Such anti-liberal solutions were never pursued. Instead, the 'unemployables' were left to the rigours of the Poor Law.

Unemployment was part of the larger problem of poverty. In response to the rising cost of poor relief, Balfour had appointed a

Royal Commission on the Poor Law in 1905. In 1909 it issued two reports. Both recommended a major transformation of the system of poor relief, including the abolition of the boards of guardians and the transfer of their responsibilities to county and city councils. Both agreed that the poor should be classified – aged, mentally ill, sick, children, able-bodied – and that treatment should differ according to the needs of each class. The fundamental difference between the reports was over whether or not pauperism should remain a distinct category. The Majority Report maintained such a distinction by transferring responsibility for poor relief to a special committee of the county or city council. This committee would provide special services for each category of pauper as they were needed. The Minority Report, which was written by Beatrice Webb, recommended the provision of specialized services – schools, hospitals, mental institutions, homes for old people – for the whole community as they were needed. A committee of the county or city council (such as the existing school and health committees) would be responsible for providing each category of service. Each classification of paupers (such as children or the sick) would be the responsibility of the relevant committee, which would attach conditions of relief as it deemed appropriate. Each committee would be subject to the oversight of a government agency (such as the Board of Education and a new Ministry of Health) which would administer national grants and have inspection powers. The attraction of the Minority Report for Liberals was that it would reduce costs by eliminating the need for two sets of services, one for paupers and one for the rest of the population. Its disadvantage was its authoritarianism; once he or she became a case for treatment, the pauper lost all freedom.[52]

In fact, the Liberal provincial press gave the Minority Report a friendly reception. Liberals were especially attracted by its emphasis on the prevention of poverty and destitution. On the other hand, they did not like the abolition of the boards of guardians. The replacement of those directly responsible to the rate-payers by nominated committees, government officials and experts challenged their liberal principles far more fundamentally than the authoritarian treatment of those who would not work.[53] Asquith and Burns were sympathetic to this rank-and-file reluctance to abolish popular control, for neither had much use for the Webbs. Since Lloyd George and Churchill were already pursuing the alternative of compulsory insurance, there was no strong force in the Cabinet to combat the Prime Minister's indifference. As a result, neither the Majority nor Minority Report was acted upon.

None the less, something had to be done about sickness, the most important remaining source of pauperism now that the aged poor had been provided for. Liberals had no difficulty justifying assisting the sick. Due to illness, a hard-working, thrifty man could see his savings disappear and be forced to turn to the Poor Law through no fault of his own. Assistance from the state would not only save the worthy poor from unwarranted destitution, it would also assure that sick workers sought proper medical care quickly. In this way, preventive action would be encouraged and worker efficiency would be increased. The benefits to both employers and the community justified contributions by both to an insurance scheme. The worker, however, also had to contribute in order to foster self-reliance and preserve his independence. Far from discouraging thrift, a state-supported insurance scheme would encourage it. Now savings would not be eliminated by a catastrophe, but would supplement the state's payment.

Lloyd George began serious work on a health insurance scheme at the end of 1910. An enormous number of interests were affected, and he wanted to reconcile all of them to his measure if possible. His most important constituency was the working class. By allowing trade unions to become approved societies for administering the plan, Lloyd George assured himself of their co-operation. He bought the support of the friendly societies in the same way. Since many of them were in a precarious financial position, they needed the state and employer contributions to make them solvent. The industrial insurance companies were more difficult. They forced Lloyd George to drop his plan for widows' and orphans' benefits, which they feared would compete with their business in selling funeral benefits.

Given the variety of institutions which had to be integrated into the scheme, as well as Lloyd George's unsystematic and even dilatory approach to deciding its final shape, the measure which was introduced to the House of Commons on 4 May 1911 was unusually complex. All manual labourers and all other workers with annual incomes of less than £160 were required to insure through an approved society. After three days of illness, the worker was entitled to a weekly payment of 10s (7s 6d for women) for the first thirteen weeks he was sick, and 5s (later increased to 10s) for the next thirteen. Thereafter, the worker was entitled to a disability benefit of 5s per week for as long as he or she was unable to work. Workers also had the right to medical treatment from a doctor who was paid a capitation fee by the approved society. Finally, a worker's wife was entitled to a 30s maternity benefit, and the worker had the right to treatment in a sanatorium for tuberculosis. Approved societies with schemes in place were able to offer additional benefits as a result of the state and employer contributions they would now receive.[54]

Despite the later claims to the contrary, the government clearly expected the measure to strengthen its electoral position. The ecstatic reception which the Bill received from the Liberal press reflected the same expectation. The *Leeds Mercury* called it 'a masterpiece of constructive statesmanship' which 'transcends in social and economic importance any measure ever submitted to any Parliament'.[55] Even the compulsory element did not trouble Liberals. If compulsion was necessary to assure a large enough pool, including the neediest workers, then so be it.

As the Bill made its way through the Commons, Lloyd George was more than willing to compromise with those who were still dissatisfied. In an attempt to buy off the doctors, management of the medical benefit was turned over to local insurance committees rather than the approved societies. Patients would be free to choose a doctor from a panel registered with the local committee. In response to pressure from Labour, workers earning less than 2s per day were exempted from contributing, although Lloyd George refused to eliminate the worker contribution entirely. Finally, a virtually separate scheme was created for Ireland in order to meet Irish demands.

Despite such efforts at conciliation, by the last months of 1911, it was clear to Liberals that the Insurance Bill was a major electoral liability, especially among working men and employers, who resented having to make contributions.[56] For at least a year, it was the most prominent issue at by-elections, and both sides attributed the sorry Liberal performance to its unpopularity. The government faced the additional problem that the doctors might refuse to participate in the scheme. The British Medical Association (BMA) demanded a substantial increase in the capitation fee and a substantial reduction of the maximum annual income of £160 for participants. In October 1912, Lloyd George offered to increase the capitation fee, but he remained firm on the income limit. At the same time, the government threatened to organize a national medical service if the doctors still refused to co-operate – a threat which was heartily supported by the rank and file.

By 1913 health insurance was becoming less of a focus of controversy. The rebellion of the BMA collapsed in January. Speakers had been stumping the country for a year explaining the provisions of the Act. Most importantly, benefits began to be paid. As a result, there is some evidence that working-class hostility was waning, and the government's by-election record improved significantly.[57] Nevertheless, national health insurance did not speak well for the Liberal Party's ability to anticipate the desires of its working-class constituency.

Liberal social legislation was directed at promoting social harmony. By reconciling the poor and working class to the existing social and economic systems, Liberals sought to combat the attractions of more extreme solutions – such as socialism. The relations between capital and labour therefore posed a major challenge to liberalism. Liberals could not admit any inherent conflict between the two. On the contrary, they asserted that both had a common interest in the prosperity of industry. Strikes and lock-outs were doubly disastrous, for they destroyed both industrial prosperity and social harmony. Because industrial relations were so closely linked to the market mechanism which fixed the price of labour, Liberals shied away from compulsion to prevent disputes. Instead, the role of government was to facilitate voluntary agreements. The favoured method which evolved between 1893 and 1908 was the conciliation board, with representatives of employers and workers in an industry under an independent chairman. To encourage the conciliation process, the Conciliation Act of 1896 created a conciliation service at the Board of Trade. The immediate objective of the service was to facilitate the settlement of an industrial dispute when both parties requested its intervention. Its ultimate objective was to encourage the creation of conciliation boards whenever it was practicable.

Conciliation could only succeed if both capital and labour were sufficiently well organized to be able to impose discipline on their constituencies. Thus, strong trade unions were essential to harmonious industrial relations. As Asquith explained to a Liberal audience at Stockton, they offered 'the greatest safeguard against industrial warfare and aggressive acts on one side or the other which bred bad blood between classes and brought material loss to the community at large'.[58] For this reason, the government (responding to pressure from both Labour MPs and its own back-benchers) reversed the Taff Vale decision with the Trade Disputes Act of 1906. Only when unions were freed from liability for actions during a strike could they effectively perform their constructive role in industrial matters.

The perception that strong trade unions and effective conciliation machinery were vital to the community's interest shaped the Liberal response to the problem posed by sweated industries. These were trades whose labour force was employed in small workshops or worked at home. They were characterized by unsanitary working conditions, extremely long hours and wages insufficient to maintain a minimum level of subsistence. Liberals believed that sweating resulted from the inability of the workers to organize in trade unions for their mutual protection. Between 1906 and 1908 a Liberal consensus developed in favour of wages boards as a solution to the problem. Each board would be like a conciliation board, consisting of representatives of the workers and employers in the trade, as well as independent members, all appointed by the government. The board would provide the means for capital and labour to meet and bargain about wages, hours and conditions of work.

131

The Trade Boards Act of 1909 provided for both central and local wages boards in four trades with large numbers of female workers. It also gave the Board of Trade ultimate power to enforce under the law the minimum wage rates determined by the boards. As with the government's unemployment legislation, the Liberal and Non-conformist press gave little attention to the new Bill. They could see a clear case for assisting these poor workers. As George Toulmin pointed out, 'so far as the victims are concerned there is no necessity to ask for any proof of their willingness to work. There is no need to beware of shirkers'. Given this fact, the problem simply was to devise a means to restore to them the 'power of self-help'.[59] Liberals were not troubled that this involved Parliament's creating machinery to establish minimum wages. Since the workers could not form trade unions to give them equal bargaining power with capital, government intervention offered the only practical remedy to an exceptional situation. The experiment was so successful that in 1913 Sydney Buxton extended the Act to five more trades.

Even as Liberals were adapting traditional conciliation machinery to sweated trades, its effectiveness in better organized industries was breaking down. After 1907, and especially between 1910 and 1913, there was a dramatic increase in strike activity to a level unknown since the period 1889–94. Wages had not been keeping up with rising prices for some time. The revival of economic prosperity after 1909, and the tremendous expansion of trade union membership which followed in its wake, created ideal conditions for strikes. Beyond the economic problem, however, there appears to have been a broader working-class discontent. It was reflected in growing dissatisfaction with the working of the established institutions of capitalism and parliamentary democracy, which seemed to discriminate against the workers. It was reflected in a growing sense of class solidarity, encouraged by trades councils which brought together representatives of the organized workers of a community, whatever their skill level. It was reflected in the attraction of younger workers to the language and principles of socialism or syndicalism.[60]

One manifestation of this broader discontent was a rejection of industrial conciliation. Among the rank and file, there was a sense that conciliation boards were unfair, and a growing dissatisfaction with leaders who insisted on adhering to them.[61] The result was a series of strikes or threatened strikes in Britain's major industries. Often the disputes were triggered by seemingly minor issues, and many were sustained after the leaders had agreed upon a settlement. Virtually all the strikes were over wages. Other issues included conditions of work, the working of conciliation boards in settling grievances, and recognition of the union as a bargaining agent.

Liberals were troubled by this wave of strike activity. They recognized that there were legitimate grievances and even frustration which underlay so much working-class unrest. They had little patience with employers who resisted justified claims and forced their employees to strike. None the less, the provincial press tended to focus on how the workers' actions were undermining constructive industrial relations. Liberals reaffirmed that the role of trade unions was to prevent strikes, not to promote them; therefore, negotiation was the proper course to pursue. All issues were resolvable by discussions if both parties showed good sense and good will. Strikes should be a last resort, for, like any form of warfare, they merely resulted in waste, resentment and suffering. They accentuated the hostility between capital and labour rather than promoting the mutual understanding which was central to the industrial world which Liberals desired to create.

Most trade union leaders shared the Liberals' preference for negotiation rather than direct action. Thus, the trend among workers to ignore the advice of their leaders disturbed Liberals. If leaders could no longer ensure the discipline of their men, then unions would cease to provide a mechanism for the orderly resolution of differences between capital and labour. Most dangerous of all was the rash of unauthorized strikes in violation of existing collective bargaining agreements. Such anarchic and irresponsible actions were a negation of the rule of law. Liberals rightly perceived that these striking workers were repudiating the liberal view of industrial relations, which was defined by the *British Congregationalist and Examiner* on 24 August 1911: 'Discipline, restraint, loyalty to covenants made by representatives, respect for the rights and liberties of others – these are the only qualities that can prevent Democracy passing into chaos, from which a despotism will be the only escape.'

With the railway strike of August 1911 Liberals saw a new danger: a sectional interest opposing the general good. The railway strike followed two months of industrial action at most of the major ports. The nation's ability to move goods was being threatened. The result could be enormous suffering for people who had no interest in the immediate issues of the strike. Liberals supported the railwaymen's demands for better wages and recognition of the union, but the *Methodist Recorder* warned on 12 October.

> This does not mean that the public . . . consent to the view that to right the wrongs of the few they [the railwaymen] may cause the suffering of the many . . . The nation is larger than any given class, and its interests are therefore of prior importance; to allow any one class so to act as to cause detriment to the larger interests of the people is to produce anarchy and national strife.

Liberals had difficulty, however, in defining how the government was to defend the public interest. The conciliation service of the Board of Trade had helped resolve many industrial disputes during the past four years. Furthermore, following Lloyd George's dramatic and successful intervention to prevent a railway strike in 1907, there were occasional forays by ministers into the world of industrial conciliation – with mixed results. Now the Cabinet created an Industrial Council at the Board of Trade to investigate any dispute referred to it and recommend terms of settlement. The Council, however, amounted to little. It was a gesture to demonstrate to Liberals that the government was dealing with the crisis. In fact, the Cabinet agreed with Pease that the best response was to 'rely on conferences, conciliation, compromise and *common sense*'.[62] These could not be imposed by the government. All it could do was remain impartial and assure that conciliation machinery was available if the parties desired to use it.

Thus, the only response which the government could offer to growing working-class unrest was to reaffirm the liberal views of trade unionism and industrial relations which the strikers were rejecting. This was one indication that, despite two electoral triumphs and the enactment of an imaginative programmne of social reform, Liberals had only a limited understanding of their party's working-class constituency. Another was the indifference or even hostility with which workers greeted some of the government's social legislation. While antipathy eventually might be overcome, such reactions suggest that these measures did little to consolidate the party's position with working-class voters.

There is no cause for surprise in this failure. Most Liberals had no experience of what the workers wanted. They would support any policies which dealt with the problems at hand and could be reconciled with liberal principles. As a result, the policies which were developed often were more effective at satisfying the desires of Liberals than those of working people. At the same time, social reform was not the primary concern of the Liberal rank and file. Their priorities continued to be the safeguarding of free trade and the limitation of the privileges of Church, land and liquor. For them, the real achievements of 1909–11 were the Budget of 1909, which provided an alternative to tariff reform and launched the assault on the landlord, and the Parliament Act, which limited the veto of the House of Lords and opened the way to legislation dealing with a wide range of traditional concerns. As the Liberals set to work to use the Parliament Act, the limitations which their traditional liberalism imposed on the party's ability to respond to working-class aspirations would become even more patent.

7

Domestic Policies:
The Years of Frustration,
1912–1914

The paramount importance of traditional issues for Liberals became unmistakable between 1912 and 1914. This was not only because the Parliament Act at last made possible the accomplishment of key policies in the Newcastle Programme. Just as importantly, with policies enacted to relieve poverty and unemployment, Liberals again turned to the traditional issues in their search for social reforms. Liberals perceived their policies of land reform and education reform to be central to the social question. None the less, Liberals had great difficulty in transcending the traditional focus of both issues so that they would generate enthusiasm among the party's working-class constituency. Land reform remained most successful in the rural context in which it had been spawned, while urban workers showed little interest in it. At the same time, Nonconformists persevered in their insistence that any measure of education reform must remove their grievances, thereby restricting the government's efforts to give its policy a broader appeal.

Its failure to develop a credible social reform policy during the last years before the First World War was just one source of Liberal weakness. The Marconi Scandal undermined the party's claim to place moral propriety before political expediency. In March 1912, the British Marconi Company was awarded a contract to build a chain of wireless stations throughout the empire. In April Sir Rufus Isaacs, the Attorney General, bought 10,000 shares in the American Marconi Company at the urging of his brother, who was managing director of the independent British company. Isaacs then sold 1,000 shares to both Lloyd George and the Master of Elibank (the Chief Whip), and the latter later used Liberal Party funds to buy more shares. Although there was no corruption in the awarding of the contract or the purchase of the shares, rumours of impropriety forced the government to agree to an investigation by a select committee of the House of Commons. During the ensuing debate in October 1912, Lloyd George and Isaacs denied owning any shares in the British company, while failing to mention their American shares.

The ministers' behaviour throughout reflected questionable judgement. Their colleagues had little choice but to support them, but privately they found the actions of the three men 'thoughtless', 'unwise', 'certainly indiscreet and very nearly improper', 'lamentable' and 'difficult to defend'.[1] Some among the party's Nonconformist constituency were especially disturbed by the affair. Although Silvester Horne was unswerving in his support of Lloyd George, the *British Congregationalist and Examiner* believed that the Chancellor's 'want of judgement has shaken the confidence of many of his sincerest admirers and friends, though it has not destroyed their faith in him'.[2] Overall, the incident could not help but weaken the credibility of the party with those who took seriously its claim to embody principle and righteousness.

Such doubts concerning the Cabinet's commitment to principle rather than political expediency were reinforced by its vacillating response to the crisis in Ireland. The first measure to benefit from the Parliament Act was to be an Irish Home Rule bill. Liberals were elated by the prospect that their twenty-five-year commitment to justice for Ireland at last was to bear fruit, and they were outraged when the Ulster Protestants threatened to rob them of their triumph by resorting to force to resist a constitutionally passed act of Parliament. Yet the government did nothing when faced with the organization of the Ulster Volunteers and the seditious speeches of Sir Edward Carson, the Protestants' leader. Such passivity seemed feeble to some Liberal activists, especially when contrasted with the arrest and forced-feeding of suffragettes who employed violence and hunger strikes to express their demand for votes for women, or with the arrest of labour leaders like Tom Mann and James Larkin for seditious speeches during strikes. When, in 1914, the Cabinet began to explore a compromise with the Ulster leaders – thus justifying their threat to use force – there was a crisis of confidence among its supporters both in Parliament and in the constituencies. Thus, by July 1914, the Liberal government was faced with both working-class indifference to its policies and a collapse of morale among the rank and file.

THE LANGUISHING OF SOCIAL REFORM

The continuing wave of strike activity provided the initial focus for Liberal social policies after 1911. In particular, the coal strike of 1912 raised the issue of the minimum wage. In October 1911, the Miners' Federation of Great Britain (MFGB) declared in favour of district minimum wages. The MFGB drew up district schedules, subject to a national minimum of 5s a day for men and 2s for boys. The owners in most districts were prepared to concede a minimum, but those in Scotland, North-East England and South Wales refused.

Liberals viewed the threat of a national coal strike in cataclysmic terms. The provincial press feared the disruption of the economy and the suffering which would result. Although sympathetic to the miners' claims, Liberals believed that all issues could be resolved by good sense and reasonableness.[3] On the other hand, nothing could justify the national disaster which a strike would entail. 'There is something wrong', the *Leicester Daily Mercury* argued on 24 February, 'with the state of mind which suggests that the welfare of the nation should be subservient to the quarrels of sections . . . it is of paramount importance that the national welfare should have the first consideration.' For this reason, Liberals endorsed the government's decision to intervene. On 28 February a Cabinet committee proposed a compromise based on recognition of the principle of the minimum wage in the coal industry, but with the minimum to be negotiated on a district basis. The MFGB, however, insisted on a national minimum of 5s and 2s, and on 29 February its members went out on strike.

With its efforts at conciliation having broken down, the Cabinet decided to proceed by legislation. Because the circumstances were unique, and there was a real danger of disorder if the strike was prolonged, they concluded that a measure for a limited period on an experimental basis was justified. The provincial press concurred. The Bill which Asquith introduced on 19 March employed the familiar system of conciliation boards – with representatives of owners and miners and an independent chairman – to set minimum wages for underground workers on a district basis. The miners continued to strive to have the 5s and 2s national minimum fixed in the Bill. Some Liberals were prepared to concede this. Forty-seven Liberal MPs voted for an amendment fixing the national minimum, and it was endorsed by the *Manchester Guardian* and the *Daily News*. On the other hand, A. C. Murray found 'strong objections amongst our moderate and business Liberals'. The provincial press, fearing the precedent of Parliament setting wages, supported the government in resisting the miners' demands. Furthermore, Asquith insisted that the Act would not serve as a precedent to be extended to other industries. It was, he told the House of Commons, 'an experimental measure to meet a special emergency in regard to a particular class of workers working under peculiar conditions in one great industry. It does not purport to lay down any general principle'.[4]

The Trade Boards Act of 1909 and the Coal Mines Act of 1912 embodied the Liberal approach to the minimum wage. Liberals had no difficulty embracing the principle. They recognized that some men and women could not earn enough to maintain themselves and their families, not because of their own failings, but because of the structure of the economic system. At the same time, Liberals saw all sorts of problems with the state fixing a *national* minimum, for a wage set above that which prevailed locally would merely lead to inefficiency or unemployment. Some in the parliamentary party supported Labour resolutions favourable to the principle on a national basis; however, these remained a minority. When an MFGB deputation asked Asquith in 1914 to extend the minimum wage in the coal mines to surface workers, he firmly refused. Once the exceptional nature of the 1912 Act was breached, he feared it would have to be extended to factory workers.[5] Thus, Liberal minimum wage legislation would continue to be limited to those with special problems. Furthermore, when a measure was justified, Liberals sought to minimize parliamentary interference. They preferred that wages be agreed upon by those in the industry, using a conciliation board arrangement which would maximize regional flexibility.

The minimum wage was just one issue raised by the coal strike. Another was nationalization. Railway nationalization had been under discussion for some time. The railways had been regulated by Parliament since the 1840s. Furthermore, the recent trend towards amalgamation was destroying railway competition and creating a series of monopolies. Nationalization, the *Leicester Daily Post* argued, was 'the only solution that will enable the State to possess and use its monopoly in the paramount interests of the public, and the public alone'. Liberals were more doubtful about nationalization of the coal mines. Still, when the Leicester Town Council carried a favourable resolution, the majority of Liberals on the Council supported it, and the *Daily Post* concluded that 'the balance of fact and argument is on the side of nationalisation at no remote date'.[6] Thus, while Liberals were in no hurry to nationalize either the railways or the coal mines, they clearly could accept nationalization if a Liberal government decided it was justified in the public interest.

Of more immediate concern to Liberals was the problem of protecting the public interest when it was threatened by a national strike in a vital industry. The issue was given greater urgency by another major stoppage on the London docks, the second in two years. Many among the rank and file were clearly getting tired of union failures to adhere to agreements and resented these attempts to coerce the public by threatening the poor with starvation. They wanted the government to do something to prevent such occurrences.

Asquith responded by asking the Industrial Council which had been created in 1911 to make recommendations concerning how the fulfilment of industrial agreements could best be secured. Most breaches of agreements were the result of differences of interpretation as to what the agreement meant. Ambiguities, however, were often crucial to securing compromise. To eliminate them could make agreements more difficult to reach. Furthermore, the loss of flexibility could lead to disputes later which might have been avoided. The Industrial Council therefore recommended only that all agreements should include provisions for dealing with differences over interpretation – that is, a conciliation mechanism. Another reason workers struck in defiance of agreements was that employers who were not party to the agreement undercut it. This had been one cause of the 1912 London dockers' strike. The Council recommended that, under certain conditions, the Board of Trade could extend such an agreement to everyone in a trade if both parties requested it. The Board of Trade should do so, however, only if the agreement included provisions for no changes without reasonable notice and no stoppages without an investigation. Trade unionists, however, would not countenance any measure which limited their right to strike.

The government also sent Sir George Askwith, the chairman of the Industrial Council, to Canada to investigate the Lemieux Act. This Act required that in key industries, thirty days' notice had to be given of desired changes in wages and hours. Any dispute in one of these industries had to be submitted to a board with powers to investigate the issues and make recommendations before a strike or lock-out could occur. Askwith was attracted by the possibilities which the Act offered in assuring that conciliation was attempted, that the public was fully informed and that its interests were considered before an industrial action could occur. Again, however, trade union resistance to any restriction of the right to strike led the government to do nothing.

In truth, the government did not want to act because it did not believe the state should be involved further in the settlement of industrial disputes. First, as Buxton told the Cabinet in April 1912, people could not be forced to work. Nor could the government throw one million people in jail. So there were clear limitations on what could be achieved by a stricter law. Furthermore, Liberals still believed that the best formula for peaceful industrial relations was that defined by Asquith when he spoke to the Association of Chambers of Commerce in March 1914: there should be strong employer and labour organizations; on both sides 'there should be a growing disposition to subordinate particular and individual and local interests to the general interest; and . . . in the free interchange of opinion between the two is to be found the best hope of a real industrial settlement.'[7] When the parties turned away from rational discourse, liberalism saw little that could be done beyond waiting until common sense reasserted itself and the existing voluntary machinery for conciliation could once more be effective.

Thus, there were clear limitations as to how far most Liberals were prepared to go when considering state intervention in strikes or the setting of wages. The years 1912–14 also revealed limitations in the Liberal approach to poverty and unemployment. In seeking ways to attack the root causes of these evils, Liberals increasingly turned to their traditional policies dealing with temperance, education and land.

Temperance reform was less important than it had been. Many Liberals were approaching the problem of drink with greater sympathy. The *Eastern Daily Press*, for example, emphasized that poverty often led to drinking in order to relieve the dreary lives of the poor and called for greater 'opportunities for intelligent pleasures and healthy enjoyments'. At the same time, the situation was improving. Between 1899 and 1909 the national drink bill dropped from £186 million to £155 million, a per capita decrease of over 20 per cent. There was a comparable fall in convictions for drunkenness from 1905 to 1909. Finally, the Licensing Act of 1904 had led to a reduction in the number of licensed houses by nearly 10,000.[8]

None the less, the government's Nonconformist supporters still believed that 'the curse of intemperance . . . is responsible for more poverty and destitution than all other causes put together'.[9] Temperance reformers, however, remained divided over what to do about it. Some, like Eliot Crawshay-Williams, the Liberal MP for Leicester from 1910 to 1913, favoured a system of disinterested management which would break the power of 'the trade' by removing the profit motive. Others, like Clifford, continued to favour local option because it embodied the democratic principle. Most were willing to accept partial measures which reduced hours, imposed Sunday closing and regulated clubs. Still, there was growing impatience over the delays in introducing a new licensing bill. At the annual meeting of the Free Church Council in March 1914, Rev. J. Tolefree Parr 'warned the Government that if they went back to the electors without having attempted to redeem their explicit pledge on this matter they would certainly lose the support of many who had not only voted, but worked for them enthusiastically in the past'.[10]

For most Nonconformists, education was a more important issue than temperance. As with temperance, the severity of the grievances had been mitigated. Balfour's Act had not stopped the transfer of denominational schools to public control. By 1911, three-fifths of the five million students in elementary school attended council schools, reversing the ratio of ten years earlier. The Liberals had made it easier for Nonconformists to become teachers by opening up the Anglican teacher training colleges to non-Anglicans and building new non-sectarian colleges. As a result, by 1909 9,500 of 12,000 places at such colleges were not subject to religious tests. The expansion of the colleges also had obliterated the pupil-teacher system which had discriminated against Nonconformists at Anglican schools. Whereas in 1906–7 there had been over 11,000 pupil teachers, by 1913–14 there were under 1,500.[11] Still, the basic grievances remained. Sectarian schools which received public money were not under public control, yet they subjected their teachers to religious tests. There were over 5,700 districts whose only school was denominational – usually Anglican – and another 1,200 with more than one Anglican school, but no other. These single school areas increasingly became the focus of efforts to satisfy the Nonconformists.

The Nonconformists themselves remained divided on the education question. Moderates like Horne and the Wesleyan leader Scott Lidgett wanted to see the matter settled and were prepared to compromise. Extremists like Clifford and John Massie, the chairman of the Education Committee of the Congregational Union, rejected any proposal which perpetuated rate aid to sectarian schools. The Parliament Act gave Nonconformists new hope that their grievances could be removed without any need to compromise. When instead they saw that the Irish were to be given Home Rule without having to support education reform as a *quid pro quo*, Nonconformist fury boiled over. There were charges of broken faith by the government and threats of indifference to Home Rule and abstention at the next general election.[12]

In October 1911, Runciman was replaced at the Board of Education by Pease. Although he was a Quaker, Pease had no sympathy with Nonconformist grievances. He approached education as an instrument of social reform, reaffirming the traditional liberal belief that education was the crucial means for individual development and thus for genuine equality of opportunity. The moment was opportune for a more comprehensive approach to the education issue. Some Liberals were growing impatient with the religious extremists and passive resisters.[13] At the same time, the Royal Commission on the Poor Law had drawn public attention to the relationship between early school leaving and unemployment and poverty. Finally, there had been mounting pressure from local authorities for a revision of the grant system. With rates increasing, the limit on local initiatives for educational improvement was being reached.

Pease's objectives were 'to ensure that the best brains of the whole community should get to the top, and to provide that there should be a general diffusion of knowledge, so that we should possess an educated democracy'. This required the organization of a national system of education at all levels (not just elementary), with the opportunity for all students to progress through the system to the level and in the direction that interest and ability justified. The local education authori-

141

ties (LEAs) would provide elementary, secondary and continuing education. They would have the powers to build, shut down, or combine schools (including denominational schools) as efficiency demanded, and the government would subsidize building loans so that LEAs would use these powers. Regional councils would co-ordinate the activities of the LEAs and determine the provision of specialized institutions like universities, technical or agricultural schools, and teacher training colleges. The Board of Education would set standards. The revised grant system would be based on effort as well as need, thus encouraging LEAs to improve education. Money would also be provided to upgrade the teaching profession by improving pay and pensions. Finally, the school-leaving age was to be raised to fourteen; the half-time system, which allowed children below the school-leaving age to work part-time, was to be phased out; and children would be encouraged or required to attend continuing education classes after they left school. In this way, Pease hoped to end children leaving school for jobs which offered no training and no future, and thus to cut off the supply of casual labour and unemployables at its source.[14]

Pease knew that the Nonconformist grievances could not be ignored. He hoped to relieve them indirectly through his broader programme of educational improvement. First, by giving the LEAs the power (and the money) to build schools where they were needed and to close or combine unnecessary schools, he hoped many single school areas would be eliminated. Secondly, if the LEAs were to be able to assure educational efficiency, they needed greater control over secular education in the denominational schools, including the power to appoint and dismiss all head teachers. By thus subsuming relief of Nonconformist grievances in provisions for improving education, Pease hoped to mobilize the support of the LEAs and the teachers and secure passage by the House of Lords.[15]

The Liberal press responded sympathetically when Pease outlined his proposals in the House of Commons on 22 July 1913. Thereafter, it lost interest. This apathy confirmed the conclusions of educational enthusiasts like Haldane, F. D. Acland and C. P. Trevelyan: the public was indifferent to education reform, while Liberal activists would not support it unless the Nonconformists affirmed that the proposals were worth fighting for.[16] In short, education reform as social reform had no electoral appeal. Furthermore, the Nonconformists would not accept the partial and indirect relief which Pease offered. On 17 November, W. Robertson Nicoll wrote to Asquith stating that the Nonconformists expected the single school areas to be eliminated by the LEAs either taking over the denominational schools or building new council schools. At the Free Church Council's annual meeting on 11 March

1914, Rev. J. Pickett warned the government to 'be careful that they did not provoke, not simply the beginnings of revolt, but of a sense of betrayal'. At a concurrent meeting of the National Passive Resistance League, Rev. A. F. Guttery argued that a government which caved in before the threats of Sir Edward Carson should be able to redress the constitutionally expressed grievances of Dr John Clifford.[17] In July 1914, Pease finally accepted the inevitable and circulated to the Cabinet a bill dealing with single school areas which met the Nonconformist demands. Thus, the government was back where it had been in 1906 – trying to satisfy the Nonconformists on education. All attempts to broaden the context in which the education issue was discussed so as to promote a major measure of social reform had failed. For Nonconformists and most Liberals, education reform continued to mean resolving the religious question, and all else was secondary.

Land reform, rather than education reform, was the real Liberal panacea for resolving the nation's social problems. Policies to benefit the tenant farmer and rural labourer would revive British agriculture and end the exodus from the countryside to the cities or overseas. Urban policies would encourage better housing and a healthier living environment while facilitating entrepreneurship. The effects of both together would be to reduce poverty, unemployment and industrial unrest as workers were able to live better at lower cost. Business would also benefit from reduced costs as well as increased labour productivity. All that was required to achieve this millenium was to break the land monopoly, that last remnant of feudalism which allowed land to be treated as a vehicle for achieving social status and political power rather than as an economic resource to be developed.

In 1912 the government's popularity was waning, while the Irish question threatened to dominate politics for the next three years. Lloyd George was looking for a policy of social reform which would rally the Liberal troops as the Budget had in 1909. Land reform was ideal for his purpose. It was an issue he cared about deeply. Furthermore, as Sir George Riddell shrewdly noted,

> While it deals with present-day economic troubles, it is framed to appeal to the Liberal politician who is not prepared to attack the commercial classes, but will rejoice in attacking the pockets and privileges of his traditional bugbears and enemies, the squires and ground lords.[18]

Initially, Lloyd George contemplated an independent land campaign. He changed his mind, however, and decided to secure Cabinet approval so that he could go to the country with the policy of the government.[19] To strengthen his position with both his colleagues and the public, Lloyd George appointed a Land Inquiry Committee to document various aspects of the land problem. Its evidence would serve as a resource for Lloyd George and the Cabinet as they developed their proposals, and its reports would provide Liberal speakers and editors with a source of 'objective' information with which to justify Liberal policy. Thus, the land campaign could be presented as a proven necessity for the well-being of the community rather than as a vendetta against the landlords.

The Committee's rural report was nearly completed before the Cabinet got to work on developing its proposals in the summer of 1913. Haldane was the only person who had thought out a coherent policy, and his proposal for a land commission to adjudicate a wide range of issues – such as wages, rents, leaseholds, tenancies – provided the basis of subsequent discussions. There was disagreement in the Cabinet over how to deal with minimum wages for agricultural labourers, and the rating of land values was even more intractable. As a result, when Lloyd George opened the land campaign at Bedford on 11 October, there was still no government policy. After the Bedford speech, however, Charles Hobhouse noted that the Cabinet meetings which finally decided on a rural programme were 'friendly, harmonious, unanimous'.[20] Lloyd George had succeeded in winning the confidence of his colleagues by being patient and allowing them to help shape the policy.

The foundations of the Liberals' rural land programme were two: to secure a decent life and reasonable future prospects for the agricultural labourer so that he would stay on the land, and to provide reasonable security for the farmer so that he would develop the land for optimal use. The first required a minimum wage. This was easily justified, since agricultural labourers had been unable to organize effective trade unions. The Cabinet still had not agreed on how the minimum wage was to be fixed by the summer of 1914. The preference seemed to be to use wages boards, which would reassure farmers that their views were adequately represented and provide for maximum variation according to local conditions. The agricultural labourer also needed a decent cottage, free from the tied-cottage system which Liberals believed destroyed his independence. The government proposed that the state should build 120,000 cottages to be let directly to the labourers at economic rents, which the minimum wage would assure they could pay. Finally, the labourer needed the prospect of improving himself. The government proposed that a new Ministry of Land, which would replace the Board of Agriculture, should have the power to purchase land for small holdings at fair prices.

To win the support of the farmer, the government proposed to create a body of Land Commissioners under the Ministry of Land. If a farmer felt that he was unable to pay the minimum wage, he could appeal to the Commissioners to have his rent lowered. Farmers would be given security of tenure, and they could appeal to the Commissioners on issues of compensation. The farmers also would have greater protection against damage done by game. Again, the Commissioners could fix compensation. The Commissioners also would determine the price at which land would be purchased for public purposes, and they offered an alternative to wages boards as a means of fixing minimum wages.[21]

In order to mobilize support for the government's land programme, Lloyd George created the Central Land and Housing Council. During the peak of the campaign from May to July 1914, Council speakers addressed 90 to 120 meetings each day. The Council also printed massive quantities of literature for distribution. Runciman organized a concurrent campaign by the National League of Young Liberals, while F. E. Hamer of the *Manchester Guardian* undertook to organize the Liberal press.[22]

All indications were that the rural campaign was succeeding. There were some problems with the farmers, who did not like the minimum wage, wanted to retain tied cottages, and were attracted by the Unionist policy of land purchase. On the other hand, they welcomed Liberal proposals for security of tenure and compensation for damage by game. Even more, they welcomed the proposals for rate relief which were incorporated into the 1914 Budget. The support among rural labourers appeared overwhelming. The favourable reports from Liberal organizers were confirmed by Unionist observers: the workers welcomed the promise of a minimum wage, shorter hours, a weekly half-holiday and a cottage. Yet the response of the Liberal rank and file to the land campaign was curiously uncertain. All the reports Lloyd George received indicated unreserved enthusiasm.[23] Yet, while the Norwich and Leicester papers used each Lloyd George speech to restate the case for land reform, there were few other leading articles on the subject. The *Eastern Daily Press* never even formally endorsed the government's proposals. Furthermore, the Leeds papers, which did not serve a rural constituency, rarely commented on the campaign at all.

Unlike the rural campaign, the urban land campaign was beset by problems. The Cabinet had great difficulty agreeing on a policy. As a result, whereas Lloyd George had introduced the rural programme as a coherent whole at Swindon, the urban programme had to be introduced piecemeal. The most clearly articulated aspect of the urban programme was the protection of leaseholders. Any new leaseholder would have the right to appeal to the Land Commissioners to secure renewal of his lease on fair terms. His new rent would not include the value of improvements he had undertaken or goodwill he had created. Renewal could be denied only if the land was to be put to better use, and the leaseholder must then be compensated for improvements and goodwill. All told, this policy represented a direct appeal to the middle-class small businessmen whom the government always was trying to woo.

The second part of the urban programme aimed at encouraging housing and urban development. Implicitly, it recognized the failure of the 1909 Housing and Town Planning Act. The government would undertake a national housing survey (also necessary for its rural programme) to determine the needs of each municipality. The machinery by which local authorities could purchase land compulsorily for public purposes would be simplified, and the Land Commissioners would determine a fair price for the land. Finally, local authorities would have the right to purchase land in anticipation of future development.[24]

The government, however, could not agree on a land tax policy. In May 1911, Asquith and Lloyd George had received a memorial signed by 173 Liberal and Labour MPs calling for the rating and taxation of land values. While the Cabinet favoured some form of land value taxation, no one had any sympathy for the single-taxers, who believed that the rating and taxation of land values was a sufficient policy for solving all social problems. The uncompromising views of the single-taxers threatened to alienate moderate Liberals. As a result, Asquith, Lloyd George and Runciman (the President of the Board of Agriculture since October 1911) had publicly repudiated the single tax long before the campaign was launched.[25]

Popular pressure was far greater for rating reform than for tax reform. The Liberal rank and file had been crying for rate relief for years. One of the objectives of Liberal social legislation had been to relieve the poor rate. As a result of old-age pensions, for example, the number of people over seventy in receipt of outdoor relief had plummeted from 168,000 in March 1906 to 8,500 in January 1913. Insurance, too, was expected to reduce the number of people who had to enter the workhouse, the most expensive form of relief. In 1913 the government turned to the education rate. In 1900–1 the rates had accounted for 43.6 per cent of LEA expenditures; by 1910–11 they accounted for 51.5 per cent. Pease's proposed reform of the grant system provided for the Exchequer to pick up a larger share of the costs.[26]

The pressures to relieve the rates, combined with the broad support in the party for the rating of land values, assured that Lloyd George would include rating reform in the 1914 Budget. Political distractions, however, caused the Budget proposals to be thrown together haphazardly, even by Lloyd George's lax standards. An annoyed Cabinet saw them for the first time on 30 April, too late to modify them.[27] The

Budget proposed a new system of grants, based on need and effort, in support of education, roads, police and health. At the same time, local authorities eventually would be required to introduce the rating of site values and to use the new grants to relieve the rate on buildings. Since the land valuation would not be completed until 1915, the Budget provided temporary grants for 1914–15. Finally, these reforms were financed, not by a national land values tax as the single-taxers demanded, but by increases in the graduation of the income tax, super-tax and death duties.

Some forty Liberal MPs rebelled against the Budget on the grounds that Parliament was being asked to raise money for grants which would not go into effect until 1915. Asquith and other financial purists found the constitutional argument unanswerable. As a result, the Cabinet abandoned rating reform for a year, dropping the temporary grants (except for those for education and insurance) and reducing the income tax by 1d. The new grant proposals would be introduced in a separate bill in the autumn. This in turn led to a second rebellion by land taxers and other radicals: the government's majority on the second reading on 22 June fell to thirty-eight. Its majority on an opposition amendment on 8 July fell to twenty-three when Liberals opposed to the Budget abstained.[28]

The provincial press accepted all this turmoil in the parliamentary party stoically. None the less, there was no gainsaying the seriousness of the situation. As Richard Holt, one of the leaders of the Liberal rebels, made clear, their protest was

> a combined remonstrance by businessmen and some survivors of the Cobden-Bright school of thought against the ill-considered and socialistic tendencies of the Government finance . . . We have certainly travelled a long way from the old Liberal principle of 'retrenchment', and I deeply regret it.

Worse still, there seemed to be no compensating advantage in the form of working-class enthusiasm. On the contrary, all reports indicated that the urban working class was indifferent to the land campaign. Observers told Lloyd George that the way to mobilize the support of urban workers was to promise to extend the Trade Boards Act to all low-paid town workers.[29] There could hardly have been a more explicit confession that land reform had no appeal to the urban working class as a policy of social reform. Thus, land reform was effective only in its traditional rural context, just as education reform was effective only in its traditional Nonconformist context. The working class could see nothing central to its interests in the Liberals' treatment of either issue.

THE FUTURE OF THE PROGRESSIVE ALLIANCE

During the years preceding the First World War, the Labour Party was unable to mount any meaningful challenge to the Liberals' supremacy as the party of the left. Labour contested twelve Liberal seats in by-elections from 1911 to 1914 and came in last every time. Labour also lost four of its own seats, two to Liberals and two to Unionists. At best, the Labour vote in new constituencies reached 20 to 30 per cent of the total, sufficient to threaten to cost the Liberals the seat. The Unionists won six on a minority vote. As had been the case in the general elections of 1910, however, Labour could not wrest a seat from the Liberals.

One problem facing Labour was that the Osborne Judgement hampered its political activity. This decision of the House of Lords in December 1909 declared that trade unions could not use their funds for political purposes. As a result, they could no longer contribute money for MPs' or town councillors' salaries, support trades council political activities nor contribute to national or local campaign funds. In part, Liberals had no doubt how to respond to the Osborne Judgement. Payment of MPs had been enshrined in the Newcastle Programme as the means of assuring that the House of Commons was accessible to all men of ability. Also, it would allow Labour MPs to be spokesmen for their constituencies rather than for sectional interests represented by the trade unions. Thus, there was overwhelming Liberal support for the government's 1911 Act which gave MPs an annual salary of £400.

The Cabinet was divided, however, as to how much further it should proceed. Liberals sympathized with the West Fife miners who complained of having to pay 'for the spread of Socialist doctrines of which they altogether disapproved' through their trade union contributions. As a result, although most members of the Cabinet favoured restoring trade unions' rights to engage in political activities, they believed that some provision must be made to protect the consciences of the minority.[30] The measure which they finally agreed on allowed a trade union to use its funds for political purposes if a majority voted in favour of doing so, if a separate political fund was created, and if individual members were allowed to contract out of the political fund without losing any benefits or suffering any disability. Although this solution did not altogether satisfy the TUC, most Liberals welcomed it as just and consistent with liberal principles. It was finally enacted in January 1913.

The Osborne Judgement had not hampered Labour unduly in the 1910 general elections. Thereafter the party's continued inability to gain new seats tempted the Liberals to take the offensive in by-elections. In mining constituencies, where MFGB candidates continued to work closely with the local Liberal organizations, Liberals were not prepared to give up the seats when sitting members died. With the land-taxers in the vanguard, they wrested Hanley from Labour in a July 1912 by-election, even though Labour's candidate was president of the Staffordshire Miners' Association. A Lib-Lab won Chesterfield in 1913, while in May 1914 Liberal intervention allowed the Unionists to win North-East Derbyshire. By 1913 Liberals were preparing to contest a number of Labour seats at the next general election – including Chester-le-Street, East and North-East Manchester, and Keir Hardie's seat at Merthyr Tydfil. An article in the *Westminster Gazette* – the voice of official liberalism – supported such local initiatives. The policy of the whips, it said, which sought to prevent Liberals from challenging socialist seats, 'can only result in the suicide of Liberalism. We have, or ought to have, no more in common with Socialism than we have with Toryism.'[31] Similarly, while the provincial press continued to pay lip service to progressive unity, it always justified Liberal interventions while condemning those of Labour.

Municipal elections confirmed that in many cases the progressive alliance was little more than a hollow aspiration. Labour continued the attacks on Liberal seats which had been evident from 1906–9. While the party made substantial cumulative gains annually over the whole country, there were few cities in which it achieved a significant breakthrough. As a result, Labour had only a small foothold on the councils of most English cities by 1913 – eight of 120 seats in Birmingham, seven of fifty-one in Halifax, two of sixty-four in Sheffield, five of thirty-six in Northampton. There were, however, some notable exceptions. In Bradford, Labour won 43 per cent of the vote in the 1913 municipal elections and held twenty of eighty-four seats. In Leeds, Labour had fourteen elected councillors after the 1913 municipal elections, while the Liberals had twelve. Only the aldermen allowed the Liberals to continue as the second party on the City Council. In Leicester, by 1913 the elected representatives on the Town Council were eighteen Liberals, sixteen Conservatives and fourteen Labour. On the Board of Guardians, it was even closer: sixteen Liberals and fifteen each for the Conservatives and Labour.[32]

The persistence of the Labour attack played havoc with the progressive alliance. Occasionally, as in Wigan, Wakefield and Derby, local progressive alliances were forged to the benefit of both parties of the left in municipal elections. More often, however, local struggles between Liberals and Labour merely allowed the Conservatives to consolidate their control of municipal councils in most of the larger cities, including London, Birmingham, Manchester and Liverpool.

The Liberals' weakness in London was especially unsettling. They represented a viable party of government in only four of the county's twenty-eight boroughs. In cities (or wards) where liberalism became too weak or socialism too strong, many Liberals abandoned their withering organizations and turned to anti-socialist pacts with the Conservatives. Such agreements, which were a negation of progressivism, occurred in Glasgow, Bradford, Liverpool, Crewe and the London boroughs of Poplar and West Ham.[33]

Eventually, Labour hostility and Liberal ambiguity towards cooperation at the municipal level was going to effect the alliance for parliamentary elections. By 1914 Labour was organizing for a major bid to increase its parliamentary representation. The partial reversal of the Osborne Judgement assured that the financial means once more were available. Furthermore, the growth of trade union membership from 2.6 to 4.1 million between 1910 and 1914 meant the party's potential financial resources were expanding. The greater aggressiveness of the younger generation of trade unionists also offered hope to those who wanted to attack liberalism. In 1912 the supporters of the Labour Party gained control of the MFGB. Thereafter, increasing pressure was placed on the district federations to break their ties with the Liberals and build their own organizations. By 1914 only financial restraints prevented the MFGB from running twenty-three candidates in addition to its eleven sitting members at the next general election. In London, the socialist organizations and the trade unions were finally able to bury their differences in 1914 to form the London Labour Party. Local Labour parties and trades councils with progressive sympathies affiliated. Overall, by June 1914 Labour was ready to contest some 120 seats in a general election, and by 1915 it might have contested over 150. In the face of such activity, Lloyd George hinted at a more formal alliance which would give Labour a substantial increase in seats as well as representation in the Cabinet. It is unlikely, however, that the rank and file on either side would have accepted such a bargain.[34] In truth, the progressive alliance already was being killed in the constituencies, and if the municipal results were any indication, the implications were as ominous for the Liberals as they were hopeful for the Unionists.

THE CRISIS OF TRADITIONAL LIBERALISM

Every tradition of liberalism dictated that the Liberal Party should have been sympathetic to the extension of the franchise to women. Most of the party did support some form of women's suffrage. They recognized it to be part of their historical commitment to democracy and the extension of liberty. They understood that the vote traditionally had embodied the symbol of full citizenship. Since women had the duties and responsibilities of citizens, they should also have a citizen's rights. Fairness also dictated that women should have the vote, since the laws passed by Parliament affected women as much as men. Most important of all, the well-being of the nation demanded women's involvement in political affairs. Liberal supporters of the franchise argued that women had a distinct point of view. The national life could only be enriched by the contribution of that viewpoint to public affairs, especially on matters relating to children and home life, social problems and the civilizing of the nation. Women, these Liberals concluded, had proved their responsibility and worthiness by raising families and managing the home. It was therefore a matter of justice that they be given the vote.

Support for women's suffrage was strongest among Liberal women. The Women's Liberal Federation was committed to attaining the vote as one of its principal objectives; the National Women Liberals Association, while unwilling to put undue pressure on the party's leaders, also included many suffragists. Among the men, the NLF had overwhelmingly endorsed women's suffrage in 1905, while the Scottish Liberal Association called on the government to grant facilities for the suffrage bill of 1910. Among Nonconformists, too, there was considerable support for female emancipation. It was not merely that their most radical leaders like Clifford and Horne endorsed votes for women. In 1909 the Wesleyan Methodist Conference reflected the new spirit which recognized female equality when it voted by 224 to 136 that women should be able to be elected as representatives to the Conference. The following spring, nineteen District Synods endorsed the recommendation while twelve opposed it. The *Methodist Recorder* on 29 July 1909 supported an action by which 'women will win the right to use all their powers in the service of the nation and the Church'.[35]

There was, however, considerable opposition to women's suffrage among Liberals. While the *Leicester Daily Mercury*, *Leeds Mercury*, and *Yorkshire Evening News* never explicitly opposed votes for women, their leading articles tended to adopt the language of the opposition. Most commonly, these Liberals claimed either that the majority of the women did not want the vote, or that such an experiment, whose consequences were so difficult to predict, could not be undertaken unless the nation (that is the male electorate) were properly consulted and approved. A second line of argument was that each sex had its proper sphere, and politics was the sphere of men. Women were weaker, naturally dependent, and temperamentally unstable; therefore, they were unsuited to participate in public affairs. The community would lose by giving the vote to women because women would be diverted from their proper sphere. Nor, opponents argued, was a limited extension of the franchise possible. Once the principle was admitted, there was no logical stopping point short of universal suffrage with a female majority of the electorate.

By emphasizing the experimental nature of such a change, by questioning whether the community would benefit and whether the majority of women wanted it, and by insisting that the nation must be properly consulted, these Liberal opponents of women's suffrage were using arguments which might lead even some Liberal supporters to hesitate. Liberal supporters were all the more hesitant because of uncertainty about the electoral effects of extending the suffrage. Conciliation Bills in 1910 and 1911 proposed to give the franchise to women on the same basis as men. Liberal constitutency organizers were convinced that this would give the vote to unmarried or widowed property owners who would vote Conservative. Liberals thus had a plausible reason for opposing specific measures of enfranchisement without having to come out openly against the principle.[36]

These ambiguities and divisions were reflected in the parliamentary party. Liberal MPs supported the Conciliation Bills: 131 voted or paired for the 1910 Bill, with fifty voting or pairing against; the division of Liberals on the 1911 Bill was 150 to 47.[37] The Cabinet initially contained a large majority of supporters of women's suffrage; however, by 1912 changes had left it fairly evenly divided. Given these divisions, the Cabinet was reluctant to touch the issue. The 1910 and 1911 Conciliation Bills died after receiving a second reading because the government would give them no more time. Asquith then promised that if a similar bill, capable of amendment so as to be made more democratic, passed its second reading in 1912, it would be given facilities to complete its passage through the Commons.

The government's refusal to introduce its own women's suffrage bill gave a powerful impetus to the militant suffragettes. Militancy had been initiated by the Women's Social and Political Union (WSPU) in 1904. In 1906 WSPU members began heckling speakers at Liberal meetings. During the summer of 1909 they began breaking windows and sometimes attacking Cabinet ministers and policemen. When they were arrested and imprisoned as common criminals, they resorted to hunger strikes to protest that they be treated as political prisoners. Prison officials responded with forced feeding. The result of these militant activities was to give new vigour to the suffrage movement by forcing both the press and the politicians to take it seriously.

Virtually all Liberals were offended by the actions of the militants. Some condemned violence but refused to waver in their support of women's suffrage. These 'candid friends' warned that militant activity was alienating public opinion and thus delaying achievement of their goal. Only rational argument and constitutional agitation would win the cause. Those who were more ambiguous about votes for women went even further. They treated the behaviour of the militants as evidence that women might not be fit for the vote. It demonstrated irresponsibility and the emotionalism which opponents claimed rendered women temperamentally unsuited to participate in settling the affairs of the nation. The *Yorkshire Evening News* became hysterical about the subject: following an attack on Asquith, on 23 November 1910 it called the suffragettes 'maniac women', 'lunatic females', the 'shrieking sisterhood', and concluded, 'They should be put into a home and kept there until they have learned to forget the ways of the brute and have approximated to some degree of civilization.' Forced feeding created special problems for Liberals because of the violence it entailed. Generally, they accepted it as a regrettable necessity; the women could not be allowed to starve themselves to death. There were, however, vocal minorities representing both extremes – those who opposed forcible feeding, and those who believed the home secretaries were being too lenient.[38]

During 1910 and 1911, there was a sharp reduction of militant activity in an effort to facilitate passage of the Conciliation Bill. In November 1911, however, the WSPU resumed its violent ways. The result was a political reaction against women's suffrage. Already, Haldane had told C. P. Scott that the balance in the Cabinet had become 'distinctly less favourable'. Now, so was the balance in the House of Commons. When the Conciliation Bill came up for its second reading in 1912, thirty-four MPs (of whom nineteen were Liberals) who had supported it in 1911 voted against it, and seventy more 1911 supporters (including seventeen Liberals) abstained. As a result, the Bill was defeated by a vote of 222 to 208. Support among Liberal activists also was waning. In May 1912 the Lancashire and Cheshire Liberal Federation narrowly voted not to allow a women's suffrage resolution to be placed before its annual meeting. When Arthur Richardson tried to make a statement in favour of women's suffrage at the NLF's annual meeting in November, the tumult raised by both supporters and opponents was so great that he had to sit down.[39]

One reason the WSPU revived militancy in November 1911 was to protest against a new government policy which undercut the Conciliation Bill. The Cabinet had announced that it would introduce a comprehensive reform bill in 1912 granting manhood suffrage. The bill would be open to amendment by the Commons to extend the franchise to women. There were a variety of political factors influencing this decision. First, amendment of a manhood suffrage bill made it easier to assure that, if women got the vote, the Liberals would not be hurt electorally. Second, there was enormous pressure from the Liberal rank and file for a measure to eliminate plural voting. Liberals believed that plural voting cost the party between twenty and forty seats in the general election of December 1910. The government had tried to pass a bill abolishing plural voting in 1906, but it had been vetoed by the House of Lords. In 1911, Pease told the Cabinet that Liberal agents were again pressing for a bill.[40] The urgency was all the greater with a Home Rule bill imminent, for the substantial reduction of the Irish representation which it envisioned meant a *net* loss of some thirty-five MPs who normally voted with the Liberals. This prospective loss of Irish support also reinforced the importance of assuring that women's suffrage did not hurt the Liberals.

The central proposal of the 1912 Franchise Reform Bill was to give all men the vote, subject to a six-months' residency requirement and the necessity of their registering. What was the anticipated electoral impact of enfranchising some 2.5 million working men for the first time? Historians disagree as to whether these new voters would have provided an untapped pool of Labour support, or if they would have behaved like other working-class voters. Secretaries of the regional Liberal federations, however, had no doubt that their party would benefit from such a reform.[41] A greater concern was the continued loss of seats on a minority vote due to Labour intervention. The NLF was beginning to urge either the alternative vote or the second ballot to remedy this. Feeling was not yet strong enough, however, for the government to act.

The rank and file was delighted by the government's Reform Bill. The Cabinet, however, was plagued by growing dissension over the women's suffrage issue. Lord Loreburn told the Unionist MP F. E. Smith that he would introduce a wrecking amendment in the House of Lords if a women's suffrage amendment were passed, while Grey told C. P. Scott that he supported the Bill only on the understanding that, even with women's suffrage, it would still be supported by the whole government. The Cabinet was saved from having to resolve these differences on 25 January 1913 when the Speaker ruled that a women's suffrage amendment would change the Bill and force the government to reintroduce it. Although the ruling took the Cabinet by surprise, members were relieved to have been extricated from an awkward position.[42] The government withdrew the Bill and in the new session introduced another to abolish plural voting. In that way, the Parliament Act could be used to assure that the one electoral grievance which the Liberal rank and file really cared about was removed before a general election in late 1915.

The women's suffrage issue could not be resolved so easily.

Liberals accepted that the government had done its best to redeem its pledges, given the Speaker's unexpected ruling. Women were not so charitable. Many felt they had been betrayed, and some felt they had been tricked. As a result, Liberal women organized for political action. The objective of the new Liberal Women's Suffrage Union was to persuade the Liberal Party to adopt women's suffrage as part of its programme, and to promote this goal the Union would only support pro-suffrage candidates. With the women adopting the familiar tactics of Liberal pressure groups, it would be increasingly difficult to keep women's suffrage an open question. The result, as Sir John Barran warned Lloyd George, could 'lead ... as surely to disruption and disaster as did the similar policy of the Unionist Party on Tariff Reform'.[43] This decision by Liberal women was paralleled by that of the National Union of Women's Suffrage Societies to end its non-party position and support Labour as the one party committed to women's suffrage. It intervened in eight by-elections from 1912 to 1914, while by 1914 its members were speaking on Labour Party platforms.[44] Thus, the prospects were for increasing trouble for the Liberals from the constitutional women's movement.

At the same time, the militants resorted to more extreme actions. On 18 July 1912 a hatchet was thrown into Asquith's carriage in Dublin. In February 1913 the house being built for Lloyd George on Walton Heath was blown up, inaugurating an arson campaign which continued until the war. Such acts of criminal violence outraged Liberal sensibilities. Liberals concurred with Reginald McKenna, the Home Secretary since October 1911, that the duty of government was to 'enforce the respect for the laws without which our civilization and the whole social fabric must be shattered'.[45] Most Liberals therefore endorsed the so-called 'Cat-and-Mouse' Act, which allowed the Home Secretary to release hunger-strikers from prison if their lives were in danger and then rearrest them when their health was restored. The government and most of its supporters were united in their determination to resist all attempts to use violence to coerce the government into conceding women's suffrage.

Women's suffrage was not a party issue between Liberals and Unionists; Welsh disestablishment was a source of intense bitterness between them. Like education, it enabled the Unionists to charge the Liberals with destroying religion and spoliation of the Church. Lloyd George responded in kind, reminding Lord Hugh Cecil of the origin of some tory family fortunes.

> Look at the whole story of the pillage of the Reformation. They robbed the Catholic Church, they robbed the monasteries, they robbed the altars, they robbed the almshouses, they robbed the poor, and they

robbed the dead. Then they come here when we are trying . . . to recover some part of this pillaged property for the poor for whom it was originally given, and they venture, with hands dripping with the fat of sacrilege, to accuse us of robbery of God.[46]

The establishment of the Anglican Church in Wales offended some of the most basic liberal principles: democracy, equality, liberty and justice. Some three-fourths of Welsh church-goers were Nonconformists. For these people, it was an offense to their sense of nationality that a sectional church of a wealthy minority should be established as the Church of the nation. For forty years Welshmen had returned a majority of MPs in favour of disestablishment. In 1906 not a single Unionist had been elected; after December 1910 they were only three of thirty-four Welsh MPs. For Liberals, the voice of Welsh democracy was clear and unambiguous.

Disestablishment, however, was not merely a Welsh concern. To Liberals, it was an injustice for the state, which comprised people of many faiths, to give one religion a privileged position. It was not the business of the state, Lloyd George told his Carnarvon constituents, 'to thrust itself into the domain of conscience nor to meddle with a man's religious belief.'[47] For this reason, Liberals claimed that disestablishment did not represent an attack on religion at all. The lesson of Irish Church disestablishment had been that the Church benefited when it was forced to rely on its own resources and to get back in touch with the people. Thus disestablishment did not weaken religion, but made it more vital.

Welsh disestablishment had been second only to Irish Home Rule on the Newcastle Programme. After years of postponement and increasing Welsh impatience, McKenna finally introduced a bill on 23 April 1912. The reception was mixed. The provincial Liberal press and the *British Congregationalist and Examiner* showed considerable enthusiasm; however, the *Methodist Recorder* was indifferent. Furthermore, many Liberals were uncomfortable with the disendowment proposals. The government's Bill, while safeguarding incumbents, ultimately would leave the Church only with those endowments which had come to it since 1662 – about one-third of the total. The rest would be allocated for secular purposes, primarily education and poor relief. Liberals argued that earlier endowments had been given to the Church when it had discharged those national duties. Now that they were the responsibility of the state, disendowment merely restored those resources to the people of Wales, to be used once more for the purposes for which they had been intended.

Still, many Liberals were sensitive to tory charges of plundering religion for secular purposes. On 11 December 1912 Asquith received a memorial signed by forty-four Liberal MPs supporting a Liberal amendment giving the Church more generous terms. In response, the Cabinet decided to make further concessions, depriving the Church only of tithes and glebes. This merely offended the Welsh and radical Nonconformists. John Massie condemned the spirit of compromise which sought to avoid embittering the 'promoters of ecclesiastical ascendency ... Surely we must remedy injustice even though the unjust be embittered.'[48] The frustration of these opponents of compromise was all the greater because once again it was to no avail. The House of Lords vetoed the Disestablishment Bill. In 1913 and 1914 it would have to repeat the ritual of passage through the Commons so that the Parliament Act could be applied. By then, however, attention was focused on the explosive situation in Ireland.

For more than twenty-five years, Liberals had believed that Home Rule would resolve the centuries-old Irish question by the application of the most basic of liberal principles – the right of the people to manage their own affairs. Since 1885 Home Rule had embodied the demands of Irish nationalism, supported at every election by four-fifths of Ireland's MPs. Liberals believed Home Rule would reconcile the Irish with the British connection because, as Sir John Simon told the annual meeting of the NLF in 1911, 'the cure for discontent is freedom'. People could not be governed against their will; they must be trusted to govern themselves. Liberals dismissed Unionist claims that Home Rule would threaten British security. Britain would retain control of the army and navy in Ireland. In any case, the economic ties between Great Britain and Ireland were too many for Irish separation to be a danger. Liberals similarly dismissed Protestant fears that Home Rule would mean papal domination. On the contrary, the *British Congregationalist and Examiner* affirmed its belief that 'political freedom and independence mean ultimate emancipation from the priest'.[49]

Some Liberals viewed Irish Home Rule as the first step towards a broader policy of devolution for the four parts of the United Kingdom. The most compelling argument for devolution was the need to relieve the over-burdened Westminster Parliament so that it would have more time to deal with imperial affairs. It also offered a logical justification for continuing Irish representation at Westminster after Home Rule. Finally, it attracted the many supporters of Scottish Home Rule within the Scottish Liberal Association and among Scottish Liberal MPs. On the other hand, many Liberals and Irish Nationalists feared that Unionists were using devolution to kill Home Rule. Their suspicions ensured that there would be no devolution proposal in 1912. In introducing the government's Bill, however, Asquith made clear that they viewed it as the first step towards a general scheme of devolution. For the moment, this was sufficient to satisfy its Cabinet supporters and the Scottish Home Rulers.

The Home Rule Bill which Asquith introduced on 11 April 1912 was similar to the amended Bill of 1893. An Irish executive would be responsible to a two-chamber Parliament – an elected House of Commons and a nominated Senate. (The latter was later changed to election by proportional representation.) In addition, forty-two Irish MPs would continue to sit in the Imperial Parliament. The Irish Parliament could legislate on all matters except those specifically excluded, for example, foreign policy, defence, police, religion, foreign trade, land purchase. The Irish Parliament would have limited taxing powers, while the Irish government would receive a block grant based on Irish tax receipts in the Imperial Exchequer. The Protestant minority was protected in several ways. The Imperial Parliament retained control of the armed forces. Furthermore, the Irish Parliament was prohibited from passing any measure favourable to a particular religious denomination. Most important of all, not only did the Lord Lieutenant retain the right to veto any measure passed by the Irish Parliament, but the Imperial Parliament also could repeal Irish acts. It is unlikely either of these powers would have been used except against acts prejudicial to the Protestants.

The Cabinet discussed whether to go further and allow those counties of Ulster which had a Protestant majority to opt out of Home Rule temporarily. Lloyd George, Churchill and Haldane favoured such a scheme, but the Cabinet decided against it. Historians have censured Asquith for his failure to impose a compromise settlement during the Bill's first passage through the House of Commons.[50] Thereafter, any compromise would require the consent of the opposition, which would have to pass it through the House of Lords. This, however, was precisely what Asquith wanted. The Unionist and Ulster leaders gave no indication in 1912 that they were interested in a settlement. Liberals rightly believed they were using the threat of rebellion in Ulster to try to force a general election and destroy both Home Rule and the Parliament Act. For Asquith to have forced unpalatable concessions on his supporters while receiving nothing in return would have weakened his party while leaving the opposition stronger than ever. This was the lesson of the abortive education compromise of 1908. This time, Asquith would impose a compromise on his extremists only if the Unionist leaders would do likewise by securing its passage through the House of Lords. His strategy, therefore, was to persevere with the Home Rule Bill which his supporters wanted. Only after it had passed the Commons the first time would the opposition be faced with the alternative of taking the responsibility for enacting a compromise or seeing Home Rule passed in its unadulterated form.

Both Liberal and Unionist observers agreed that the public would no longer be roused by the Home Rule battle. It would be a mistake, however, to assume such indifference was shared by Liberal activists. It may have been true that Lloyd George and Churchill wanted to get Home Rule out of the way. The *Nation*, one of the organs of new liberalism, may have seen it as nothing more than a debt which had to be paid to the Irish.[51] But this view was not shared by the rank and file. The cheers and enthusiasm with which they greeted Asquith's Albert Hall pledge in December 1909 reflected their continued commitment to a cause which so embodied liberal principles. The subject dominated the leader columns of the provincial Liberal press in 1912. Local Liberals speaking at political meetings that year did not avoid the subject as an embarrassment. On the contrary, they reaffirmed their commitment at every opportunity. As he prepared for the coming campaign, Fred Burn, secretary of the Lancashire, Cheshire and North-Western Liberal Federation (the home of the new liberalism) told Runciman, 'It is pleasant to get back to an agitation with a spice of idealism in it.'[52] Such enthusiasm, however, was difficult to sustain over three years, especially as the threat of rebellion in Ulster came to dominate the political debate.

Ulster Protestants based their case against Home Rule first on the threat it might pose to religious liberty. Catholic Ireland, they claimed, would be dominated by the clergy and ultimately by Rome. In addition, given Ulster's strong economic ties with Britain, they feared for their prosperity under a Home Rule Parliament. Finally, they simply wanted to remain part of the United Kingdom, and they challenged the right of anyone to deprive them of their British citizenship against their will. For these reasons, Ulster Protestants, under the leadership of Sir Edward Carson and Captain James Craig, organized to resist Home Rule. Their objective was not separate treatment for Ulster; it was to use the threat of armed rebellion to force the government to drop the Home Rule Bill.[53] In case the government did not back down, they prepared to form a provisional government when Home Rule was enacted. They raised an army, the Ulster Volunteer Force, and organized support services in the event of war.

The Ulster resistance received the support of the Unionist leadership. On 27 July 1912, speaking at a mass demonstration at Blenheim, Andrew Bonar Law, who had replaced Balfour as the Unionist leader in November 1911, made clear how far he was prepared to take his party:

> I say now, with a full sense of the responsibility which attaches to my position, that if the attempt be made under present conditions [to force Home Rule through Parliament], I can imagine no length of resistance to which Ulster will go in which I shall not be ready to support them.

This determination to destroy Home Rule led the Unionist leaders along paths of dubious constitutional propriety. In 1913 they sought to persuade the King that he might veto the Home Rule Bill or dismiss his ministers before it passed. They publicly threatened that the army in Ulster might not obey orders which involved enforcing Home Rule, while privately officers were informed that there was money available for those who chose to resign their commissions rather than coerce Ulster. Finally, only the threat of a back-bench rebellion prevented the leadership from having the House of Lords amend the annual Army Act in 1914 – an action which would have killed the Act and ended the government's authority to discipline the army.[54]

Liberals acknowledged the concerns of Ulster Protestants, but they had little sympathy with the Ulster cause. The Protestant minority could hardly be allowed to dictate to the four-fifths of Ireland which demanded Home Rule. Indeed, half of Ulster favoured it. Liberals questioned the legitimacy of Ulster's fears. The protections built into the Home Rule Bill seemed to them more than sufficient to secure Irish Protestants against injustice or persecution. The best evidence of this was the Protestants' inability to suggest ways of improving the Bill. Liberals could only conclude that Ulstermen were not motivated by fears for religious toleration and civil liberty at all. On the contrary, they were seeking to retain their own privileged position based on religious ascendency and a monopoly of political power. Ulstermen, according to Silvester Horne, had tainted and distorted the true character of Protestantism, so that it 'means the denial of freedom of speech . . . the reign of unreason, and the triumph of prejudice'.[55]

Most of all, Liberals were appalled and outraged by the threat of violence. Initially, they tended to dismiss the reality of the threats. They assumed that the real goal of the Unionist and Ulster leaders was to destroy the Home Rule Bill and thus render the Parliament Act nugatory. The tories were trying to reclaim their veto over Liberal legislation by threatening civil war. Thus, as in the struggle against the House of Lords, Liberals believed their right and ability to govern were at stake, and the successful use of the Parliament Act became the test of that right and ability. More than the Liberal Party was at stake, however. To give way before threats of violence was to undermine the rule of law and destroy the bases of democratic and constitutional government. Most of all, Liberal anger was directed against the Unionist leaders, who belied their claim to be the party of the constitution and law and order by 'playing with treason',[56] promoting anarchy, encouraging the King to become embroiled in a party issue, and making government impossible – all for party purposes.

These were the views of the Cabinet as well as the rank and file. The Cabinet, however, did nothing. Like Carson, Asquith did not believe that the situation would end in civil war. Unlike Carson, he made no preparations for strengthening the army in Ulster in case force should be necessary. The government also made no attempt to prosecute either the Ulster Volunteers or Carson and the other Ulster leaders. There were good political reasons for such inaction. The government had no desire to make a martyr of Carson and further inflame the situation in Ulster, especially when it was unlikely an Irish jury would convict. The Nationalist leaders opposed prosecution.[57] None the less, by leaving unpunished actions and statements which appeared treasonous, ministers made nonsense of claims that the law must be upheld. They were allowing political expediency to take precedence over principle, and weakened the moral case they sought to build against the Unionists accordingly. More importantly, they sent a clear message to Carson that he could do his worst with impunity.

With the danger of an explosion in Ireland growing daily, the pressure began to mount for a settlement by consent. On 30 August 1913 Birrell, the Chief Secretary, warned Asquith that Home Rule would bring violence and that the army would have to be used. He concluded by suggesting they consider excluding parts of Ulster from the Bill. Two weeks later, Lord Loreburn, the former Lord Chancellor and a known Home Ruler, wrote a letter to *The Times* calling for a conference among the leaders to seek out a compromise. The King, too, was urging a conference on Asquith. In response to these pressures, Asquith met Bonar Law secretly on 14 October, 6 November and 10 December. They easily agreed on a compromise which conceded Home Rule with the exclusion of the four Protestant counties of Ulster. They could not agree, however, on what to do about Tyrone and Fermanagh, which had very small Catholic majorities. Furthermore, while Asquith insisted that exclusion should be temporary, Bonar Law maintained that it must be permanent. These were the issues which would hang up all future efforts to resolve the Irish crisis.[58]

Asquith did not inform the Cabinet of his talks with Bonar Law until 12 November. Members were divided on the question of a compromise based on the exclusion of Ulster. Some believed exclusion was unworkable; they saw it as another attempt to kill Home Rule and opposed it. Others believed violence in Ulster would kill Home Rule; they supported exclusion. Conflicting liberal principles were also involved. The principle of nationality dictated that Ireland should not be divided; however, the principle that Liberals did not coerce people dictated a solution by consent. Finally, conflicting political considerations had to be weighed. Those who feared the political implications in the country if there was violence in Ulster saw the dangers in failing to compromise. Those who feared the political consequences among the Irish and the Liberal rank and file if there were too many concessions saw the danger in compromise.[59]

The last concern was a real one. When the Irish leaders were consulted about the possibility of exclusion, they were emphatic that it would be very unpopular in Ireland and could split their party. The provincial Liberal press, while continuing to insist that Parliament could not be coerced by the threat of force, concurred that a settlement by consent was desirable. The press reluctantly would accept temporary exclusion of Ulster as the price of peace. Liberal activists, however, were less conciliatory than the press. Sir W. Smith told J. E. B. Seely, the War Secretary since 1912, that Nottinghamshire Liberals wanted the government to 'stand firm and deal with Ulster rebellion *if* it comes *when* it comes'. The executive of the Harborough Division Liberal Association opposed 'any attempt to confer on the subject of Home Rule with a party who regard Ireland only as a valuable electioneering weapon, and urges the Government to waste no more time in futile efforts at conciliation, which Conservatives set forth as signs of weakness and hesitation'.[60]

The unsettled state of Liberal opinion became manifest following the arrest and imprisonment of James Larkin, the Dublin labour leader, for seditious remarks during the Dublin transport strike. Liberals and Nonconformists were appalled by the flagrant contrast in the treatment of Larkin and Carson. The *Methodist Recorder* could see 'no difference whatever in principle between the militant oratory of the Ulster leader and the criminal and revolutionary incitements of Mr. Larkin. They both mean that a party may justly resort to violence either to get what it desires or to resist what it dislikes.'[61] Larkin's imprisonment also angered the working class. All observers agreed that even moderate trade unionists were alienated by the seemingly discriminatory treatment of the two Irish leaders.[62] The Cabinet could not afford to estrange workers and activists alike. It released Larkin, and two weeks later it decided not to pursue a negotiated settlement.

It was just a matter of time, however, before the government made an offer to Ulster. The proposal which they finally agreed on was one suggested by Lloyd George – that Ulster counties should be able to opt out of Home Rule immediately, but would come under the Irish Parliament after a stated number of years unless the Imperial Parliament made other arrangements during the interim. Very reluctantly, the Irish Nationalists accepted the temporary exclusion of Ulster, but only as the price of a settlement by consent. Thus, they would abstain from voting for it in the House of Commons. If it were to pass, it would have to be with Unionist votes.[63]

In opening the debate on the second reading on 9 March 1914, Asquith outlined the government's proposals. Each county could vote to opt out of Home Rule for six years, long enough to require two British general elections. Carson immediately rejected the plan as a 'sentence of death with a stay of execution for six years' and called for indefinite exclusion. Liberals, however, found the government more than generous. Even the *Leeds Mercury*, which insisted that there could be no coercion of Ulster, believed that the 'Government have gone to unprecedented lengths in order to secure a peaceful settlement . . . it is impossible to disguise the fact that feeling in the Liberal party is hardening'. Robertson Nicoll found the same among Nonconformists. Most of those at the annual Free Church Council, he told Lloyd George, were disappointed that the government had made concess-ions.[64] Liberals agreed that there could be no more, and that per-manent exclusion was out of the question.

Thus, there were already rumblings of discontent among the rank and file when word came of resignations by some army officers at the Curragh. As a precaution, the government had decided to move troops to protect ammunition depots in Ulster. As a result of incom-petence and misunderstanding, some officers thought that the government was preparing to move against the Ulster Volunteers, and that they were being given the option of resigning their commissions instead. Neither was so. Matters were made worse when General Sir Hubert Gough, the foremost of the resigning officers, came to London to clarify what had happened. He persuaded Seely and Morley to alter a Cabinet memorandum to state that the government had no intention of imposing Home Rule on Ulster by force. The result was Seely's resignation and Asquith's succession to the War Office. At the same time, the officers were reinstated, and the matter was dropped.

Liberals were outraged. They believed that the officers, a privileged elite from the aristocracy, had tried to thwart the efforts of a democrati-cally elected government to do its duty. Furthermore, the Unionist leaders were justifying the officers' behaviour. Once again, the Union-ists were undermining constitutional government for party purposes. Grey, usually the embodiment of calm, wrote 'I am inwardly boiling with indignation at this stupid prejudiced attempt to dictate policy to us and break us.' One of Lewis Harcourt's constituents did not see how the government could have 'allowed itself to be dictated to by a military Junta . . . Why did you receive these men at all, why did you listen to one word of explanation?' Every Liberal he met, he con-cluded, 'was indignant at this betrayal of our principles'.[65]

The Curragh incident exposed the government's weakness. The Ulster Unionists saw that it would back down if they stood firm. This view was confirmed when on 24 April the Ulster Volunteers success-fully landed 35,000 rifles at Larne, thus flaunting the government's ban on the import of weapons. Asquith told the King that the Cabinet was unanimous in its belief that the gun-running required a firm response. Yet the considerations which had prevented their proceeding against the Ulster Volunteers earlier still applied, and now there was an additional one. Asquith was convinced that 'if we were to order a march upon Ulster that about half the officers in the Army – the Navy is more uncertain – would strike'. As a result, not only did the Cabinet ignore the Larne gun-running, but it refused to do anything to bolster the military position in Ireland. As late as 24 July, when all hope of a negotiated settlement seemed gone, Asquith still would not consider what the army should do if Carson proclaimed a provisional government.[66]

The Cabinet could not decide on such contingent action because several members were not prepared to use force to impose Home Rule on Ulster. Thus, even as it decided to proceed with temporary exclusion, the Cabinet was prepared to make further concessions. There were two possibilities: to exclude the Protestant counties indefinitely, and to exclude the mixed counties of Tyrone and Fermanagh. The Nationalist leaders were prepared to compromise on the former but not the latter. The Ulster leaders would compromise on neither. Thus, when the leaders of the two British and two Irish parties met at Buckingham Palace from 21 to 24 July, they failed to reach an agreement.

Once again, the government's proclivity for compromise exasperated many of its followers. The *Eastern Daily Press* saw the Buckingham Palace conference as 'a triumph for those who threaten civil war, and an acknowledgement that menaces of violence and disorder may be made with impunity'.[67] On 21 July, 112 Liberal MPs supported a resolution calling on the government to use the Parliament Act to pass the Home Rule Bill. The next day, Sir John Logan of Harborough sent Asquith a telegram that he would resign his seat if further concessions were made. Robert Harcourt told his brother that there was a real danger of a back-bench rebellion if the government appeared to force compromise on the Irish Nationalists. Charles Trevelyan warned Runciman that the Yorkshire working class had lost confidence in the government and was on the verge of revolt.[68] The Irish crisis seemed to be threatening the Liberal Party as well as Ireland with dissolution.

The Liberal government has been much criticized for allowing Ireland to reach the brink of civil war in the summer of 1914. It chose not to make immediate political concessions to Ulster in 1912 when they would not lead to a settlement. This decision was at least as justifiable as that of the Unionist leadership in repudiating settlement and seeking to use the threatened Ulster rebellion to destroy Home Rule. The Cabinet then refused to face up to the consequences of its decision. It made no effort either to suppress Ulster opposition or to meet it militarily should that prove necessary. Here is the true criticism of Asquith's preference for waiting on events. He placed the constitutionally elected government in a position of weakness rather than strength when faced with the possibility of dealing with rebellion. None the less it is equally clear that the ultimate responsibility for the disastrous situation in Ireland rested with those who promoted rebellion. These men preferred to risk destroying the constitution rather than be limited by the restraints which it imposed on the methods they could use to oppose and reverse a policy they disagreed with.

Thus, the failure of liberalism in Ireland was not a failure of policy. It was the same as its failure in dealing with militant women and striking workers, a failure first identified by George Dangerfield some sixty years ago.[69] An ideology rooted in the supremacy of rational discourse could not succeed when others had rejected reason, moderation and common sense as a means of resolving problems. Nor was this the Liberal Party's only failure by 1914. Its strategy for consolidating its position as the party of the working class also seemed to be failing. The policies of new liberalism, such as health insurance, education reform and land reform, had no significant appeal for working men. The progressive alliance was being abandoned by the party activists on both sides. This was not the only sign of disaffection among Liberal activists. There was also deep dissatisfaction with the government's failure to relieve education and temperance grievances, and outrage at the compromises it had made on the Welsh Church endowments and Ulster. Already, there had been rebellions on both the right and the left over the 1914 Budget, and the Ulster crisis threatened more. On top of all this came the failure of the government's external policies. Over many years, retrenchment was sacrificed in the name of peace. Yet in the end, the Liberal Party did the unthinkable and took the nation into a continental war.

8

Liberalism and External Affairs

Liberals believed that their principles defined a unique approach to international relations. They began from the premiss that nations formed a community with a common interest, just as domestic society did. That interest resulted from the economic interdependence of states and their common need to assure the continued growth of the world economy. It was best secured by the Concert of European powers acting together to resolve differences which might threaten the peace and thus the prosperity of Europe. Liberals rejected the preservation of peace through a balance of power, for that assumed the opposition rather than the mutuality of national interests. At the international as at the national level, narrow sectional interests must give way before the broader interest of the community as a whole.

The principles of liberal external policy which followed from these premisses were similar to those of liberal domestic policy. Liberals affirmed the equality of nations as of individuals. They supported the right of people to manage their own affairs overseas as well as at home. They recognized the principle of nationality in the Balkans as in Ireland and Wales. They opposed oppression and tyranny wherever these occurred. Most important of all, force was no more justifiable as a means of settling disagreements among nations than among men. Conciliation and the rule of law must prevail in both instances. Liberals preferred international arbitration as the means of resolving disputes among states. In the absence of arbitration machinery, however, differences must be settled by negotiation. Treaties embodied the liberal contention that the affairs of states could be regulated by the rule of law; therefore, like industrial agreements, they must be observed. To assure that nations were not tempted to resort to force, spending on the army and navy must be limited. Expansion of the armed services merely provoked other nations to follow suit, thus endangering world peace. Furthermore, expenditure on armaments diverted money from social reform, endangering domestic peace as well. Thus peace, retrenchment and reform were intimately related as the watchwords of liberal policy.

Inevitably, the realities of Britain's role as a world and imperial

power forced a responsible leadership to compromise these principles. Most importantly, the empire and Britain's trade routes had to
be protected. This meant that Britain must maintain naval supremacy.
The accepted definition of this was the two-power standard: Britain
must have sufficient battleships to give her a 10 per cent margin over
the next two largest naval powers. There was much disagreement in
practice over how the standard was to be calculated. Many Liberals,
for example, saw no need to include countries like the United States or
(after 1904) France, with whom Britain was on friendly terms. The fact
remained that no government could risk losing either naval superiority or the freedom to use the navy as the exigencies of war demanded.
This reality limited how far the Liberals could go, either in the
direction of retrenchment or arms agreements, and the Unionist
opposition was always vigilant in assuring that they did not go too far.
Reality also dictated that Britain retain its influence in the affairs of
Europe – not only to protect its interests on the continent, but also to
protect the empire. The scramble for empire in Africa, Asia and the
Pacific, however, plus the conflicting continental ambitions of
Germany and France as well as those of Russia and Austria–Hungary,
were limiting Britain's options. The Concert of Europe hardly seemed
to exist, while a policy of isolation was leaving the empire vulnerable
in the face of the hostility of Europe's other expansionist powers. The
Unionist governments of 1895–1905 had adapted – most significantly
with the Japanese alliance in 1902 and the French entente in 1904. The
flexibility of any Liberal government would also be limited by the
European realities which it had to face.

As was the case in domestic affairs, any time the Liberal leaders
compromised liberal principles while defending Britain's external
interests, some among the radical rank and file resisted and threatened rebellion. Between 1882 and 1902, it had been imperial policy
which had strained party unity as Liberals had sought to define what
compromises were justifiable in maintaining the empire. The policies
of 1905–14 revealed the bases of a liberal consensus on imperial affairs:
self-government for whites, voluntary co-operation between Britain
and the white dominions, a cautious application of liberal principles in
response to violence in India. Now it was defence and foreign policies
which threatened to divide the party. Differences revolved around the
government's attitude towards Germany. First, political necessity
dictated that the government expand and modernize the navy to meet
the perceived threat to British security posed by the growing German
navy. Second, Sir Edward Grey, the Foreign Secretary, sought to
restrain Germany and protect British interests by maintaining a
balance of power in Europe. In doing so, he seemed to discard all
liberal principles – allying with tsarist Russia; planning for military

intervention on the continent; sacrificing Persia, Morocco and Tripoli to diplomatic expediency.

While all of these policies generated significant opposition within the Liberal Party, the divisions should not be exaggerated. As during the Boer War, the number of people representing the little-England or Liberal Imperialist extremes was relatively few. Within the Cabinet, only Grey was an extreme Liberal Imperialist. Haldane might have been, but his fondness for Germany modified his position. Asquith, on the other hand, was a natural moderate whose confidence in Grey's judgement drew him towards the extreme. On the other side, John Morley, John Burns, Lewis Harcourt and (before his retirement in 1912) Lord Loreburn were extreme little-Englanders, opposed to any British involvement on the continent. Everyone else held an inter-mediate position. Certain offices dictated the attitude a man adopted on external issues. The chancellor of the Exchequer had to fight for economy. This was as true of Asquith as of Lloyd George. The First Lord of the Admiralty was an advocate for the navy. This was true of both Reginald McKenna, who otherwise had a Treasury outlook, and Churchill, who jumped from one extreme to the other after his transfer. Others similarly varied their positions. Some of Churchill's leading critics in 1914 – McKenna, Herbert Samuel, Walter Runciman, C. P. Trevelyan – had been perceived as moderate Liberal Imperialists during and after the Boer War.

Among the rank and file, the critics of government policies were more vocal than the supporters. Although well represented in the House of Commons, they rarely could muster more than twenty or thirty votes against the government. The extreme radicals were supported in the country by the *Daily News*, the *Manchester Guardian* and the *Nation*. This base among the elite Liberal press exaggerated their strength, just as it exaggerated the strength of the new liberalism. The ordinary Liberal was likely to trust the government and follow its lead, if at times regretfully. Furthermore, Liberals cared much more about retrenchment than the Concert of Europe. Thus, while the annual leap in the naval estimates which commenced in 1909 triggered a real crisis of conscience, most Liberals trusted Grey and defended him against his critics. All told, the forces for unity in the party were more powerful than differences on external issues, just as they transcended differences on domestic policies.

Liberal Imperialism

Liberals had no interest in expanding the empire any more. Their primary concern was to consolidate what Britain already had. When dealing with white colonists, they were agreed on how this should be done: give the people control over their own affairs. Even when confronted with emerging nationalism in India, Liberals saw the solution in terms of associating the people more directly with government. In India, however, as in Ireland, the resort to violence to express dissent, as well as the presence of a British bureaucracy and a latent doubt over whether Indians really could govern themselves, mitigated against a fuller application of liberal principles.

The immediate problems facing the new Liberal government in December 1905 were in South Africa. One of the most devastating counts in the Liberals' indictment of their predecessors had been the decision to import cheap Chinese labourers, whose liberties were restricted. While the government wanted to end the practice immediately, it was hampered because the Unionists had just approved 14,700 additional licenses to import. Recognizing the necessities imposed by due process of law, the government decided upon a policy which was more modest than its supporters had been led to expect. Holders of valid licenses could use them; however, no new licenses would be issued, and all indentured Chinese would be repatriated when their contracts expired.[1] Liberal opinion accepted that the government was doing the best it could, given that to revoke the licenses already approved would require it to suspend the law. The first Chinese returned home in July 1907, the last in 1910.

Chinese labour was only one embarrassing Unionist legacy to the Liberals. Early in 1905 the Colonial Secretary, Alfred Lyttelton, had issued a constitution giving the Transvaal a representative assembly without responsible government. Since all Liberals were committed to responsible government for the Transvaal, Boer demands were likely to be received sympathetically by the rank and file. At the same time, it would be more difficult to reduce the military establishment in South Africa in the face of continued Boer hostility. The Cabinet therefore decided to try to conciliate the Boers by conceding responsible government immediately. They also decided to drop the Lyttelton constitution and send a committee of inquiry to South Africa to consult opinion there.[2] For the first time, the Boers saw a government in Britain which was interested in their views.

The problem in constructing a constitution for the Transvaal was to strike an appropriate balance between Briton and Boer. As the *Eastern Daily Press* pointed out, Liberals had no desire to establish an ascendency party in South Africa; that would merely convert the Transvaal into a new Ireland.[3] The Boers were prepared to accept a British majority, but not a majority for the Rand mining interests. This enabled the committee of inquiry to recommend a compromise on suffrage and the apportionment of seats in the new assembly, which satisfied everyone but the Rand capitalists. The allocation of seats assured that, despite the British majority, the opponents of the mining interests were able to combine to elect the Boer leader, Louis Botha, the first Prime Minister in 1907. By 1909 Liberals looked upon the Transvaal constitution as one of the great achievements of the Campbell-Bannerman ministry. It was, the NLF boasted in its annual report, 'a bold experiment, possible only at the hands of those who believed in Liberal principles ... that freedom and self-government can alone create a loyal and contented community'.[4]

The decision of the four South African colonies to form the Union of South Africa in 1909 was, for Liberals, the ultimate vindication of their policy. At the same time, it forced them to accept the consequences of that policy for South African blacks. The proposed constitution for the Union prevented election of non-whites to the Union Parliament; it also provided a mechanism whereby the Union Parliament could withdraw the franchise from those non-whites in Cape Colony who held it. Liberals and Unionists alike condemned these provisions. The government, however, feared that any interference with the decision of self-governing colonies would destroy the bill, alienate the Boers and create a crisis with the other dominions. In the end, the Cabinet's desire for peaceful colonial relations took precedence over any concern they may have had for South Africa's blacks. These matters, they said, must be left to the South Africans to settle for themselves. Twenty-six Liberal MPs voted for an amendment to permit the election of non-whites from Cape Colony and Natal to the Union Parliament. Most Liberals, while regretting the colour bar, accepted that there was nothing the government could do.[5]

This commitment to autonomy shaped the Liberal approach to relations with the white dominions. Liberals were not unalterably opposed to imperial federation. The problem was, as Lord Crewe wrote Herbert (now Lord) Gladstone, 'forty years of consideration has produced no scheme by which such a system can decide matters of common interest without trenching on the self-government of the component parts'.[6] As a result, most Liberals believed that any development towards closer union must evolve gradually from a relationship based upon the voluntary co-operation of independent states. This view was shared by Canada and South Africa. As Sir Richard Soloman, South Africa's High Commissioner in London, wrote Botha concerning New Zealand's 1911 proposal to create an Imperial Council of State, it was 'likely to lead to interference in that full control of their local affairs, which they naturally regard with the greatest jealousy'.[7]

The area of imperial co-operation which proceeded the furthest under the Liberals was defence. Haldane, the War Secretary from

1905–12, made some progress in developing a system which would promote military co-ordination without threatening autonomy. He envisioned the General Staff in London serving as an Imperial General Staff with responsibilities for strategic planning. As much as possible, Britain and the dominions would use the same systems of military organization and training and the same equipment. To facilitate this, the dominions could send officers to the British staff college for training, and there would be a regular exchange of officers between Britain and the dominions. Britain, however, would have no authority over dominion armies. While there was progress towards making the British and dominion armies more compatible, there was less success in centralizing strategic planning. British military experts worked with dominion general staffs on war planning when requested by a dominion. In the end, however, movement towards effective military co-operation remained slow.[8]

The Admiralty had difficulty achieving even this limited success. Because a unified navy under a single command was so clearly the optimal fighting force, the Admiralty was reluctant to make concessions to colonial nationalism. With McKenna as First Lord, however, the Admiralty finally developed a plan which would satisfy dominion desires to have their own navies. Three self-contained fleet units would be built – one Australian, one Canadian, and one New Zealander and British. Each would be under the control of the dominion government and manned (as much as possible) by dominion sailors, but subject to the regulations and discipline of the Royal Navy. In the event of a general war, all would come under Admiralty command.

The McKenna proposals were never fully implemented. The Australian fleet unit was built; however, political divisions within Canada rendered it impossible for that dominion to agree on a naval policy. At the same time, the arrival of Churchill at the Admiralty in October 1911 marked a revival of efforts to use the dominion naval contribution to meet British needs. Churchill encouraged the new Conservative government in Canada to scrap the 1909 proposal and contribute three new dreadnought battleships to the Royal Navy. Implementation of this plan, however, was delayed by opposition in the Canadian Parliament. At the same time, Churchill insisted on retaining the battle cruiser *New Zealand* for home defence. As a result, by 1914 New Zealand was preparing to follow Australia in building its own fleet unit. Both dominions were angry that Churchill had abandoned the 1909 agreement without consultation – the more so when the First Lord announced to the Commons in 1914 that it was a waste to use battleships and battle cruisers in the Pacific.[9]

Haldane and McKenna were more representative of the liberal

approach to imperial defence than was Churchill. Both took great pains to deny any aspirations, in Haldane's words 'to interfere with the absolute right of the governments of the Dominions by dictating to them their military organization or to seek to interfere with their own home defence'. Churchill's approach, on the other hand, made Liberals nervous. They feared that if dominions made a direct contribution to imperial defence, such as the three Canadian dreadnoughts, they would rightly demand to influence imperial defence and foreign policy. Such fears of intrusion were not all on one side. By 1913 the Canadian opposition was accusing Churchill of interfering in Canada's internal affairs, and even the First Lord was wondering if he had not been mistaken in trying to guide Canadian policy according to British interests.[10] Indeed, the fiasco of the Canadian dreadnoughts merely emphasized the wisdom of the usual caution with which Liberals approached any imperial policy which touched the freedom of action of either the dominions or the mother country.

It was more difficult for Liberals to arrive at a liberal policy for colonies with no significant European settlement. Still, by 1906 it was not merely radical fanatics who desired to apply liberal principles to the government of non-Europeans. India provided the test of how far Liberals were prepared to go in this direction. From 1905–10, the Indian Secretary was John Morley. Morley was a nineteenth-century radical who had entered politics to implement Gladstone's Home Rule policy as Chief Secretary for Ireland in 1886 and 1892–95. During the 1890s he also had been one of the foremost critics of expansionist imperialism, and he had been a leader of the pro-Boers. Thus, Morley had the ideal credentials to be a sympathetic Indian administrator.

Britain could not withdraw from India. Strategic and economic considerations alike dictated that it remain. Yet by the twentieth century, Britain was faced with an active nationalist movement which was demanding self-government, while increasing terrorism expressed the growing social and political discontent there. Morley's approach to these problems was quintessentially liberal. He believed Britain's role in India was 'to implant – slowly, prudently, judiciously – those ideas of justice, law, humanity, which are the foundation of our civilisation'.[11] To achieve this goal, he resisted the instinct of the English in India to meet violence with coercion. Morley did not oppose coercive measures when they were necessary to maintain order. He resented, however, the tendency of Indian administrators to treat the suspension of civil liberties and the rule of law as the solution to all problems. He therefore did what he could to prevent the abuse of powers of deportation, imprisonment without trial, suppression of meetings and regulation of the press.

Like any liberal, Morley believed that coercion offered no long-run solution to India's problems. It was useful only if accompanied by reforms to remove legitimate grievances. This meant trying to involve Indians more directly in managing their own affairs. 'Governments become useless', he wrote Sir George Clarke, the Governor of Bombay, 'whenever the governed are voiceless. That's the very root of liberalism in its widest and deepest sense.'[12] First, Morley encouraged the appointment of more Indians to positions of power in the judiciary, officer corps and administration. He set the pace in 1907 by appointing two Indians to his own advisory council, and in 1909 by appointing the first Indian to the Viceroy's executive council. Second, the Government of India Act of 1909 made governmental institutions in India more representative. Morley was under no illusion that such reforms would reconcile Indians to British rule. He was firmly convinced, however, that reform was preferable to bureaucratic autocracy and coercion as a means of keeping India governable.

This belief reflected Liberal opinion in general. Liberals welcomed the Morley–Minto reforms as a cautious, prudent step towards self-government. They hoped these reforms would end Indian violence and blunt the growing resentment of British rule. Thus, Liberals looked with satisfaction upon the government's management of Indian affairs. It was one of many affirmations during the years of Liberal rule that liberal principles could be applied successfully to the government of the empire.

THE FIGHT FOR PEACE AND RETRENCHMENT

Peace and retrenchment were cornerstones of the Gladstonian gospel which Edwardian Liberals cherished. War was 'a thousand times accursed', John Clifford told his congregation on 16 August 1914. 'It is anti-Christian, inhuman, wicked, devilish, a tool of savages and not of men.'[13] Liberals and Nonconformists were appalled by the devastation which warfare with modern weapons would bring. Schooled in Norman Angell's *The Great Illusion*, they believed the next war not only would take a horrible toll in human life, but it would destroy the world economy, ruining victor and vanquished alike. Liberals saw two sources of hope in the struggle for peace. One was international arbitration. The *Eastern Daily Press* on 1 April 1911 called it 'one of the grandest steps forward in human civilisation – the most striking effort yet made to substitute the human method of reason and arbitration for the brute method of tooth and claw in the settlement of international disputes'. The other was democracy. It was working people who fought and paid for wars. Surely they would use their influence on the side of peace.

The greatest threat to peace which Liberals saw was the accumulation of armaments. An arms race merely increased the level of tension and mutual suspicion, and thus the danger of war. At the same time, the financial burden impoverished the nation while diverting vital resources away from productive output and social reform. Liberals believed that nothing was done to stop this perversion of the national interest because privileged groups had a vested interest in armaments and even war: the aristocracy who provided the officers in the army and navy, the jingo press which sought to use war and invasion scares to increase circulation, and the armaments firms which manufactured these instruments of destruction.

The Liberal government elected in 1906 was committed to reducing expenditure on the army and navy. During the first three years of its existence, it was successful. R. B. Haldane, the Secretary for War, had a genuine commitment to the principles of national efficiency which led him to seek out ways of eliminating waste. It also led him to rationalize the organization of the army so that it would be better prepared to go to war. Thus, Haldane served liberalism well. He minimized the growth in the army estimates while securing better value for the money spent and preserving voluntarism.

The Boer War had revealed an imperative need to reform the organization of the army. Haldane started from several premises: the navy was responsible for home defence; the regular army was needed for rapid deployment overseas, especially in defence of the empire; peacetime organization should be directed towards assuring efficiency and expansion in war. First, he reorganized the regular army, along with the army reserve and the militia, into an expeditionary force of six infantry divisions with artillery and cavalry, ready for mobilization at the outbreak of war. Unnecessary infantry and artillery units were eliminated. Furthermore, the army would not duplicate services like transport and medicine which, during a war, could be provided by trained civilians. In these ways, Haldane believed he could reduce the overall size and cost of the army while increasing its fighting strength by 50 per cent. Secondly, Haldane reorganized the volunteers into a new territorial army. In the event of war, the territorials initially would be responsible for home defence. Furthermore, after six months' training, they would be ready for service overseas, providing the means of expanding and replenishing the regular army.

Once Haldane won Campbell-Bannerman's support, he had no difficulty getting his proposals through the Cabinet or Parliament. Most Liberals had little interest in army reform. Their main concern was retrenchment. Although Haldane reduced the estimates by £2 million during his first two years in office, radicals like Silvester Horne found the sum 'paltry'. A saving of £5–10 million seemed to Horne 'a reasonable expectation'.[14] Haldane, however, saw no propsects for further reductions. After successfully resisting an attack on his 1908 estimates, which called for a £200,000 increase, he was left in relative peace. Beginning in 1909 the economists turned their attention to the more substantial increases in the cost of the navy.

Prior to 1908 there was substantial progress towards naval retrenchment. Admiral Sir John Fisher, the First Sea Lord from 1904–10, already was doing for the navy what Haldane would do for the army: eliminating the wasteful and superfluous while improving efficiency and increasing strength at home. As a result, the 1905 estimates were £3.5 million below those of 1904, and a further saving of £1.5 million was projected for 1906. The Liberals were able to reduce the 1906 estimates further by reducing the building programme which the Unionists had planned. Furthermore, the government promised to drop one battleship from the 1907 programme of four, while it made a second contingent on the outcome of arms reduction negotiations at the 1907 Hague Conference.

Liberals were not only pleased to see the estimates going down; they were also delighted by a gesture which showed the government was taking the Hague Conference seriously. Liberals hoped that Conference would produce important steps in the direction of both arms limitation and international arbitration. Germany, however, had no interest in either. Its leaders regarded arbitration as little more than pious sentimentality, while they construed a limit on naval construction as a device for perpetuating Britain's supremacy (and thus Germany's vulnerability). As a result, the conference achieved little in forwarding the causes which were most dear to the Liberal rank and file.

Radical frustration began to surface in 1908. The navy estimates were increased by £900,000, although once again the building programme projected by the Unionists was reduced. Fifty-three Liberal MPs supported a 2 March motion calling for further reductions. The provincial press, however, was adamant that the government must maintain naval supremacy and congratulated it on the economies already achieved. In fact, the government's policies (along with those of its Unionist predecessor) had reduced the average spending per person on armaments by more than 20 per cent between 1904–5 and 1907–9. Furthermore, upon becoming Prime Minister, Asquith had made Reginald McKenna, a former Financial Secretary to the Treasury, First Lord of the Admiralty. McKenna was a cold and aloof figure, a man of little tact or facility for conciliation. He tended to be unbending on policy matters, and Asquith hoped that his adherence to Treasury views on spending would assure continued restraint in the navy estimates.[15]

It was not to be. In 1909 a naval scare triggered a leap in the estimates which would continue unabated until the outbreak of war in 1914. The British believed they needed naval supremacy for three reasons: as their principal defence against an invasion and to protect both the empire and the commerce upon which the survival of the country would depend in time of war. In 1907 the Admiralty launched the battleship *Dreadnought* and the battle cruiser *Invincible*. Both of these ships were so much faster and more powerful than previous battleships or armoured cruisers that they came to define the standard of naval strength. In 1908 Germany, which had launched its naval programme in 1898, responded by passing a new Navy Law accelerating its rate of building. Furthermore, by the end of the year there was evidence that Germany was laying down new battleships faster than its Navy Law permitted. Most dangerous of all, the Admiralty believed Germany now had the capacity to build battleships as rapidly as Britain. Thus, if Britain ever fell behind, it could no longer be assured of catching up. The Admiralty, which was rent by divisions over both strategic planning and building policy, suddenly had to respond to a major German naval challenge and even the possible loss of British supremacy in capital ships (dreadnoughts and battle cruisers). By July 1908 Fisher, who earlier had been dismissing the German threat, was urging McKenna to include six dreadnoughts in his 1909 estimates; by December, he was supporting a call for eight.[16]

Asquith and Grey were persuaded by the Admiralty's case. Asquith told McKenna he could see no reason why Germany should need so many dreadnoughts 'unless for aggressive purposes, and primarily against ourselves'. Grey was prepared to resign if McKenna did not get what he wanted.[17] Lloyd George and Churchill led the opposition in the Cabinet to McKenna's proposal for six new dreadnoughts and an increase in the naval estimates of £2.9 million. Lloyd George was worried that, given the discontent among the rank and file over the government's failure to confront the House of Lords, an increase of £3 million in the naval estimates would 'chill their zeal for the Government', while more could lead to rebellion. Asquith, who would not carry on without Grey, eventually was able to persuade both sides to accept a compromise committing the government to build four dreadnoughts, while reserving the power to begin gathering the materials for another four later in the year should it prove necessary. In fact, it was no compromise at all. The Sea Lords insisted they needed all eight, and Asquith promised them that the four contingent dreadnoughts would be built as part of the 1909 programme.[18]

As rumours spread of a substantial increase in the naval estimates, the radicals mobilized to resist. At a meeting of the general committee of the NLF on 26 February, the resolution on naval expenditure claimed that a sufficient case had not been made for larger estimates. None the less, while the provincial newspapers opposed unnecessary increases, they were firmly committed to maintaining Britain's naval supremacy and were quite willing to trust the judgement of the government. Indeed, they quickly rallied to its defence in the face of the Unionist demand for all eight dreadnoughts. Some radicals, however, remained dissatisfied. When the government announced in July that it was proceeding with the four contingent dreadnoughts, Silvester Horne launched a bitter attack, charging it with pursuing an 'aggressive and militaristic policy' which was wasteful and provocative towards Germany. Still, only thirty-seven Liberal MPs voted against the government.[19]

The navy estimates continued to soar, from £35.1 million in 1909 to £44.4 million in 1911. In the face of such increases, the Liberal Party remained divided. At one extreme was the *Leeds Mercury*, which believed 'Germany seeks pre-eminence on sea as on land' and urged the government to lay down eight battleships in 1911 to achieve a two-to-one supremacy. At the other extreme was J. M. Hogge of York, who condemned 'the stupendous folly of the Liberal Government in attempting to impose upon the nation these inflated, unnecessary, and wasteful armaments'. Most Liberals were between these extremes. Like the press of Norwich and Leicester, they believed reductions were only possible if there were an international agreement to limit construction. Still, they were troubled. The *Leicester Daily Mercury* began to wonder whether the Admiralty was contributing to the arms race by demanding so much, while the *Eastern Daily Press* thought 'the margin left for a policy of retrenchment is exceptionally large'.[20]

In part, these Liberals accepted more dreadnoughts because they were unwilling to jeopardize the domestic policies of the government. At the same time, they saw plenty of evidence that the Cabinet remained committed to the cause of peace. The government, for example, supported the Declaration of London of 1909 which defined the rights of neutral shipping in wartime. By defining contraband and establishing an International Prize Court to adjudicate claims for compensation, the declaration was an attempt to substitute the rule of law for the existing anarchy which allowed each belligerent to decide for itself. More important, in March 1911 Grey welcomed an initiative by the United States to negotiate a new and more complete arbitration treaty. Ecstatic Liberals welcomed the prospect as 'a triumph for the eternal forces of justice and reason'. If other nations followed Britain and America, the result could be a League of Peace, with 'nations, like individuals, deciding their differences by law instead of by force'.[21]

Another reason why Liberals acquiesced in the government's naval programme was that it strengthened the case against conscription, which they hated even more. The advocates of four months of compulsory training claimed it was essential if Britain were to be adequately protected against invasion. Haldane replied that the navy would stop any substantial invasion force. A short service conscript army, he added, would divert men and money away from Britain's first lines of defence – the navy and a professional army ready for service overseas to defend the empire. As a result, Britain would be more vulnerable to attack.[22] Liberals and Nonconformists were appalled by the prospect of any form of compulsory training. They looked to the navy and the territorial army to render conscription unnecessary. Thus, having greeted the territorials with such indifference, Liberals now saw their success as vital. Most of the generals, however, had little use for the territorials and hoped they could be used as a step towards conscription. By 1911 the territorial force had stabilized at about 265,000 men – some 50,000 short of its establishment as provided by law. In 1913, a Unionist MP introduced a bill (which was defeated) to bring the force up to strength by compulsion.[23]

Thus, the threat of conscription appeared real, and it left ordinary Liberals more reluctant than ever to attack the government's naval policy. The on-going accumulation of more capital ships provided them with a powerful retort to charges that Liberal policies were leaving the country vulnerable to attack. The moderate press increasingly reiterated the government's contention that Britain had no choice but to respond to what other nations did. If Germany insisted on building, Britain could only do likewise.[24]

In 1912 Germany passed a new Navy Law which would allow it to keep 50 per cent more battleships active year-round. Churchill, the new First Lord, was convinced that the purpose of Germany's North Sea fleet was to attack the British navy at a moment when it was unable to mobilize its whole force because of commitments elsewhere. To thwart this, he sought to concentrate more battleships in home waters. This required removing the Mediterranean battle fleet so that the crews could man more modern ships at home. In the event of war, Churchill argued, the decisive battle would be fought in the North Sea. If Britain won, it could take care of the Mediterranean later; if it lost, all other theatres were irrelevant.[25]

The proposal to denude the Mediterranean of battleships met with considerable resistance. Within the Cabinet, McKenna led those who opposed redeployment because it would force Britain into an alliance with France to protect its interests in the region. Reinforced by opposition from the Foreign and War Offices as well, the Committee of Imperial Defence (CID) recommended that Britain maintain a one-power standard in the Mediterranean apart from France. Churchill proposed to achieve this by using Canada's three dreadnoughts plus the battle cruiser *Malaya*. In this way, Britain would not have to increase its building programme. Since France already had decided to redeploy its Atlantic fleet in the Mediterranean, the two countries agreed that, if they were involved in a war together, France would protect British interests in the Mediterranean, while Britain protected French interests in the Atlantic. In this way, Britain would not be left vulnerable in the Mediterranean before the colonial dreadnoughts were completed.[26] At the same time, McKenna's fears came close to being justified.

The reorganization of the fleets was just one part of the policy towards Germany which Churchill announced in March 1912. Because of Britain's overwhelming superiority in other kinds of ships, since 1909 it had accepted a 60 per cent superiority over Germany in capital ships. Churchill now made the new standard public, while indicating that it would have to be revised upward as the older ships were retired. Furthermore, any additions to Germany's existing programme would be matched, two for one. Finally, any dominion contributions were deemed additional to the basic standard. The radicals accepted the 60 per cent standard as reasonable. In fact, it may well have been less moderate than the old two-power standard as most Liberals would have interpreted it. Judged against the most likely combination of powers, the 60 per cent standard allowed Britain to maintain more than a 10 per cent superiority over the whole Triple Alliance. Furthermore, if Britain and France were allied in a war and the dominion ships were added, the superiority over the Triple Alliance was substantial indeed.[27] Not surprisingly, the Germans took just such a view of the building programme of Britain and its allies. The German leaders resented Churchill's periodic suggestions for a naval holiday, with all powers ceasing new construction of capital ships for a year, when Canada, France and Russia all were launching major new programmes.

Churchill's offers of a naval holiday were intended to demonstrate to the Liberal rank and file that the government was exploring every avenue for ending the naval race. The radicals, however, were not impressed. As a result of the bellicosity of Churchill's language and his obvious relish for his job, as well as the continued growth of the estimates, they had lost confidence in him as a liberal and a man of peace. Thus, when Churchill warned in his November 1913 Guildhall speech that there would be another substantial increase in the naval estimates, the radicals mobilized to resist. At the annual meeting of the NLF on 27 November, Henry Vivian warned Asquith, 'Although we are loyal ... we feel on this matter that there is a point beyond which we may become troubled with regard to our loyalty.' On 17

December a deputation representing some 100 Liberal MPs waited on Asquith to express their concern. Sir John Brunner, president of the NLF, launched the new year with an appeal to all Liberal associations to pass resolutions in favour of a reduction of armaments. The radical press, of course, chimed in with its support. More significantly, so did the *Daily Chronicle*, while J. A. Spender, the recognized voice of official liberalism, warned Fisher that Churchill was extravagant and needed to learn that there was a limit to the amount of expenditure the country could undertake.[28]

In the Cabinet, too, a formidable opposition to Churchill emerged. In 1911 McKenna had promised Lloyd George that the year's estimates of £44.4 million would be reduced by £3–4.5 million over the next two years. Instead, because of the German Navy Law of 1912, Churchill's initial proposal for 1914 was £50.7 million. Furthermore, with the Canadian dreadnoughts tied up in Parliament, Churchill decided in January to accelerate Britain's programme, increasing his estimates to £54 million. The Cabinet understood the effects of such increases on the party. Sir John Simon warned Asquith that Liberal activists would believe the leaders had thrown over the causes to which they were pledged. He viewed Churchill's departure with equanimity if it convinced the party that the Cabinet *'fights for economy* but pursues Home Rule unflinchingly'.[29] Lloyd George, of course, was also attuned to the electoral implications of their actions. As in 1911, however, he was prepared to accept larger estimates in 1914 if Churchill could promise him substantial reductions next year, when there would be a general election. Nor did he share the desire of some of his colleagues to force Churchill's resignation.

Churchill had a strong case. The bulk of the estimates were the result of decisions which the Cabinet already had made and proclaimed – the 60 per cent standard against Germany, the one-power standard in the Mediterranean, building programmes already under way, the need for more men as the navy expanded. Some of the increase was the result of inflation and improved naval technology. The rest was due to increased pay for the sailors, the conversion from coal to oil and the development of an air corps.[30] There was little room for the Cabinet to cut back without reversing its public commitments. Furthermore, as in 1909, Grey was supporting the First Lord, and Asquith would not risk Grey's departure. To ensure a settlement, Asquith made clear that any resignations would mean the end of the government. It was unthinkable that Churchill's opponents would sacrifice Home Rule, Welsh disestablishment, the Parliament Act – all they had worked for over the past two years. As a result, Churchill had to yield little. He eliminated some cruisers from the building programme, reduced the estimates to £51.6 million and promised further reductions for 1915.

The rank and file accepted these estimates for the same reasons as the Cabinet: too many other issues were at stake. Clearly, retrenchment was becoming a futile cause. The cost of armaments per head had increased by nearly 30 per cent between 1907–9 and 1914–15 – more than wiping out the savings of the earlier years. Furthermore, the Cabinet had given up hope of an agreement on arms reductions. It was not even planning to raise the subject of the next Hague Conference in 1915.[31] To some degree, the radicals had recognized reality. Since 1909 their fights increasingly had been to cap arms expenditures rather than to achieve substantial reductions. None the less, they could never really accept the kind of growth which had occurred in recent years. The rebellion against Lloyd George's 1914 Budget was a reaffirmation of the Gladstonian view that the Treasury should scrutinize and limit spending rather than raise more taxes to enable government to spend at will. The fight for retrenchment was still going on when the war came.

THE TRIPLE ALLIANCE VERSUS
THE TRIPLE ENTENTE

For a Liberal like C. P. Scott of the *Manchester Guardian*, 'foreign policy is the touchstone of all policy'; it provided the ultimate test of moral righteousness. Liberals believed that the objective of British foreign policy should be to promote freedom and harmony among nations. They wanted Britain to pursue this goal in several ways. First, as Gordon Hewart told his adoption meeting at Leicester, Britain must recognize that 'the peace movements and the cause of Free Trade are intrinsically the same'.[32] Secondly, it must recognize the equal rights of all nations rather than assert the supremacy of British rights. Thirdly, it must seek to be on good terms with all nations, avoiding provocative words and actions. Finally, it must avoid needless entangling engagements which could involve it in the quarrels of others.

The man charged with implementing these principles was Sir Edward Grey. In many ways, Grey embodied the liberal ideal of a Foreign Secretary. He was universally recognized as a man of integrity, principle and righteousness. Everyone believed he was a man who could be trusted. Most Liberals also believed he was a man of peace. Furthermore, they liked Grey's style – sober, cautious, prudent. There was none of the bravado of a Palmerston, Disraeli, or Chamberlain. As a result, Liberals believed that British diplomacy under Grey's stewardship did not offend or irritate other nations, and Britain was respected rather than hated as it had been in 1899.

Despite his many qualities, Grey was subjected to a barrage of radical criticism during his tenure, especially from 1909–12. There were two aspects of Foreign Office policy which radical critics found objectionable. First, as G. M. Trevelyan told Walter Runciman, 'Their one idea seems to be friendship with Russia at all costs in order to redress the balance of power against Germany. They tell us, in effect, that we cannot make friends with Germany or meet her half way in policy'.[33] Secondly, the radicals thought Grey's concern for the balance of power in Europe was preventing him from pursuing moral and humanitarian issues more aggressively – not only in Russia and Persia, but also in the Congo, Macedonia and Tripoli.

The radicals had read Grey correctly. In January 1903 he wrote a friend, 'I have come to think that Germany is our worst enemy and our greatest danger . . . I believe the policy of Germany to be that of using us without helping us: keeping us isolated, that she may have us to fall back on'.[34] Grey was obsessed with the fear that Britain might be left friendless, as it had been in the 1890s. France or Russia, as well as Germany, could once more threaten the interests of an isolated Britain. Thus, once the ententes with France and Russia were in place, he was reluctant to do anything to upset either power. This placed strict limits on how far he would go to promote better relations with Germany, as well as on how far he would go in the cause of humanitarianism.

It is important, however, not to exaggerate the differences between Grey and his critics. Both believed that war was a catastrophe which must be avoided. Both were appalled by the growth of armaments and believed, if this continued unchecked, it could lead to financial ruin and even social revolution. Both opposed imperial expansion and hated the jingoism of the nationalist press. Both believed moral issues should be a concern of British foreign policy. There were no differences between Grey and his critics about what was happening in the Congo or Persia, only about how much Britain could do to rectify conditions there. Even in Europe, after 1911 Grey wanted to see relations with Germany improved as much as the radicals did. Like them, he had no desire to convert the ententes into an alliance. The real differences between them were two. First, Grey was acutely aware of Britain's weakness in Central Asia and so insisted upon sustaining the entente with Russia at any cost. The radicals hated the Russian regime and opposed the policies which followed from friendship with it. Secondly, Grey believed the security of France was so vital to Britain's national interest that Britain must be prepared to fight for it.

Until August 1914 the radicals were not prepared to contemplate a continental war under any circumstances.

The Congo atrocities illustrate both the shared values of Grey and his critics and their differences over method. King Leopold of Belgium had granted trade monopolies for exploitation of the Congo. The monopolists had resorted to forced labour, which resulted in an appalling record of brutality and atrocities towards the natives. The conjunction of the humanitarian and free trade issues assured that Congo reform would have enormous appeal among Liberals and Nonconformists. Grey, too, found conditions in the Congo 'so scandalous that ... we must use all the means at our disposal, short of undertaking the administration of the Congo ourselves, to put an end to it'.[35] Nevertheless, Belgium was a friendly state, and he was reluctant to do anything which might drive it closer to Germany. He accepted the reformers' policy that the Belgian Parliament should take responsibility for the Congo. The substitution of popular control for autocratic rule was a natural liberal solution to the problem. Furthermore, he refused to recognize the 1908 annexation by Belgium until the abuses had been rectified. Thereafter, he was prepared to give the Belgian government time. Grey's patience infuriated E. D. Morel, the leader of the reform movement. Morel thought Grey was allowing concerns about the balance of power to outweigh moral considerations. Yet Grey's policy of quiet pressure was vindicated. By 1913 the conditions of the natives in the Congo had improved sufficiently for Britain to recognize Belgium's annexation and for the Congo reform movement to disband, without Anglo-Belgian relations having been strained unduly.

Thus, Grey's commitment to the pursuit of moral objectives was tempered by his fear of Germany. The centrepiece of Grey's strategy for preventing Germany from dominating Europe was the 1904 entente with France. This had been part of a broader Unionist effort, which included an alliance with Japan and improved relations with the United States, to make the empire less vulnerable by reducing the demands on the British navy. It settled most of the outstanding colonial differences between the two countries. Most importantly, France accepted Britain's paramount position in Egypt, while Britain recognized France's special interest in Morocco. Liberals were delighted to see the Anglo-French colonial rivalry ended so suddenly. They especially welcomed the spirit of friendship and co-operation which the agreement seemed to represent.

Germany, however, resented Britain and France settling the fate of Morocco by themselves. It insisted on an international conference to regularize matters. Grey saw the resulting crisis as a test of Britain's worthiness as a friend and of the effectiveness of the entente as a vehicle for resisting German domination of Europe. He believed, therefore, that Britain must give France unreserved support at the forthcoming conference. Furthermore, if the conference failed, and a war between France and Germany resulted, he was convinced that Britain must support France. If it failed to do so, France would hate it, all other countries (most importantly Russia) would believe Britain's friendship was worthless and Britain would be left isolated while Germany became master of Europe.[36]

This conviction shaped Grey's dealings with the two protagonists. Often he was more prepared than France to adopt a conciliatory attitude towards Germany during the conference at Algeciras in early 1906. When necessary, however, he retreated and supported the French position. In addition, he told the French and German Ambassadors in London that he believed British public opinion would endorse military support of France should the crisis result in a war. Finally, while he firmly resisted French pressure for an alliance, he authorized formal talks between the French and British military establishments concerning contingency plans should they be involved together in a war against Germany. Grey made clear to Paul Cambon, the French Ambassador, that these talks in no way committed Britain to participate in the event of a war.[37] Given Grey's behaviour in subsequent years, it is clear he believed Britain's freedom of action had been preserved. It is equally clear that he believed Britain's interests dictated that it support France in a war with Germany, and that he would not remain part of a government which refused to do so.

In authorizing the military talks with France, Grey consulted both Campbell-Bannerman and Lord Ripon, the leader of the House of Lords. While both had reservations, they agreed to the talks as long as Britain was not committed. Haldane at the War Office and Tweedmouth at the Admiralty also knew of them. The Cabinet, however, was not informed. Grey probably feared that opposition from radicals in the Cabinet would unsettle France and undermine his efforts to reassure the French leaders of Britain's reliability. Campbell-Bannerman and Ripon clearly were privy to the decision not to inform the Cabinet, so it was no Liberal Imperialist conspiracy to exclude the radicals – the less so as Asquith apparently did not learn of the military talks until 1911.[38] Nor was the decision to support France out of touch with Liberal and radical opinion at the time. The provincial Liberal press was favourable to France the few times it bothered to comment on the crisis. Even the radical weekly *Speaker* noted on 13 January 1906, 'If Germany is assured that Great Britain and France will act loyally together, there is little likelihood of her forcing a war upon them for Morocco's sake. If Great Britain appears to waver, the result may be otherwise.'[39]

The Morocco crisis enabled Grey to define part of his policy for containing Germany. The other part was to negotiate a parallel entente with Russia, France's ally. Grey did not fear Russian power in Europe. On the contrary, he thought that its revival following Russia's defeat by Japan in 1905 offered the surest check on German ambitions. Campbell-Bannerman endorsed Grey's desire to improve relations with Russia. For example, he feared the effects of a proposed visit to Russia by radical MPs in 1906: their hostility to the regime could enable 'the Russian Government to say if this is the sort of friends you are going to be, we prefer the Kaiser. And where should we be then?'[40] They would be faced with the prospect of Russia seemingly expanding inexorably towards India.

The British were acutely aware of their weakness in Central Asia. Russia had consolidated its hold on northern Persia and was showing interest in expanding towards Afghanistan and India from several directions. As a result, a War Office report concluded, 'the military burdens of India and the Empire will be so enormously increased that, short of recasting our whole military system, it will become a question of practical politics whether or not it is worth our while to retain India or not'.[41] During a time of retrenchment, no Liberal government could contemplate a vast military undertaking to defend India. The 1907 agreement with Russia provided an alternative. For the first time, Russia formally recognized that Afghanistan was outside its sphere of influence. Both governments undertook not to interfere in the domestic affairs of Tibet. Finally, they delineated spheres of influence in Persia. Britain recognized Russia's supremacy in the north, which included Teheran. Russia recognized Britain's paramount interest in the south, along the Afghan and Indian borders and the entrance to the Persian Gulf. In between was a neutral zone, open to the economic exploitation of all powers but the political penetration of none.

Liberals hated tsarist Russia. It was the embodiment of autocratic tyranny which suppressed liberty and oppressed its citizens. Most Liberals could give the entente begrudging support because it would reduce the cost of defending India and remove the principal sources of friction between the two powers. None the less, they were troubled to see Britain the friend of the Tsar. Even Joseph Henry of Leeds, who was no radical, thought the Tsar should not be allowed to visit England in 1909.[42] No other aspect of Grey's policy placed such a strain on the loyalties of the rank and file.

Most Liberals were far more comfortable with Germany than with Russia. Given the 'racial', religious, cultural and economic ties between the two countries, Liberals could imagine no greater catastrophe than a war between Britain and Germany. They saw no grounds for a war. They believed that Britain had no desire to deny

Germany its 'place in the sun'. They welcomed its economic prosperity (which could only benefit Britain) and recognized that Germany required a navy to protect its expanding trade. They believed the German people desired peace as much as they did, and they did what they could to foster friendly relations and promote mutual understanding between the two peoples. Most of all, they wanted an entente with Germany comparable to those with France and Russia.

Grey was more sceptical. He feared, as he told his Ambassador in Paris, that Germany 'has reached that dangerous point of strength which makes her itch to dominate.'[43] This anxiety that Germany had Napoleonic ambitions was made more acute by German naval expansion. If it were able to dictate terms to France, or Belgium and Holland, then those countries' ports would enable Germany's growing navy to threaten Britain. Grey believed that the key to peace and British security was the balance between the two European power blocs: the Triple Alliance of Germany, Austria–Hungary and Italy which had existed since 1881; and the Triple Entente of Britain, France and Russia which he had helped to create. He had no sympathy with his anti-German officials in the Foreign Office who would have liked to drive a wedge between Germany and Austria–Hungary or hasten Italy's departure from the Triple Alliance. To isolate Germany would make war more likely. At the same time, he was cautious about pursuing friendlier relations with Germany. He would do nothing to endanger the ententes with France and Russia; their collapse once more would leave Britain isolated and exposed. Too often German diplomacy seemed to him to be directed at undermining Britain's credibility with its friends.[44]

By 1908 it was becoming clear to the radicals that there was a sharp cleavage between Grey's views and theirs on European policy. The Balkan crisis of 1908–9 brought these differences into focus. When Austria–Hungary annexed Bosnia and Herzegovina, and Bulgaria declared its independence from Turkey, both nations abrogated the Treaty of Berlin of 1878. Initially, the radicals applauded Grey's stand as the guardian of the sanctity of treaties and the spirit of international law. When, however, Grey supported Russia's claim that Serbia must be compensated, and a confrontation between the Triple Entente and the Triple Alliance developed, they reversed themselves. Austria–Hungary, they claimed, merely was ratifying what had long been the reality, while Grey's anti-German diplomacy threatened to involve Britain in a war over issues which did not concern it.[45] Grey, they argued, was perverting the peaceful intent of the ententes, which could be restored only by a comparable agreement with Germany.

In the Cabinet, too, there was pressure on Grey to try to reach an understanding with Germany. In theory, Grey was amenable if an agreement limited German naval expansion. Germany, however, would not reduce its building programme. The most it would consider was to slow down the rate at which battleships were built. This provided the British with neither the savings nor the security which alone could justify the kind of political agreement Germany was demanding. The German government wanted each party to promise to remain neutral if the other were involved in a war. Grey would not consider a commitment to remain neutral if Germany attacked France, and the Cabinet supported him in this. Grey offered instead an assurance that Britain would not attack Germany nor be party to any agreement which contemplated such an attack. This promise seemed worthless to the Germans. Only a neutrality agreement could justify any modification of a naval programme which they considered vital to their security. Thus, there was an impasse. Each side thought that the other was demanding major concessions and offering very little in return. In each case, what one defined as security the other defined as a threat to its security.[46] As a result, by the spring of 1911, all efforts to negotiate an agreement had broken down

On 1 July 1911 the German warship *Panther* appeared in Agadir harbour on the Atlantic coast of Morocco. The dispatch of the *Panther* was the climax of two years of German frustration as France tightened its grip on Morocco. Now Germany was trying to assure that France gave it adequate compensation for abandoning the country altogether. As had been the case during the first Morocco crisis, Grey was determined to stand by the entente and prevent the humiliation of France. He was not, however, unsympathetic to Germany's claim to compensation. He therefore urged the French to offer concessions, arguing that Britain could support France in a war only if the public was convinced that Germany had provoked it by rejecting all reasonable efforts to settle the issue peacefully.[47]

The Cabinet agreed that if Germany and France could decide on compensation for Germany elsewhere, that would settle the issue. If they failed, then Britain's interests required that it be a party to any negotiations which altered the Algeciras agreement. This position was conveyed to the German Ambassador on 4 July. When Germany demanded the entire French Congo, however, Grey feared that if Britain remained passive, Germany would attempt to impose a settlement on France. Thus, when on 21 July Lloyd George proposed that he issue a warning to Germany during his annual speech to City financiers, Grey and Asquith jumped at the opportunity. There could be no more forceful way of reminding Germany that Britain would not stand aside than a statement by the supposedly pacifist Chancellor of the Exchequer. Both Grey and Lloyd George always maintained that the Mansion House speech had made for peace by forcing Germany to negotiate seriously with France. Its immediate effect, however, was to create a crisis in Anglo-German relations. Since the Cabinet was just as determined not to go to war to keep Germany out of Morocco as it was to prevent a German humiliation of France, Asquith made a pacific statement to the House of Commons on 26 July, and Grey started pressing France to make counter-proposals to Germany.[48] In the end, France agreed to give Germany part of the French Congo in return for a free hand in Morocco, and the crisis passed.

Most Liberals had had no difficulty in supporting British policy throughout the crisis. They had not liked Germany's method of starting a negotiation by sending a warship to Agadir; they had accepted that Britain's interests required that it be a party to a settlement; and they had believed Lloyd George's Mansion House speech was necessary and effective in promoting peace. Although radicals were more likely to be critical of French actions in Morocco, many of them initially echoed the first two sentiments. The Mansion House speech, however, led some to question whether Britain was supporting France too blindly.[49] These fears became acute when Cabinet radicals finally learned of the military conversations with France.

The Agadir crisis had revived the conversations between the two General Staffs. At a meeting of the Committee of Imperial Defence (CID) on 23 August, however, it became clear that the navy was not prepared to transport the expeditionary force to France at the outset of a war. This was the climax of a struggle which had been going on for years between the Admiralty and the War Office for control of British military policy. At the same time, McKenna was convinced that the opponents of Germany were trying to circumvent the Cabinet and force acceptance of a plan which would commit Britain to a continental war. Other Cabinet members who had not been invited to the CID meeting shared his fear that the Cabinet's freedom was being limited.[50] At the Cabinet meetings of 1 and 15 November, the radicals launched an attack on the military conversations with France. The Cabinet was overwhelmingly opposed to sending an army to the continent. Even Asquith disliked such a policy. Yet, while it reaffirmed its supremacy in all such decisions, the Cabinet did not disavow the staff talks. It merely asserted, as Grey long had done, that they did not bind Britain in any way.[51] At the same time, by replacing McKenna with Churchill in October, Asquith had ensured that the War Office plan now had Admiralty support. Thus, Grey emerged with his policy of being ready to give France military support strengthened.

At the same time Grey's policy was being challenged in the Cabinet, it also came under attack from radicals in the House of Commons and the country. The focus of the attack was not merely his German policy and his handling of the Agadir crisis. Radicals were also disturbed by his policies towards Persia and Tripoli. Persia was a constant headache for Grey. The Russians knew that he would not risk upsetting the entente over Persian matters. As a result, Russia continued to tighten its grip in the north. Grey did what he could to restrain the Russians, but his goals were strictly limited. Reality dictated that the Persian government could do nothing to threaten Russia's paramount position in its sphere of influence. Thus, Grey blocked measures which might have made the government more independent of Russian control – such as loans from British sources, or the appointment of British officers for a gendarmerie. Such policies would merely encourage Russia's suspicion of British intentions and lead it to intervene more directly.

To his radical critics, Grey's policy seemed to be a repudiation of liberalism. In order to preserve the entente with Russia, he was allowing that autocratic power to strangle constitutional government in Persia. As G. M. Trevelyan complained to Runciman, 'We exhibit ourselves before Europe as a little dog following the Czar's heels . . . It makes one feel that there is no such thing as the principle of justice and honour in these high matters.'[52] The radicals especially feared a partition of Persia. Grey fully concurred with them, for he did not want an Anglo-Russian frontier of hundreds of miles which would have to be defended. Ending the entente, however, would increase the likelihood of partition. Mutual distrust would force each power to consolidate its military position. For Britain, the result would be a vast increase in the army estimates, not only to secure its position in Persia, but to defend India as well. An argument so firmly based on liberal principles was difficult to refute. There was no Cabinet opposition to Grey's Persian policy, while his critics got little support in Parliament.[53]

The Italian invasion of Tripoli in September 1911 created similar problems for the radicals. They were disturbed that Britain did nothing in the face of this blatant act of aggression. They wanted Britain to act with other powers to stop the war, or at least to mediate the dispute. The Concert of Europe could not act, however, if the other powers were not prepared to do so. Nor could mediation be successful unless it was acceptable to both parties in the dispute. Grey therefore maintained a strict neutrality. He had no intention of doing anything which might drive Italy closer to its Triple Alliance partners.[54] Once again, some radicals were reluctant to recognize that their policy was impossible. All they could see was Grey condoning an immoral act because of concerns about the balance of power.

When in November 1911 Germany revealed how close the two countries had been to war during the Agadir crisis, Grey's opponents launched a comprehensive attack on his foreign policy. They focused on its anti-German bias and its resultant subservience to French and Russian rather than British interests. British behaviour during the Agadir crisis proved, they claimed, that Grey had converted the entente with France into a *de facto* alliance. The radicals were able to force two debates in the House of Commons. The *Nation* and the *Daily News* even urged Grey's resignation. In the Cabinet, however, there was no support for these attacks. Furthermore, the entire centre of the party supported Grey. The only Liberal associations which sent him protests were Manchester and York – the homes of two of his foremost radical critics, C. P. Scott and Arnold Rowntree. The provincial Liberal press rallied to his defence. Editors found Grey's answers to his parliamentary critics conclusive. Did the radicals, the *Eastern Daily Press* asked, want Britain to repudiate the entente with France and fight to resist encroachments by Russia in Persia, Italy in Tripoli and France in Morocco? The answer seemed self-evident. These Liberals looked back on the Agadir crisis without regrets. They were grateful, Robert Harvey, president of the Leicester Liberal Association, told the annual meeting, that it had been in the hands of a statesman with Grey's skill, judgement and experience. The whole affair, he concluded, had been well managed.[55]

Although Grey weathered the attacks on his policy with little difficulty, there was obviously a deep division between him and most of his Cabinet colleagues over a continental commitment. He could not risk remaining so divorced from their sentiments. He therefore worked harder to promote friendlier relations with Germany while continuing to involve the Cabinet in policy decisions. The rank and file, too, wanted the government to make every effort to reach an understanding with Germany that would reduce tensions. In February 1912, Haldane went to Germany to discuss the issues which divided the two countries and see if there was any basis for an agreement. In the end, however, the negotiations which began with this visit foundered on the same issues as those of 1909–11. Germany was not prepared to alter its Navy Law sufficiently to satisfy the British, while the British Cabinet would not consider a political formula which included a neutrality pledge.[56]

These negotiations were the last attempt to arrive at an Anglo-German naval agreement before the war. Instead, Grey supported negotiations with Germany over less contentious issues. During 1912–13, he encouraged Lewis Harcourt, the pro-German Colonial Secretary, to renegotiate an 1898 secret agreement allocating Portugal's colonies between Britain and Germany should the Portuguese empire collapse. Although a new treaty was agreed on which was more favourable to Germany, it had to be shelved because of disagreements over its publication. In June 1914 the Foreign Office also successfully ended years of disagreement with Germany concerning the building of the Baghdad railway through Turkey's Asian provinces. Germany agreed to terminate the railway short of the Persian Gulf, thus securing British interests in the region.[57]

Grey's greatest success in improving Anglo-German relations came with the outbreak of war in the Balkans in 1912. The Balkan states were trying to wrest Macedonia away from Turkey, and to everyone's surprise they were victorious. Then in 1913 they fell out among themselves, resulting in a second war. Grey's objective throughout was to prevent great power involvement. He sought to restrain Russia and France by warning that Britain would have difficulty going to war over a Balkan issue, while he told Germany not to count on British neutrality if war resulted. To reduce the area of possible conflict, he articulated the principle that no power should seek territorial gains from Turkey. Most importantly, he co-operated with Germany to assure that potential disagreements between Russia and Austria–Hungary did not become confrontations between the Triple Entente and the Triple Alliance. A conference of ambassadors meeting in London established the framework for a Balkan settlement which all could accept: an independent Albania, no Serbian port, and the delineation of Albania's border with Serbia and Montenegro in a manner favourable to the latter two states. The first two defined Austria–Hungary's minimum conditions, while Grey sought to assuage Russia with the latter.

Liberals, radicals and Nonconformists alike were delighted with the government's management of the crisis. Like the *Leicester Daily Post*, they supported the Balkan states' 'struggle for self-government and freedom'. Once Asquith affirmed that the victors could not be denied the fruits of their victory, the rank and file never wavered in their support. From start to finish, they viewed the ambassadors' conference as a tribute to Grey's sagacity and skill as a statesman. Most of all, they were delighted to see Britain and Germany working together to preserve the peace through the Concert of Europe. With many radicals believing Grey had adopted their policy, their opposition to him dissolved.[58] Grey had become the preserver of European peace, and the radicals turned on Churchill as their new *bête noire*.

Yet just as the radicals previously had exaggerated the differences between themselves and Grey, now they overestimated how much he had changed. Grey believed that his efforts during the Balkan crisis had borne fruit because of 'the existing grouping of the Powers, and the part which in those groups was played by the different Powers to preserve the peace, and which they could not have played so successfully if they had not belonged to those particular groups'. In short,

Germany and Britain had been able to work together successfully because each was part of a power bloc. Nor had Grey's distrust of Germany diminished. In January 1913 he told Sir Rennell Rodd, his Ambassador in Rome, that Britain could never again allow itself to be dependent on Germany's goodwill: 'The Prussian mentality is such that to be on really good terms with it one must be able to deal with it as an equal.'[59] This meant maintaining British naval supremacy and preserving the ententes with France and Russia.

The entente with France became even stronger after the Agadir crisis. As a result of the British decision to remove the Mediterranean battle fleet and the French decision to move the Atlantic fleet to Toulon, the two Admiralties worked out detailed plans for naval co-operation should they be involved in a war together. Once again, some members of the Cabinet objected that such talks might lead France to believe it could count on British support in the event of a war. To calm such fears, Grey and Paul Cambon, the French Ambassador, exchanged letters which explicitly recognized that the naval and military conversations did not 'restrict the freedom of either Government to decide at any future time whether or not to assist the other by armed force'.[60] Thus, the Cabinet radicals had a formal acknowledgement that they retained their freedom of action. In return, the Grey–Cambon letters gave the French a formal delineation of the obligations of the entente, including the promise of consultation during a crisis and the explicit recognition of the military and naval talks as a possible basis for action.

While the public knew nothing of these talks, they could see the redisposition of the fleets. The radicals did not like what seemed to be further evidence of a secret alliance. Even J. A. Spender, a friendly observer who knew of the military talks, feared (rightly) that British military leaders wanted to use them to commit Britain to raise a conscript army to fight in a continental war against Germany. If there was one thing Liberals and radicals alike were agreed upon, it was what the *Leicester Daily Post* called 'the folly of England creating and dispatching armies abroad to fight other people's battles. It is an insane proposal which can hardly be too strongly condemned.'[61]

The entente with Russia never had been as close as that with France, but it was just as important to British interests. By 1914 the agreement in Asia was in trouble. Britain had been trying to improve its position in Tibet, and Russia was demanding compensatory concessions in Afghanistan. At the same time Russia, having tightened its grip on north Persia, was beginning to move southwards towards the oil reserves. As a result, the Foreign Office was giving serious thought to a partition of Persia which would give Britain most of the neutral zone.[62] Such an agreement would mark the failure of Grey's Persian policy; however, the alternative – a collapse of the entente – was unthinkable. For this reason, when the Russians indicated they wanted to have naval conversations like those with France, the Cabinet was amenable as long as they were on the basis of the Grey–Cambon letters. Grey realized that such talks could trigger a new round in the Anglo-German naval race, but again he preferred to accept that risk rather than endanger the entente.[63]

Thus, the foundations of Grey's foreign policy in June 1914 remained what they had been in January 1906. He would do nothing which might threaten cordial relations with France and Russia. He did not want to see the ententes turned into alliances, for he wanted to preserve Britain's flexibility in the event of a war. At the same time, while he had no interest in fighting for Russian interests in Central Europe, he was convinced that British interests demanded that France not fall under German domination. This meant that if France were attacked by Germany, Britain must be prepared to give it military support.

These views shaped Grey's response to the European crisis which followed the assassination of Franz Ferdinand, the heir to the Austro-Hungarian throne, by a Serbian nationalist on 28 June. Grey wanted to work with Germany, as he had in 1912–13, to limit the area of conflict. Once he was convinced, however, that this time Germany did not want to restrain Austria–Hungary, and that France was likely to be involved in a war with Germany, then Grey was determined that Britain should fight on France's behalf. Initially, probably only Churchill among his Cabinet colleagues shared this conviction. Even Asquith, after telling Venetia Stanley on 24 July that it was likely the four continental powers would be involved in a war, concluded: 'there seems to be no reason why we should be anything more than spectators'. Similarly Haldane still believed on 2 August that Britain's 'real course' was not to 'rush in', but to be 'ready to intervene if at a decisive moment we are called on'.[64] On the other side, probably only Burns, Morley and Sir John Simon were determined to keep out. The others, with varying degrees of conviction, preferred that Britain should not fight but would not rule out the possibility altogether.

In the days following Serbia's rejection of Austria's ultimatum on 25 July, there was little division between Grey and his colleagues. His proposal to call a four-power conference to try to mediate between Russia and Austria–Hungary of course had their whole-hearted support. The Cabinet decision of 29 July to tell Germany that it could not count on British neutrality and France that it could not count on British intervention created no problems for Grey. It merely repeated the strategy which he had employed in the previous Balkan crisis to restrain those two powers. Grey also was true to the spirit of all he had been saying since January 1906 about the non-binding nature of the military conversations. He bluntly told Cambon on 1 August that Britain was under no obligation to support France, and that Parliament would not authorize the dispatch of the expeditionary force 'unless our interests and obligations were deeply and desperately involved'.[65]

By 2 August the Cabinet could no longer evade defining what those interests and obligations were. Determined to keep his government together, Asquith had sought to avoid such firm decisions until the Cabinet could arrive at a consensus. Furthermore, he saw that such a consensus must be based on British interests rather than vaguer moral commitments which might be open to debate. Thus, the Cabinet agreed on 29 July that Britain was under no obligation to act *alone* to defend Belgium's neutrality. They further agreed on 2 August that there was also no *moral* obligation to protect France's denuded coast. As a matter of national interest, however, they accepted Grey's contention that Britain could not allow Germany to occupy the coast of either country.[66] For this reason, they agreed that the navy should defend the Channel against the German fleet, and two days later, with the German army marching into Belgium, they opted for war.

There was a second reason why the waverers supported the war. If they did not, it would have meant the end of the government. Grey would have resigned, and Asquith would not have carried on without him. On 2 August the Cabinet was informed that the Unionists were united in support of the war. Thus, whatever the Cabinet did, Britain was going in. Under the circumstances, they preferred to have a Liberal rather than a Unionist or coalition government manage the war. In this way, they might be able to assure that the chauvinistic extremes, as well as the Liberal divisions, of the Boer War were avoided. As a result, even J. A. Pease, the Quaker chairman of the Peace Society – 'torn between loyalty [to his colleagues] and a desire to be rid of responsibility for this thing which is too horrible to contemplate' – decided to stay.[67] In the end, only Burns and Morley resigned from the Cabinet.

One reason for the Cabinet's extreme reluctance to commit Britain to war was the overwhelming opposition among its supporters. None the less, as in earlier crises, a central position emerged. While seeing no immediate reason for British intervention, it recognized that the invasion of Belgium or Holland, or even the need to preserve the balance of power, would provide such a justification.[68] This position was quite distinct from that of the radicals, who were still insisting on 1 August that no conceivable circumstances could justify British intervention. Most of the radicals, however, also finally rallied behind the government. Like G. M. Trevelyan, they hoped that the now inevitable war could be used for liberal purposes. Perhaps a Liberal government would be able 'to save us from Conscription, Protection and to make peace'. The defeat of Germany offered a chance to destroy militarism in Europe. The radicals hoped to secure self-determination; most of all, they wanted to liberate Belgium.[69] All Liberals could agree that the defence of a small nation struggling to be free and the sanctity of a treaty which embodied the public law of nations provided a justification for Liberals to go to war.

And so the Liberal Cabinet was able to lead a nearly united party into war. It was quite an accomplishment, considering how general the Liberal opposition to British participation had been just a week before. Yet it also marked the failure of Grey's foreign policy. Neither the balance of power nor British naval supremacy had served to restrain Germany, any more than uncertainty about what Britain would do had restrained Russia and France. The leaders of Germany and Russia seem hardly to have considered Britain at all as they made their decisions during the July crisis. In the end, Britain was helpless as a force for peace.

In no area of policy had Liberals' hopes been higher for the beneficent influence of liberal principles than external affairs. The pacification of white South Africa by the granting of responsible government confirmed their faith in the liberal approach to the world outside. Yet when it came to Europe, the government was forced to compromise. Just as the House of Lords had blocked the domestic policies Liberals most cherished, Germany blocked the realization of a truly liberal foreign and defence policy. Most Liberals were not anti-German. On the contrary, they saw no differences between Britain and Germany which could justify war, and they desperately wanted to see the government negotiate an understanding between the two countries. They did not, however, accept the radicals' contention that the failure to do so was Britain's fault. They saw that the navy was Britain's lifeline; therefore, naval supremacy had to be preserved. Once they recognized that Germany could pose a naval threat, they reluctantly accepted that retrenchment had to be sacrificed. However many ships Germany built, Britain would have to build more.

Liberals did not believe Germany wanted war. They believed, however, that there was a Prussian Junker militarist party which at times gained the upper hand, such as when Germany triggered the two Morocco crises, or when a new Navy Law was passed. Another manifestation of the pervasive influence of the military mentality was Germany's indifference to international arbitration and arms reduction. Thus, war with Germany was not inconceivable to ordinary Liberals. They could accept Grey's contention that Britain must not be friendless. They wanted no alliances, but the entente with France must be maintained. The Russian entente was more difficult to accept, but bad relations with Russia seemed even worse. They could not conceive of a British army being sent to the continent, yet gradually they were prodded into accepting, often without admitting it, the need for a balance of power. Divorced from the extremists who saw Germany as blameless for European tensions, they could envisage the militarists there triumphing, and they could recognize that British interests required keeping Germany out of Belgium and even France. Then peace would have to be sacrificed. Like the veto of the House of Lords, German militarism, the barrier to the realization of liberal policies, would have to be destroyed.

The Future of the
Liberal Party in 1914

The Liberal Party was faced with serious problems in July 1914, problems which threatened its survival as the predominant party of the left. Before assessing its weaknesses, however, certain misconceptions must be disposed of. Sectionalism did not pose a long-term threat to the party. Sectionalism is inherent to political parties in democratic societies. It beset the Unionists before the First World War and has troubled Labour throughout its existence. Liberals were able to overcome their sectional differences because they shared a commitment to a common liberalism which transcended disagreements on specific issues. That liberalism was encompassed in the phrase 'peace, retrenchment and reform'. It was embodied in the policies of the Newcastle Programme, which sought to attack the privileges of vested interests by giving more power to the people. It was realized in the measures of 1906–14 – those which were blocked by the House of Lords as well as those which were passed, those of the old liberalism as well as those of the new. This common liberalism transcended differences on external as well as domestic affairs. The divisions between liberal imperialism and little-Englandism were substantial. They posed no fundamental threat, however, because most Liberals identified with neither extreme. Even the extremists usually found that they had too much in common with other Liberals to justify a break with the party.

The importance of the divisions between Liberal Imperialists and little-Englanders was exaggerated because they became identified with a struggle for control of the party. The demise of Rosebery and Harcourt was crucial if the Liberals were to overcome sectionalism. With the succession of Campbell-Bannerman and Asquith, Liberals had two leaders who sought to contain and control the divisive forces in the party rather than to encourage and even identify with them. Campbell-Bannerman did this by building his leadership upon a commitment to party unity and traditional liberalism. As a result, the party activists provided him with his base of power, and he was reluctant to do anything which might weaken their loyalty. Asquith, by contrast, was more divorced from the rank and file and more willing to strain their loyalty. He overcame their distrust in two ways. First, recognizing that no one understood the activists better than Lloyd George, he gave the Chancellor's domestic projects unswerving support. Second, he won their confidence in his own right by giving them the one thing they really wanted – the limitation of the veto of the House of Lords.

The liberalism which was the pre-eminent force for Liberal unity was not irrelevant or out of date. Here is a second misconception about the weakness of the Liberal Party. The relevance of the Newcastle Programme was proved when its policies had to be enacted even after the Liberals had ceased to be a party of government. Ireland was given self-government, and the Welsh Church was disestablished. The worst abuses in the sale of alcoholic beverages were eliminated, as were the most serious Nonconformist grievances in education. The electoral system was made fully democratic, with the elimination of the plural vote. Only land reform has not yet been found relevant to the national well-being. Nor did liberalism prove unable to adapt to the new demands of a new era. On the contrary, between 1880 and 1914 a new liberalism evolved which provided a coherent justification for government action to relieve poverty and mitigate the most pressing concerns of the working class. Furthermore, the governments of Campbell-Bannerman and Asquith passed a series of acts which together embodied an intelligent and pragmatic attempt to deal with these problems. Because these policies, as well as the revised ideology which underlay them, were firmly rooted in the principles of traditional liberalism, most Liberals supported them without difficulty.

Thus, there was every reason to believe in 1914 that liberalism would continue to have much to offer the nation as a reforming creed. In another way, however, events of the years before the First World War called into question the relevance of the liberal approach to problems. Liberalism was an ideology of moderation, reason and restraint. Liberals believed that differences should be resolved by rational discourse, compromise and consent. Ulster (and even English) Unionists, militant suffragettes and striking trade unionists all rejected the liberal system for redressing grievances. None the less, even if liberalism really was out of touch with the temper of the times, such a disequilibrium was surely transitory. The times would change again, and the liberal virtues once more would be fashionable. When war came, however, liberalism's bafflement by unreason and violence may have left the party weakened. Its difficulties in resolving pre-war crises may have undermined public confidence in its ability to cope with this far more serious one.

There was another temporary weakness which may have rendered the Liberal Party less able to meet the challenges posed by the First World War. By 1914 there had been an enormous erosion of rank-and-file enthusiasm. Some alienation of the activists always occurred when the Liberals were in power. The leadership was conscious that it was the government for the whole nation; therefore, it sought to achieve some modicum of consent when legislating contentious issues. In doing so, however, it compromised on matters which embodied fundamental principles for the rank and file. The process had been going on for eight and a half years. Inevitably, some of the party's staunchest friends were frustrated and angry. The government's seeming indifference to education and temperance, its compromises on Home Rule and Welsh disestablishment, Lloyd George's 1914 Budget and Churchill's naval estimates all had taken their toll. Unless something was done to overcome these disappointments, Liberal prospects in a 1915 general election would be bleak. A revival was not impossible: the land campaign and the first fruits of the Parliament Act would do wonders for the spirits of the activists. Even if the Liberals lost, however, there was every reason to believe that a period of tory rule would have the same rejuvenating effect as in 1874–80 and 1902–5. Instead, the Liberals were denied the recuperative effects of opposition. The First World War required a demoralized rank and file to accept far more fundamental compromises of liberal principles than any they had accepted before the war.

Thus, some sources of Liberal weakness in 1914 would have been temporary had war not intervened. These were not, however, the limit of the party's problems in 1914. Even had there been no war, the Liberal Party was not in a strong position to retain the support of the working-class electorate in a political world which was moving towards class politics. Liberalism was an ideology rooted in two sets of conflicts: those between the privileged and the unprivileged and those between the industrial and the landed classes. More recently, Lloyd George had proved successful in making it an advocate of the poor against the rich – identifying the rich as much as possible with the privileged and the landed classes. The general elections of 1910 demonstrated how attractive such an approach still was for working-class voters.

If, however, the transition to class politics were to proceed to the point where labour saw capital as the principal enemy, then liberalism would have little to offer the workers. Liberalism was an ideology premissed upon the harmony of capital and labour. It was not equipped to defend the interests and redress the grievances of a labour movement which was hostile to capital. Already, there was much evidence that the Liberals had difficulty understanding what the workers wanted. Over and over again the working class had proved indifferent or even hostile to Liberal policies of social reform: health insurance, labour exchanges, education reform and land reform. There also were limits beyond which most Liberals would not go on issues that really mattered to the workers, like the right to work and a national minimum wage. Liberals were similarly limited by their ideology in their ability to sympathize with striking workers who rejected the processes of conciliation.

It should cause no surprise that Liberals were out of touch with the class aspirations of workers. Both in Parliament and in the constituencies, the Liberals were a party of the middle class. While most of the parliamentary party and constituency activists were more than willing to support measures of social reform in an attempt to redress working-class grievances, such issues were secondary because they embodied no fundamental liberal principles. Their principles dictated that their priorities should be the grievances of the middle class and the Nonconformists. The activists could be roused for a fight against privilege and the landed classes, not against poverty, and certainly not against capital. If the emergence of class politics meant that working people wanted a party whose first priority was the concerns of the poor and the working class, then they would have to look elsewhere. Socialism was the ideology which dictated these priorities, and the socialists were the party activists who saw these as the fighting issues.

Liberals feared socialism. It did not matter that there was little difference between the national policies of Liberals and socialists at this time. Liberals saw the ultimate objectives of socialism as antipathetic to everything they stood for: a free market economy, private property, even individual liberty itself. Furthermore, at the municipal level they already saw the socialists urging policies – such as the municipal supply of coal and milk, the right to work and better provision for the poor – which they considered extravagant and irresponsible. Finally, these socialists were leading the attack on the Liberal Party at the municipal level. As a result, in a few cities, Labour was already making substantial inroads at the expense of the Liberals, while elsewhere it was undermining their ability to resist the Conservatives. For local Liberals, socialism was not a theoretical evil which might emerge some day, but an immediate enemy which must be fought and defeated. Since the socialists viewed the Liberals in the same way, in most cities no municipal progressive alliance had been consolidated. After 1910 local Liberals were becoming increasingly hostile to progressive co-operation in general, while it was likely that Labour would challenge co-operation in the next parliamentary election. Even if another agreement could have been patched up, given the hostility of the rank and file on both sides, the progressive alliance offered no long-term basis for limiting the challenge of Labour. The implications for the Liberals of such a division of the left were already evident in the tory domination of so many municipal governments.

Thus, the best efforts of Liberal statesmanship to prepare the party to appeal more effectively to a working-class electorate in an era of class politics seemed to be failing. Neither the new liberalism nor Liberal policies of social reform represented a fundamental reorientation of the Liberal Party so that it could represent the interests of the working class rather than those of middle-class Nonconformists. The progressive alliance offered no solution to containing the challenge of Labour for the allegiance of the working-class voter. If class politics were coming, so was the decline of the Liberal Party – not imminently, perhaps, but eventually and inevitably.

List of Abbreviations
in the Notes

Manuscript Collections

AP	Asquith Papers
BrP	Bryce Papers
CBP	Campbell-Bannerman Papers
EGP	Grey Papers
EP	Elibank Papers
GP	Gainford Papers (J. A. Pease)
HGP	Herbert Gladstone Papers
HP	Haldane Papers
HSP	Samuel Papers
JSP	J. A. Spender Papers
LGP	Lloyd George Papers
LHP	Lewis Harcourt Papers
McKP	McKenna Papers
RP	Rosebery Papers
TP	C. P. Trevelyan Papers
WRP	Runciman Papers

Other Abbreviations

CAB	Cabinet Papers
FO	Foreign Office Papers
Parl. Deb.	*Parliamentary Debates* (House of Commons)

The *Leeds Mercury* (*Leeds and Yorkshire Mercury* from October 1901 to October 1907) and the *British Congregationalist* (*British Congregationalist and Examiner* from October 1909) are referred to by their shortened names throughout the notes.

Notes

INTRODUCTION

1 Elie Halévy, *A History of the English People in the Nineteenth Century*, Vol. V: *Imperialism and the Rise of Labour*; Vol. VI: *The Rule of Democracy 1905–1914*, trans E. I. Watkin (New York: Barnes & Noble, 1961), originally published in French in 1926 and 1932 respectively. George Dangerfield, *The Strange Death of Liberal England 1910–1914* (New York: Capricorn, 1961; reprint of 1935 edn).

2 Henry Pelling, *The Origins of the Labour Party 1880–1900* (Oxford: Oxford UP, 1965); *Popular Politics and Society in Late Victorian Britain* (London: Macmillan, 1979; 2nd edn). Roy Gregory, *The Miners and British Politics, 1906–1914* (Oxford: Oxford UP, 1968). Ross McKibbin, *The Evolution of the Labour Party, 1910–1924* (Oxford: Oxford UP, 1974).

3 P. F. Clarke, *Lancashire and the New Liberalism* (Cambridge: Cambridge UP, 1971). H. V. Emy, *Liberals, Radicals and Social Politics, 1892–1914* (Cambridge: Cambridge UP, 1973).

4 A systematic analysis of new liberal ideology is provided in Michael Freeden, *The New Liberalism: An Ideology of Social Reform* (Oxford: Clarendon, 1978).

5 This orthodoxy is most clearly stated in Martin Pugh, *The Making of Modern British Politics, 1867–1939* (Oxford: Blackwell, 1982), chs 6–7.

6 D. A. Hamer, *Liberal Politics in the Age of Gladstone and Rosebery: A Study in Leadership and Policy* (Oxford: Clarendon, 1972).

CHAPTER 1

1 HGP, Add. MS 46058, ff. 46–7.

2 In this regard, the Peelites more closely approximated Harold Perkin's professional ideal, while the Manchester School radicals approximated his entrepreneurial ideal. Harold Perkin, *The Origins of Modern English Society, 1780–1880* (Toronto: University of Toronto Press, 1972), pp. 221–31, 252–70.

3 R. T. Shannon, *Gladstone and the Bulgarian Agitation, 1876* (London: Thomas Nelson, 1963), p. 23.

4 Gladstone to Bishop Hinds, 31 December 1868, quoted in John Morley, *The Life of William Ewart Gladstone*, 3 vols (London: Macmillan, 1903), II, p. 259.

5 The agitations against the Education Act of 1870 and against the Bulgarian atrocities made an enormous impression on all Nonconformists and Liberals. Both crusades came to take on mythical qualities and were looked back upon, the one with fear and the other with longing, by the Edwardians.

6 For a full discussion of the problems of sectionalism, see Hamer, *Liberal Politics*.

7 Thomas William Heyck, *The Dimensions of British Radicalism: The Case of Ireland, 1874–95* (Urbana, IL: University of Illinois Press, 1974), pp. 6–11, 154–5.

8 For a different view, see Hamer, *Liberal Politics*, chs ix and x.

9 Also included in the radical programme and omitted at Newcastle was a graduated income tax. *The Radical Programme*, with a preface by the Right Hon. J. Chamberlain, MP (London: Chapman and Hall, 1885), pp. 87–9, 230–1.

10 See Peter Stansky, *Ambitions and Strategies: The Struggle for the Leadership of the Liberal Party in the 1890s* (Oxford: Clarendon, 1964), chp. 3 for the Rosebery leadership.

11 ibid., pp. 278–82.

12 See the Commons votes cited in H. C. G. Matthew, *The Liberal Imperialists: The Ideas and Politics of a Post-Gladstonian Elite* (Oxford: Oxford UP, 1973), pp. 26–35.

13 Campbell-Bannerman to Rosebery, 6 January 1899, and Campbell-Bannerman to James Campbell, 4 January 1899, quoted in Stansky, *Ambitions and Strategies*, pp. 284–6.

14 Heyck, *Dimensions*, pp. 6–11, 154–5.

15 All of the following tables were compiled from data gathered primarily from *The Times*, *Dod's Parliamentary Companion* (London: Whittaker, 1895–1914), and *The Liberal Yearbook* (London: Liberal Publication Department) for selected years. All classify MPs according to the year in which they were first elected to the House of Commons. Former Unionists, however, are classified according to the year they were first elected as Liberals. Working-class MPs were ignored. In uncertain cases, informed guesses were made whenever possible.

16 Emy, *Liberals, Radicals, and Social Politics*, pp. 95–6, 101–2.

17 These figures are less reliable than those in the other tables.

18 Michael Kinnear, *The British Voter: An Atlas and Survey Since 1885* (Ithaca, NY: Cornell UP, 1968), p. 16.

19 Henry Pelling, *Social Geography of British Elections, 1885–1910* (London: Macmillan, 1967), pp. 418–20. See also James Cornford, 'The transformation of conservatism in the late nineteenth century', *Victorian Studies*, VII, 1 (1963), pp. 59–60.

20 H. C. G. Matthew, R. I. McKibbin and J. A. Kay, 'The franchise factor in the rise of the Labour Party', *English Historical Review*, XCI, 361 (1976), pp. 725–35.

21 Kenneth D. Wald, *Crosses on the Ballot: Patterns of British Voter Alignment Since 1885* (Princeton, NJ: Princeton UP, 1983), pp. 37–46.

22 Clarke, *Lancashire and the New Liberalism*, chs 2, 3 and 11. For the importance of religion in general, see Pelling, *Social Geography*, pp. 426–8; Kinnear, *British Voter*, p. 82; Wald, *Crosses on the Ballot*, pp. 142–51.

23 Pelling, *Social Geography*, ch. 16. Kinnear, *British Voter*, pp. 18, 31–4.

24 Clarke, *Lancashire and the New Liberalism*, pp. 213–16. Joseph Henry (president, West Leeds Liberal Association) to Herbert Gladstone, 23 June 1905, HGP, Add. MS 46036, ff. 168–9. Moisei Ostrogorski, *Democracy and the Organization of Political Parties*, trans Frederick Clarke, 2 vols (New York: Macmillan, 1902), I, pp. 334–7.

25 Because the calculations are to an important degree dependent on city directories which were not comprehensive, there may be an under-

statement of labour members. Of greater importance, however, is the exclusion of some of the most prominent Liberal leaders in the three cities – men who had been businessmen or professionals but now were gentlemen and thus were not listed in the occupational directories. Thus, it is unlikely that there is an overall bias against working-class Liberals in the table.

26 HGP, Add. MSS 46062 and 46063. Clarke, *Lancashire and the New Liberalism*, chs 8 and 9. T. O. Lloyd, 'The Whip as paymaster: Herbert Gladstone and party organization', *English Historical Review*, LXXXIX, 353 (1974), pp. 789–93, 805–7. Neal Blewett, *The Peers, the Parties and the People: The British General Elections of 1910* (Toronto: University of Toronto Press, 1972), pp. 289–93. J. A. Pease diary, 7 April, 5 June 1908, GP, MS 38. Asquith told Pease to stop tying honours to party contributions.

27 Eliot Crawshay-Williams at the organizational meeting of the East Midlands District Council of the National League of Young Liberals, *Leicester Daily Mercury*, 19 February 1912, p. 3.

28 Cecil Beck to Charles Masterman, 26 May 1914; David Lloyd George to Asquith, 5 June 1914 (copy), LGP, C/5/15/5, C/6/11/15.

CHAPTER 2

1 This section is an abridged version of George L. Bernstein, 'Sir Henry Campbell-Bannerman and the Liberal Imperialists', *Journal of British Studies*, XXIII, 1 (1983), pp. 108–17.

2 *Parl. Deb.*, 4, LXXVII, 157–60, 367–72.

3 Thomas Pakenham, *The Boer War* (New York: Random House, 1979), p. 548.

4 Acland to Asquith, 17 July 1901, AP, MS10, ff.27–32. See also Alfred Emmott to Walter Runciman, 10 January 1901 [1902], J. A. Pease to Runciman, 12 January 1902, WRP, WR5; J. A. Spender to Rosebery, 2 October 1901, C. P. Trevelyan to Rosebery, 17 December 1901, RP, MSS 10115, ff. 107–10, 10029, ff. 151–4; Joseph Henry to Herbert Gladstone, 1 February 1902, HGP, Add. MS 46036, ff. 88–9.

5 *The Times*, 7 and 20 November 1901, p. 10. National Liberal Federation (NLF), *Proceedings in Connection with the 24th Annual Meeting of the Federation* (London: Liberal Publication Department, 1902), p. 37.

6 *The Times*, 17 December 1901, pp. 10–11.

7 *The Times*, 20 February 1902, p. 7.

8 Matthew, *Liberal Imperialists*, pp. 127–35.

9 See copy in CBP, Add. MS 41221, f. 45. See also Theodore C. Taylor, MP, to Gladstone, 23 March 1902, HGP, Add. MS 46059, ff. 152–3; Joseph Smith to J. A. Pease, 25 February 1902, GP, MS 77; and C. Silvester Horne in the *Examiner*, 23 January 1902, p. 67.

10 Campbell-Bannerman to the electors of Montrose Burghs, *The Times*, 3 January 1903, p. 11.

11 RP, MS 10168.

12 Morley at Manchester, *The Times*, 13 March 1902, p. 11. *Leicester Daily Mercury*, 3 March 1902, p. 2. *Eastern Daily Press*, 3 November 1902, p. 4.

13 Matthew, *Liberal Imperialists*, p. 139. For the movement in support of national efficiency, see Geoffrey Russell Searle, *The Quest for National Efficiency: A Study in British Politics and Political Thought, 1899–1914* (Berkeley, CA: University of California Press, 1971).

14 See, for example, the *Examiner*, 14 June 1900, p. 302; and *Eastern Daily Press*, 14 April 1908, p. 4. For a different view, see Bernard Semmel, *Imperialism and Social Reform: English Social-Imperial Thought, 1895–1914* (Garden City, NY; Anchor, 1968), chs 3 and 6.

15 Matthew, *Liberal Imperialists*, pp. 238–42. See this book, ch. 3, for the Minority Report on liquor licensing.

16 Matthew, *Liberal Imperialists*, pp. 242–57. For the traditional Liberal approach to these issues, see this book, ch. 4.

17 Matthew, *Liberal Imperialists*, pp. 228–35. Haldane always remained an object of suspicion among Nonconformists because of his views on education. See this book, ch. 3, for the education controversy.

18 *The Times*, 9 March 1899, p. 6.

19 Matthew, *Liberal Imperialists*, chs 5–6. For Campbell-Bannerman's views on defence, see his speech at Inverkeithing, *The Times*, 25 December 1902, p. 5.

20 Gladstone memorandum [1905?], HGP, Add. MS 46109, ff. 28–35.

21 CBP, Add. MS 41215, ff. 162–4.

22 *The Times*, 3 March 1902, p. 10. See also Matthew, *Liberal Imperialists*, pp. 268–75.

23 Rosebery at Liverpool and Glasgow, *The Times*, 15 February 1902, 11 March 1902, p. 11.

24 See, for example, *Leeds Mercury*, 6 February, 9 March 1903, p. 4.

25 Matthew, *Liberal Imperialists*, pp. 276–86.

26 Examples of radical alienation due to Irish support of the Education Bill are Sir William Brampton Gurdon, MP, *Eastern Daily Press*, 17 April 1903, p. 6; H. J. Wilson, MP, *Leeds Mercury*, 19 January 1903, p. 8. For further evidence of Nonconformist and Liberal support of Asquith's position on Home Rule and the Irish Alliance, see *Examiner*, 21 January 1904, p. 51, 16 June 1904, p. 575; *Eastern Daily Press*, 4 February 1904, p. 4; *Leicester Daily Mercury*, 18 July 1904, p. 2.

27 Lough to Campbell-Bannerman (CB), 20 November 1904; Lough's memorandum; Gladstone to CB, 27 November 1904; CBP, Add. MSS 41222, ff. 228–31, 233–54; 41217, ff. 139–40. CB to Gladstone, 5 December 1904, HGP, Add. MS 45988, ff. 132–3.

28 Denis Gwynn, *The Life of John Redmond* (Freeport, NY: Books for Libraries, 1971), pp. 114–16.

29 Both Campbell-Bannerman's and Rosebery's speeches are quoted in John Alfred Spender, *The Life of the Right Hon. Sir Henry Campbell-Bannerman, G.C.B.*, 2 vols (London: Hodder & Stoughton, 1923), II, pp. 182–3. Grey at Newcastle-under-Lyme, Augustine Birrell at Birmingham, Sydney Buxton at Weymouth, James Bryce at Aberdeen, Haldane at Salisbury, *The Times*, 28 November 1905, p. 11; 30 November 1905, p. 7; 1 December 1905, p. 10. John Alfred Spender, *Life, Journalism, and Politics*, 2 vols (London: Cassell, 1927), I, p. 126.

30 Perks to Rosebery, 2 February, 23 August 1901, RP, MS 10050, ff. 142–5, 170–1. Matthew, *Liberal Imperialists*, p. 84.

31 John Fuller, MP, to Rosebery, 22 February 1902; Lord Crewe to Rosebery, 23 February 1902; William Allard to Rosebery, 25 June 1902; RP, MS 10168. Jesse Herbert to Gladstone, 29 September 1902; J. Martin White to Gladstone, 17 February 1904; HGP, Add. MSS 46025, ff. 107–8; 46061, ff. 165–6.

32 Gibson-Carmichael to Rosebery, 3 July 1902, RP, MS 10168.

33 Ferguson to Rosebery, 22 January 1903, Allard to Rosebery, 27 January

1903, RP, MSS 10019, ff. 167–8; 10169. Gladstone to Campbell-Bannerman, 18 May, 16 November 1903, CBP, Add. MSS 41216, ff. 262–3; 41217, ff. 35–6.

34 *Leeds Mercury*, 27 June to 17 July 1902. George Cockburn to Gladstone, 13 July 1902; Campbell-Bannerman to Gladstone, 18 [July 1902]; HGP, Add. MSS 46059, ff. 254–6; 45987, f. 186.

35 Allard to Rosebery, 2 June 1905, RP, MS 10170.

36 In a memorandum following the general election of 1906, Gladstone indicated that eighteen of forty-one Liberal League candidates who were not MPs at the time of the election received some financial aid from Parliament Street. Although the list is not entirely accurate as to who were Liberal Leaguers, it is a fair indication of the importance of League funds in supporting League candidates. HGP, Add. MS 46107, ff. 36–8.

37 For Perks's list of Liberal League candidates, upon which these calculations are based, see Matthew, *Liberal Imperialists*, p. 300.

38 Kay-Shuttleworth to Campbell-Bannerman, 23 February 1902, CBP, Add. MS 41221, ff. 46–9.

39 Correspondence between Campbell-Bannerman and Gladstone, 18–25 May 1902, HGP, Add. MS 45988, ff. 14–19; CBP, Add. MS 41216, ff. 208–19.

40 *Westminster Gazette*, 19–22 May 1903, pp. 1–2.

41 15 August 1903, p. 2.

42 *The Times*, 18 November 1903, p. 7.

43 Birrell to Rosebery, 19 November 1903, RP, MS 10117, f. 181. Spencer to Rosebery, 17, 25, 30 December 1903; Rosebery to Spencer, 22 December 1903, 4 January 1904 (copies); Ripon to Rosebery, 7 January 1904; Rosebery to Ripon, 8 January 1904 (copy); RP, MSS 10062, ff. 278–83, 286–7, 290; 10059, ff. 285–7.

44 Gladstone to Asquith, 29 October 1903, quoted in Roy Jenkins, *Asquith: Portrait of a Man and an Era* (New York: Dutton 1966), p. 142.

45 Grey to Campbell-Bannerman, 13 December 1907, CBP, Add. MS 41218, f. 126. Haldane to his mother, 22 April 1908, HP, MS 5979, ff. 177–8.

46 Rev. C. Silvester Horne, *British Congregationalist*, 30 April 1908, p. 411. Horne was referring to Rosebery's preface to the published edition of the Chesterfield speech, where he called on his supporters to do the spade-work to secure acceptance of its policy.

Chapter 3

1 *The Times*, 8 August 1901, p. 8. See Asquith's speech at Levan, *The Times*, 14 October 1904, p. 8, for similar language by the leader of the next generation.

2 At the Albert Hall, *The Times*, 22 December 1905, p. 7.

3 See letters to Campbell-Bannerman from Gladstone, 14 June 1899, Spencer, 21 June 1899, Asquith, 22 June 1899; CBP, Add. MSS 41215, ff. 70–2; 41229, f. 57; 41210, ff. 169–70.

4 *Examiner*, 18 December 1902, p. 590; 28 December 1905, pp. 597–8. D. W. Bebbington, *The Nonconformist Conscience: Chapel and Politics, 1870–1914* (London: Allen & Unwin, 1982), pp. 22–30.

5 See the *Examiner*, April, July–September 1902.

6 See *Methodist Recorder*, April–June 1902; 24 July 1902, pp. 5–6.

7 *Leeds Mercury*, 21 October 1902, p. 4 (reporting on the *Daily News* list).

Memorandum to Campbell-Bannerman by Liberal back-benchers, 31 October 1902, CBP, Add. MS 41237, ff. 54–5. Wemyss Reid to Rosebery, 20 November 1902, RP, MS 10058, ff. 81–4.

8   *Examiner*, 22 May 1902, p. 450. *Methodist Recorder*, 18 September 1902, p. 3; 23 July 1903, pp. 3–4; 30 July 1903, pp. 4–5.
9   Chamberlain's priority always was to strengthen imperial unity. See Alan Sykes, *Tariff Reform in British Politics 1903–1913* (Oxford: Clarendon, 1979), pp. 24–62, on the evolution of Chamberlain's proposals.
10   At the 80 Club, *The Times*, 23 January 1904, p. 9.
11   George Leveson-Gower to Gladstone, 27 April 1902; Gladstone to Richard Rigg, 7 July 1903 (draft); HGP, Add. MSS 46059, ff. 169–70; 46060, ff. 241–2.
12   Robert Hudson to Gladstone, 1 January 1904, Gladstone memorandum, 9 May 1904; HGP, Add. MSS 46021, ff. 31–4; 46106, ff. 140–1. A. K. Russell, *Liberal Landslide: The General Election of 1906* (Newton Abbot: David & Charles; Hamden, CT: Archon, 1973), p. 41.
13   *Examiner*, 21 May 1903, p. 490. *Methodist Recorder*, 4 June 1903, p. 12.
14   Free Church Council manual, 'Organising for the Elections', LGP, A/2/3/1. Stephen E. Koss, *Nonconformity in Modern British Politics* (Hamden, CT: Archon, 1975), pp. 57–65. Gladstone's whip's diary, 9 July, 29 September 1903; HGP, Add. MS 46484.
15   Campbell-Bannerman to John Sinclair, 6 September 1902 (copy), CBP, Add. MS 41230, ff. 43–5. Perks to Rosebery, 12 December 1903, RP, MS 10051, ff. 161–4. *Examiner*, 29 October 1903, p. 427.
16   Jesse Herbert to Gladstone, 19 September, 21 December 1903, HGP, Add. MSS 46025, ff. 170–1; 46026, ff. 36–7. J. F. Cheetham to James Bryce, 25 December 1904, BrP, Box 4. Bryce to Campbell-Bannerman, 28 December 1903, Campbell-Bannerman to Bryce, 29 December 1903 (copy), CBP, Add. MS 41211, ff. 254–60.
17   Bryce to Clifford, 29 January 1904 (copy), CBP, Add. MS 41211, ff. 276–9. Clifford to Bryce, 2 February 1904; A. M. Fairbairn to Bryce, 26 January 1904; BrP, Box 21.
18   Bryce to Campbell-Bannerman (CB), [December 1903?]; Thomas R. Buchanan to CB, 15 January 1905; CBP, Add. MSS 41211, ff. 252–3; 41242, ff. 51–4. Gladstone's constituency estimates, HGP, Add. MS 46107, ff. 1–15.
19   *The Times*, 22 November 1904, p. 4.
20   *Leeds Mercury*, 7 October 1905, p. 4.
21   The full land reform programme had been accepted by the rank and file well before Chamberlain launched tariff reform. *Leicester Daily Mercury*, 11 February, 17 July 1899, p. 2. *Eastern Daily Press*, 2 July 1901, p. 5. *Leeds Mercury*, 25 November 1899, p. 4. Roy Douglas, *Land, People and Politics: A History of the Land Question in the United Kingdom, 1878–1952* (New York: St Martin's, 1976), chs 3, 7.
22   *Examiner*, 25 February 1904, pp. 169–70; 24 March 1904, p. 267. The *Methodist Recorder* was reluctant to take a stand against Chinese labour and published correspondence presenting both sides of the issue. In the 'Editorial Notes' of 7 April 1904, p. 3, however, it expressed its 'intense and growing aversion to the whole scheme of imported Chinese labour'.
23   *Leeds Mercury*, 28 February 1904, p. 4. *Leicester Daily Mercury*, 7 January 1904, p. 2. *Eastern Weekly Press*, 5 March 1904, p. 3.
24   Pelling, *Popular Politics and Society*, pp. 97–9.
25   Gladstone's 'Note on the Veto', [1898], HGP, Add. MS 46092, ff. 160–71.

26 *Daily News*, 7 December 1899. Campbell-Bannerman's speeches at Manchester and Birmingham, *The Times*, 16 November 1899, p. 10; 25 November 1899, p. 8.

27 Campbell-Bannerman to Lawson, 21 December 1899 (copy), CBP, Add. MS 41235, ff. 157–9. Liberal and Nonconformist opinion rallied behind the Peel Report. *Leicester Daily Mercury*, 7 December 1899, p. 2. *Leeds Mercury*, 17 November 1899, p. 4. *Eastern Daily Press*, 8 December 1899, p. 4. Meeting of the Congregational Union, *Independent*, 26 October 1899, p. 293. Meeting of the London Methodist Council, *Methodist Recorder*, 2 November 1899, p. 6.

28 *Methodist Recorder*, 28 April 1904, pp. 14–15; 12 May 1904, p. 3; 28 July 1904, pp. 4–5 (annual conference).

29 NLF, *Proceedings* (1905), p. 59. Campbell-Bannerman, Asquith and Gladstone to a temperance deputation, *The Times*, 22 March 1905, p. 11.

30 Russell, *Liberal Landslide*, p. 65.

31 ibid., pp. 172–85. Koss, *Nonconformity*, pp. 73–4, 226–7; *Examiner*, 15 February 1906, p. 150. Twenty-eight of the Nonconformist MPs in the 1900 House of Commons were Unionists, while only six Unionist Nonconformists were elected in 1906.

32 Even as Nonconformists were achieving greater political power than they had known since the seventeenth century, membership in the Nonconformist Churches already was beginning its slow but steady decline (despite a religious revival in Wales in 1904–5). See John F. Glaser, 'English Nonconformity and the decline of liberalism', *American Historical Review*, LXIII, 1 (1958), pp. 352–63.

CHAPTER 4

1 See Pelling, *The Origins of the Labour Party*.

2 *Leicester Daily Mercury*, 5 January, 20 December 1899, 2 March 1900, p. 2. *Leeds Mercury*, 25 October 1900, 9 October 1901, p. 4.

3 *Leeds Mercury*, 12, 26 March 1902, p. 4. Philip P. Poirier, *The Advent of the British Labour Party* (New York: Columbia UP, 1958), p. 128. Frank Bealey and Henry Pelling, *Labour and Politics, 1900–1906: A History of the Labour Representation Committee* (London: Macmillan; New York: St Martin's, 1958), pp. 132–3.

4 Bealey and Pelling, *Labour and Politics*, ch. 5. Clarke, *Lancashire and the New Liberalism*, pp. 84–95. Gladstone's whip's diary, 10 July 1902, HGP, Add. MS 46484, f. 17.

5 Undated notes by Gladstone, HGP, Add. MS 46106, f. 27.

6 Jesse Herbert's memorandum to Gladstone, 6 March 1903, HGP, Add. MS 46025, ff. 127–36.

7 ibid.

8 Gladstone's memorandum, 13 March 1903, HGP, Add. MS 46106, ff. 7–9.

9 *The Times*, 2 May 1903, p. 12.

10 George L. Bernstein, 'Liberalism and the progressive alliance in the constituencies, 1900–1914: Three case studies', *Historical Journal*, XXVI, 3 (1983), pp. 630–3.

11 Herbert's memorandum to Gladstone, 6 September 1903, HGP, Add. MS 46106, ff. 2–6.

12 Bealey and Pelling, *Labour and Politics*, p. 137. Alfred Billson to Gladstone, 23 September 1902, 5 May 1903; Billson to Broadhurst, 20 October 1902;

HGP, Add. MS 46060, ff. 26, 191–2, 57–9.

13 Bealey and Pelling, *Labour and Politics*, pp. 144–5. Paul Thompson, *Socialists, Liberals and Labour: The Struggle for London, 1885–1914* (London: Routledge & Kegan Paul; Toronto: University of Toronto Press, 1967), pp. 250–8. *Leeds Mercury*, 7, 12 March 1903, p. 4. *Eastern Daily Press*, 12 March 1903, p. 4. *Examiner*, 19 March 1903, p. 266. Liberals similarly concluded that John Hodge was defeated at Preston in May because of his refusal to accept their co-operation. *Leeds Mercury, Leicester Daily Mercury*, 15 May 1903.

14 Paulton to Gladstone, 14 April [1903], HGP, Add. MS 46060, ff. 174–5.

15 Pease to Gladstone, 29 June [1903]; Rowntree to Gladstone, n.d. (ca. 30 June 1903); C. P. Trevelyan to Gladstone, 7 July 1903; HGP, Add. MSS 46022, ff. 132–5; 46060, ff. 220–1, 243–4.

16 T. Catterall to Beaumont's chairman, 2 July 1903 (copy), HGP, Add. MS 46060, f. 239. *Leeds Mercury*, 9 July 1903, p. 4.

17 Bealey and Pelling, *Labour and Politics*, pp. 152–5. Poirier, *Advent*, pp. 199–203. Koss, *Nonconformity*, pp. 63–4.

18 *Leicester Daily Post*, 23, 27 July 1903, p. 4. See *Eastern Daily Press*, 27 July 1903, p. 4; and the *Examiner*, 30 July 1903, p. 98. Three weeks earlier, the *Examiner* had attacked the LRC and endorsed Storey's position; 9 July 1903, p. 26.

19 Gladstone to Runciman, 16 January 1904, WRP, WR9.

20 Bernstein, 'Three case studies', pp. 621–2.

21 Bealey and Pelling, *Labour and Politics*, pp. 205–11. For Liberal acknowledgement of these changes, see *Leeds Mercury*, 20 June 1904, p. 4; *Leicester Daily Mercury*, 17, 20 February 1905, p. 2.

22 *Leeds Mercury*, 7 September 1904, p. 4. *Eastern Daily Press*, 6 October 1904, p. 5. *Examiner*, 14 September 1905, p. 219.

23 Bealey and Pelling, *Labour and Politics*, pp. 15–16, 96–7, 194, and ch. 9.

24 Herbert's notes on an interview with A. J. Williams of South Glamorgan, 7 November 1903 (copy), HGP, Add. MS 46106, ff. 38–42. Bealey and Pelling, *Labour and Politics*, pp. 227–31, 262.

25 A. W. Purdue, 'The Liberal and Labour Parties in North-Eastern politics 1900–14: The struggle for supremacy', *International Review of Social History*, XXVI, 1 (1981), pp. 7–15. Bernstein, 'Three case studies', pp. 625–7. Joseph Henry to Gladstone, 22 April, 12 September 1904, 19 December 1905, HGP, Add. MS 46036, ff. 150–4, 179–80.

26 Hatch to Gladstone, 19, 27 November 1905; Hatch to A. H. Wainwright, 1 December 1905 (copy); HGP, Add. MS 46063, ff. 117–18, 127–8, 141–2. Henry Vivian, the Liberal candidate for Deptford in London, had the same problem; HGP, Add. MS 45986, f. 122.

27 Many of the seats turned over to Labour had virtually no Liberal organization. Even in Manchester, however, there was difficulty extending the progressive alliance to municipal elections. Clarke, *Lancashire and the New Liberalism*, pp. 186–7, 316–23.

28 *The Times*, 12 October 1905, p. 10.

29 Kenneth Stanley Inglis, *Churches and the Working Class in Victorian England* (London: Routledge & Kegan Paul; Toronto: University of Toronto Press, 1963), pp. 70–1, 287–308, ch. 4. Pelling, *Popular Politics*, ch. 2.

30 Russell, *Liberal Landslide*, pp. 65, 79. Pelling, *Origins*, pp. 119–20.

31 Campbell-Bannerman at Birmingham, *The Times*, 25 November 1899, p. 8. Letter from Sir William Brampton Gurdon, MP, *Eastern Daily Press*, 7 March 1903, p. 6. *Leeds Mercury*, 18 May 1900, p. 4. *Leicester Daily Mercury*,

6 September 1901, p. 2.

32 *Methodist Recorder*, 9 November 1905, p. 16. *Examiner*, 23 November 1905, p. 475. Russell, *Liberal Landslide*, p. 71.

33 *Examiner*, 13 October 1904, p. 335.

34 *Leicester Daily Mercury*, 2 December 1902, 31 August 1904, 21 November 1904, 30 June 1905, p. 2.

35 Gladstone at Leeds; Campbell-Bannerman (CB) at Limehouse and Stirling; Bryce at Weston-super-Mare; Asquith at Basingstoke; *The Times*, 6 December 1904, p. 7; 21 December 1904, p. 5; 18 January 1905, p. 4; 25 January 1905, p. 12; 8 November 1905, p. 10. Gladstone to Fowler, 1 January 1905 (copy); Spencer to CB, 16 December 1904; Bryce to CB, 19 December 1904; Fowler to CB, 26 December 1904; CBP, Add. MSS 41217, ff. 164–6; 41229, ff. 286–90; 41211, ff. 290–1; 41214, ff. 258–60.

CHAPTER 5

1 Memorandum, 17 February 1906, CAB 37/82/28.

2 Campbell-Bannerman to Ripon, 7 April 1906, quoted in Peter Rowland, *The Last Liberal Governments*, Vol. 1: *The Promised Land, 1905–1910* (London: Barrie and Rockliff, 1968), p. 348. See also, p. 77. Sir Almeric Fitzroy, *Memoirs*, 2 vols (London: Hutchinson [1925]), I, p. 287. Wilfred Scawen Blunt, *My Diaries: Being a Personal Narrative of Events, 1888–1914*, 2 vols (London: Martin Secker, 1919–20), II, p. 149. John Burns's diary, 21 March, 9 April 1906, Burns Papers, Add. MS 46324, pp. 22, 30. Birrell memorandum, 27 March 1906, CAB 37/83/39.

3 Free Church Council deputation to Birrell, *The Times*, 19 June 1906, p. 5.

4 CAB 37/85/92. Birrell feared intolerable administrative difficulties due to a court decision (the West Riding judgement), which was soon reversed by the House of Lords, and continued passive resistance.

5 George Kennedy Allin Bell, *Randall Davidson, Archbishop of Canterbury*, 2 vols (New York: Oxford UP, 1935), I, pp. 523–7. Acland to Campbell-Bannerman, 8 December 1906; Perks, Mansfield and Hay Morgan to Campbell-Bannerman, 12 December 1906; CBP, Add. MS 41239, ff. 182–3, 189–90.

6 Roy Jenkins, *Mr. Balfour's Poodle: An Account of the Struggle Between the House of Lords and the Government of Mr. Asquith* (New York: Chilmark, 1954), p. 24.

7 Told to C. F. G. Masterman, 21 October 1908; Lucy Masterman, *C. F. G. Masterman: A Biography* (London: Cass, 1968), pp. 111–12.

8 Corinne Comstock Weston, 'The Liberal leadership and the Lords' veto, 1907–1910', *Historical Journal*, XI, 3 (1968), pp. 508–22. Spender, *Campbell-Bannerman*, II, pp. 351–5.

9 Resolutions of the Free Church Council, *The Times*, 28 May 1907, p. 10. *British Congregationalist*, 30 May 1907, pp. 541, 553–4; 6 June 1907, p. 565. Koss, *Nonconformity*, pp. 86–90.

10 *British Congregationalist*, 30 May 1907, p. 541.

11 Campbell-Bannerman and McKenna to deputations of Anglicans, Catholics and Nonconformists, *The Times*, 22 July 1907, p. 18; 26 July 1907, p. 4; 3 August 1907, p. 8. McKenna's successor reached a temporary compromise with the Archbishop of Canterbury in June 1908 which assured that at least 50 per cent of the students accepted at any Anglican college would be members of the Anglican Church; ibid., 29 June 1908, p. 10.

12 Dillon to Bryce, 19 December 1905 (extract, copy), CBP, Add. MS 41211, f. 33. A. C. Hepburn, 'The Irish Council Bill and the fall of Sir Antony MacDonnell, 1906–7', *Irish Historical Studies*, XVII, 68 (1971), p. 474.

13 CBP, Add. MS 41211, ff. 344–6. CAB 37/83/54, 58, 61, 64, 70, 71 show the evolution of Bryce's proposals. For Nationalist suspicions of Mac-Donnell, see Redmond at Coalisland, 14 October 1906; Dillon to Morley, 19 December 1906; quoted in Hepburn, 'The Irish Council Bill', pp. 477, 479.

14 CAB 37/85/97.

15 See CAB 37/87/26, 37/88/54, 57, for the various proposals.

16 *Leicester Daily Mercury*, 8, 22 May 1907, p. 2. *Leeds Mercury*, 8, 22 May 1907, p. 4. *Eastern Daily Press*, 20, 23, 24 May 1907, p. 4. *British Congregationalist*, 16 May 1907, p. 475; 30 May 1907, p. 541. H. G. Jones to Walter Runciman, 2 July 1907, WRP, WR 17.

17 Birrell to Campbell-Bannerman, 30 October 1907, CBP, Add. MS 41240, ff. 127–32. Birrell memorandum, 3 June 1908, CAB 37/93/71.

18 *Leicester Daily Mercury*, 26 January 1899, p. 2.

19 CAB 37/90/99, 37/91/12. David W. Miller, *Church, State and Nation in Ireland, 1898–1921* (Dublin: Gill and Macmillan, 1973), ch. 9.

20 *Methodist Recorder*, 9 April 1908, p. 2; 14 May 1908, p. 3. Clifford to Asquith, 23 September 1908, AP, MS 20, ff. 25–7. The *British Congregationalist*, however, was prepared to accept the consequences of its liberalism; 9 April 1908, pp. 337–8.

21 Gwynn, *The Life of John Redmond*, pp. 150–6, 159.

22 *Eastern Daily Press*, 9 November 1907, p. 4. *British Congregationalist*, 30 April 1908, p. 411.

23 Whittaker to Gladstone [February or March 1907], UKA memorandum on licensing reform [1904 or 1905], HGP, Add. MSS 46064, ff. 149–50; 46092, ff. 36–9.

24 *British Congregationalist*, 5 March 1908, p. 229; 19 March 1908, p. 266; 14 May 1908, p. 450. *Methodist Recorder*, 5 March 1908, pp. 3, 6, 12–13; 16 July 1908, p. 20.

25 See, for example, Fred Horne, *British Congregationalist*, 13 August 1908, p. 143. Asquith's speech at London, *The Times*, 2 April 1908, p. 10, provides a good example of the themes he developed.

26 *British Congregationalist*, 27 February 1908, pp. 193–4; 2 April 1908, p. 318. *Methodist Recorder*, 27 February 1908, pp. 3–4; 5 March 1908, p. 5; 26 March 1908, p. 15.

27 J. Guinness Rogers to McKenna, 25 February 1908, McKP, MCKN 2/1/7. Joseph Henry (president, West Leeds Liberal Association) to Gladstone, 7 May 1908, HGP, Add. MS 46037, f. 83. Henry Havelock-Allan (aspiring Liberal candidate) to J. A. Pease, 21 May 1908, GP, MS 86.

28 This account of the 1908 education compromise is based on: WRP, WR 24(1) and WR 25(1); AP, MS 20, ff. 1–80; CAB 37/95/129, 37/96/155, 156; and leaders and articles in the *British Congregationalist* and the *Methodist Recorder*, November and early December 1908. Among the Liberal papers, only the *Eastern Daily Press* was enthusiastic in its support of Runciman's Bill.

29 See the following works on the new liberalism: Freeden, *New Liberalism*; Stefan Collini, *Liberalism and Sociology: L. T. Hobhouse and Political Argument in England 1880–1914* (Cambridge and New York: Cambridge UP, 1979); Peter Weiler, *The New Liberalism: Liberal Social Theory in Great Britain 1889–1914* (New York, London: Garland, 1982); P. F. Clarke, 'The Pro-

gressive Movement in England', *Transactions of the Royal Historical Society*, Fifth Series, XXIV (1974), pp. 159–81; P. F. Clarke, *Liberals and Social Democrats* (Cambridge and New York: Cambridge UP, 1978); Emy, *Social Politics*.

30 Weiler, *New Liberalism*, p. 104.

31 Emy, *Social Politics*, pp. 142–4, 185–7, 279.

32 *Leicester Daily Mercury*, 25 August 1904, p. 2. *Eastern Daily Press*, 21 September 1904, p. 6. *Leeds Mercury*, 20 October 1904, p. 4.

33 *Leeds Mercury*, 8–14 December 1904. Fenner Brockway, *Socialism Over Sixty Years: The Life of Jowett of Bradford (1864–1944)* (London: Allen & Unwin, 1946), pp. 53–6.

34 *Leicester Daily Mercury*, 3 March 1906, p. 2. *Examiner*, 8 March 1906, p. 229. *Leeds Mercury*, 20 July 1906, p. 4. *Eastern Daily Press*, 22 December 1906, p. 5. The *Methodist Recorder* never could overcome its doubts about rate-aided meals; 22 November 1906, p. 3.

35 See Bentley B. Gilbert, *The Evolution of National Insurance in Great Britain: The Origins of the Welfare State* (London: Michael Joseph, 1966), ch. 3, for the administrative origins of the measure, which were unrelated to socialism.

36 *The Times*, 16 February 1906, p. 15. Emy, *Social Politics*, pp. 200–1.

37 Asquith in Wiltshire and at the National Liberal Club, *The Times*, 26 August 1907, p. 6; 11 December 1908, p. 10.

38 Quoted in Maurice Bruce, *The Coming of the Welfare State* (New York: Schocken, 1966), pp. 155–6.

39 *The Times*, 12 December 1907, p. 6. *Eastern Daily Press*, 8 May 1908, p. 4; 4, 23 January 1909, p. 5. *Leicester Daily Mercury*, 8 May 1908, p. 2; 4 June 1910, p. 4. *Leeds Mercury*, 7 January 1908, p. 4.

40 See HGP, Add. MS 46093, for documents laying out arguments for and against an eight hours bill.

41 HGP, Add. MS 46093, ff. 134–5.

42 A 'bank-to-bank' bill provided that no miner should spend more than eight hours underground, including the time required to wind the men into and up from the pits. The bill considered by the Rea Committee provided that the average miner would spend no more than eight hours underground. It assumed that each miner would spend seven and one-half hours in the pits and that each winding required one hour, so that the average miner would have an eight-hour day if one winding were excluded from the calculation of the time spent underground.

43 CAB 37/91/34.

44 *The Times*, 18 March 1908, p. 9. Runciman to Gladstone, 10 March 1908; Lord Airedale to Gladstone, 20 December 1908; statement by the deputation from the Mining Association of Great Britain, 16 February 1910; HGP, Add. MSS 46065, ff. 166–7; 46028, ff. 154–5; 46093, ff. 140–51.

45 *Eastern Daily Press*, 28 February, 13 June 1901, p. 4 (unqualified support); 12 May 1906, 13 April 1907, p. 4 (implied opposition); 23 June 1908, p. 4 (unqualified opposition); 12 October 1908, p. 4 (implied support); 17 December 1908, p. 4 (modified opposition). The *Leeds Mercury* was most consistent, recognizing the humanitarian arguments for the measure, but feeling these were somewhat outweighed by the economic arguments against it; see 28 February 1901, 28 March, 24 June 1908, p. 4. Emy, *Social Politics*, pp. 242–3.

CHAPTER 6

1 Bruce K. Murray, *The People's Budget 1909/10: Lloyd George and Liberal Politics* (Oxford: Clarendon, 1980), pp. 46–8, 101–3. *Leeds Mercury*, 17 November 1908, p. 4.

2 *The Times*, 12 December 1908, p. 10. Pease's diary, 8, 10 December 1908, GP, MS 38. Murray, *People's Budget*, pp. 114–17. Jenkins, *Mr. Balfour's Poodle*, pp. 65–9.

3 See this book, ch. 8, for the crisis over the naval estimates.

4 Lucy Masterman's diary, 31 May 1909, April 1910; Masterman, *Masterman*, pp. 129, 161. Pease's diary, 21 October 1908, GP, MS 38. Edward David (ed.), *Inside Asquith's Cabinet: From the Diaries of Charles Hobhouse* (New York: St Martin's, 1977), pp. 72–6, 82, 88 (10 July, 5 August 1908, 7 March, 21 November 1909, 6 April 1910). Murray, *People's Budget*, pp. 76–81, 123–31.

5 Asquith to Edward VII, 19, 24 March 1909 (copies), AP, MS 5, ff. 94–5. Asquith to Harcourt, 14 April 1909, LHP, MS 510, ff. 64–5. Murray, *People's Budget*, pp. 98–108, 148–69. Lloyd George Cabinet memoranda, 29 January, 13 March 1909; CAB 37/97/16, 37/98/44.

6 Murray, *People's Budget*, pp. 293–6. Blewett, *General Elections of 1910*, p. 70. Since insurance contributions were a regressive tax, it is unlikely that the poor gained much in the end.

7 Asquith at the Holborn Restaurant, *The Times*, 25 June 1909, p. 8. *Leicester Daily Mercury*, 25 June 1909, p. 2. Mansfield at Southport, NLF, *Proceedings* (1909), pp. 66–7. Only the *Leeds Mercury*, which was in its anti-government phase, condemned the new direct taxation as excessive, robbery and an invasion of liberty; 30 April 1909, p. 4. By the autumn, it was supporting the Budget.

8 *Eastern Daily Press*, 23 July 1909, p. 5. Asquith at Sheffield, *The Times*, 22 May 1909, p. 7. The justification of taxation of monopolies and unearned increments reflected the influence of the new liberalism; Freeden, *New Liberalism*, pp. 20–1, 42–6, 134–7.

9 *Eastern Daily Press*, 23 September 1909, p. 7. *Yorkshire Evening News*, 25 September 1909, p. 2.

10 Murray, *People's Budget*, pp. 174–86, 200. *The Times*, 15, 18 June 1909, p. 10. Pease's diary, 11 May 1909 (on Ellis), GP, MS 38. (Of the people mentioned, only Perks left the party). F. S. L. Lyons, *John Dillon: A Biography* (London: Routledge & Kegan Paul, 1968), pp. 308–13.

11 Lloyd George to Spender, 16 July 1909, JSP, Add MS 46388, ff. 201–4. The average swing against the Liberals in the four July by-elections was 4.6 per cent, compared with 10 per cent over the previous eighteen months. Blewett, *General Elections of 1910*, pp. 45–7.

12 Asquith quoted in John Grigg, *Lloyd George: The People's Champion 1902–1911* (Berkeley, CA: University of California Press, 1978), p. 209. *British Congregationalist*, 12 August 1909, p. 131. Samuel to his wife, 4 August 1909, HSP, A/157/469; and Haldane to his mother, 14 August 1909, HP, MS 5982, f. 73, are examples of recognition of the party's revival.

13 *The Times*, 11 October 1909, p. 6. See Churchill to his wife, 30 August 1909, in Randolph S. Churchill, *Winston S. Churchill*, Vol. II, *1901–1914, Young Statesman* (Boston: Houghton Mifflin, 1967), p. 315; and Lloyd George to his brother, 19 October 1909, in William George, *My Brother and I* (London: Eyre & Spottiswoode, 1958), p. 232, for evidence of their intentions.

14 Sykes, *Tariff Reform*, pp. 115–44, 195–209. Murray, *People's Budget*, pp. 176-80, 209–23.

15 Redmond to Morley, 27 November 1909, quoted in Gwynn, *Redmond*, pp. 166–7. Patricia Jalland, *The Liberals and Ireland: The Ulster Question in British Politics to 1914* (Brighton: Harvester, 1980), pp. 26–7. *The Times*, 11 December 1909, p. 8. Blewett, *General Elections of 1910*, pp. 350–3.

16 Pickett to Runciman, 1 March 1909, WRP, WR 28. See also the report of the annual conference of the Northern Counties Education League, 18 November 1909, ibid.

17 *Baptist Times and Freeman*, 17 September 1909, p. 662; 15 October 1909, Supplement, pp. x-xi. *The Times*, 4 November 1909, p. 4; 6 December 1909, p. 10. National Council of Evangelical Free Churches, *Free Church Year Book* (London: National Council of Evangelical Free Churches, 1910), pp. 213–14.

18 National Council, *Free Church Year Book* (1911), pp. 225–6. Blewett, *General Elections of 1910*, pp. 343–9. Koss, *Nonconformity*, pp. 105–20. Bebbington, *Nonconformist Conscience*, pp. 79–81, 157–9.

19 *The Times*, 6 October 1906, p. 12. EP, MS 8801, ff. 145–51.

20 *Leeds Mercury*, 6 October 1906, p. 4. (Two days later, the *Mercury* retreated, asserting that 'To declare war against Socialism at present would be to go forth to seek an illusory enemy . . .',) *The Times*, 22 and 23 January 1908, p. 9. Gregory, *The Miners and British Politics*, pp. 31–3.

21 Thompson, *Socialists, Liberals and Labour*, pp. 183–8, 225–8. Chris Cook, 'Labour and the downfall of the Liberal Party, 1906–14', in Alan Sked and Chris Cook (eds), *Crisis and Controversy: Essays in Honour of A. J. P. Taylor* (New York: St Martin's, 1976), pp. 48–51. Bernstein, 'Three case studies', pp. 623–4.

22 *Leicester Daily Mercury*, 13 April 1907, p. 5.

23 Bernstein, 'Three case studies', pp. 623, 627–8, 634–7. Cook, 'Labour and the downfall of the Liberal Party', in Sked and Cook, *Crisis and Controversy*, pp. 45–7. Thompson, *Socialists, Liberals and Labour*, pp. 179–82.

24 Pease to Arthur Ponsonby, MP, 25 August 1908; quoted in Martin Petter, 'The progressive alliance', *History*, LVIII, 192 (1973), pp. 49–50. Pease to his wife, 27 August 1909, GP, MS 520. *The Times*, 17 November 1909, p. 10.

25 Blewett, *General Elections of 1910*, pp. 241–65, 389–95.

26 Bertram to Pease, 29 October 1907; A. E. Pease to J. A. Pease, 3 September 1909, 14 January 1910, and to Herbert Samuel, 16 September 1909; GP, MSS 85, 87, 88. Blewett, *General Elections of 1910*, pp. 211–15.

27 These generalizations are based on speeches and leading articles in the Liberal press of Leeds, Leicester and Norwich; accounts of speeches of Cabinet members published in *The Times*; and an analysis of election addresses in Blewett, *General Elections of 1910*, pp. 317–25, as well as Blewett's analysis of the campaign in ch. 6.

28 Samuel to Asquith, 3 February 1910; Grey to Asquith, 7 February 1910; Churchill to Asquith, 14 February 1910; AP, MSS 12, ff.105–6; 23, ff. 62–6, 70–6.

29 *Leicester Daily Mercury*, 25 February 1910, p. 4; 2 March 1910 (annual meeting of the Leicester Liberal Association), p. 3. *Yorkshire Evening News*, 22, 23 February, 17 March 1910, p. 4. *Eastern Daily Press*, 2 March 1910, p. 4. Horne in *British Congregationalist*, 24 February 1910, p. 148. C. P. Scott and William Royle (officers of the Manchester Liberal Federation) to Churchill, 24 February 1910, in Randolph S. Churchill, *Winston S.*

Churchill, Companion Vol. II: *1901–1914, Young Statesman* (Boston: Houghton Mifflin, 1969), pp. 977–8. Harold Storey (secretary, Yorkshire Liberal Federation) to Percy Illingworth, MP (a junior Whip), read to the Cabinet by Pease, 11–13 April 1910, GP, MS 38, f. 95.

30 Asquith to Edward VII, 25 February 1910 (copy), AP, MS 5, ff. 192–3. Exchange between Runciman and McKenna, 27, 28 March 1910, McKP, MCKN 3/22/10–12; WRP, WR 35.

31 Letters to Asquith from Harcourt (9 May), Buxton (31 May), Pentland (31 May), and McKenna (4 June), AP, MSS 12, ff. 136–8; 23, ff. 116–22. Pease's diary, 16 May 1910, GP, MS 38.

32 J. E. Ellis to Runciman, 29 June 1910, WRP, WR 35. Samuel to Gladstone, 25 June 1910, HGP, Add MS 45992, ff. 239–41. Major Dunne to Melton division Liberals, Rudolph Lehmann to Harborough division Liberals, *Leicester Daily Mercury*, 20 June 1910, p. 5; 11 July 1910, p. 3. Horne in *British Congregationalist*, 4 August 1910, p. 88.

33 Jesse Herbert to Elibank, 16 May 1910 (on referendum), AP, MS 23, ff. 102–7. Asquith to Balfour, [3 November 1910?], quoted in J. A. Spender and Cyril Asquith, *Life of Herbert Henry Asquith, Lord Oxford and Asquith*, 2 vols (London: Hutchinson, 1932), I, p. 289.

34 Of the many accounts of these negotiations, the best is in Searle, *National Efficiency*, pp. 177–95. Lloyd George's memorandum, plus a second of 29 October, are reprinted in Robert J. Scally, *The Origins of the Lloyd George Coalition* (Princeton, NJ: Princeton UP, 1975), pp. 375–86.

35 Lucy Masterman's diary, 12 October 1910, in Masterman, *Masterman*, pp. 164–5. *Westminster Gazette*, quoted in Searle, *National Efficiency*, p. 201.

36 See note 27 above. Blewett, *General Elections of 1910*, ch. 9, pp. 326–8.

37 At the Methodist Assembly, *Methodist Recorder*, 7 October 1909, p. 5. There are many examples of the increasing Nonconformist interest in social reform. See addresses to the Free Church Council by Rev. J. Scott Lidgett, 10 March 1909 and 12 March 1914, and by Rev. Thomas Mitchell, 5 March 1912, *Free Church Year Book* (1909), pp. 63–4, (1914), pp. 136–9, (1912), pp. 10–13; John Clifford, *Socialism and the Churches* (London: Fabian Society, 1908); and Silvester Horne to the Congregational Union, *British Congregationalist*, 12 May 1910, pp. 378–82.

38 *Eastern Daily Press*, 5 November 1908, p. 5. For a superb exposition of the nature and role of liberal social reform, see Asquith at Ladybank, *The Times*, 21 October 1907, p. 9.

39 *British Congregationalist*, 1 June 1911, p. 461.

40 *British Congregationalist*, 27 April 1911, p. 336; 2 February 1911, p. 88. *Methodist Recorder*, 19 October 1911, pp. 12–13. George L. Bernstein, 'The limitations of the new liberalism: The politics and political thought of John Clifford', *Albion*, XVI, 1 (1984), pp. 29–38.

41 Martin D. Pugh, 'Yorkshire and the new liberalism', *Journal of Modern History*, L, 3 (1978), pp. D 1151–3. Kenneth O. Morgan, 'The new liberalism and the challenge of Labour: The Welsh experience', *Welsh History Review*, VI, 3 (1973), pp. 294–300. *Eastern Daily Press*, 1 May 1912, p. 5.

42 Burns at Battersea, *The Times*, 15 April 1907, p. 4. Jose Harris, *Unemployment and Politics: A Study in English Social Policy, 1886–1914* (Oxford: Clarendon, 1972), pp. 135–44, 187–99.

43 Buxton to Ripon, 19 August 1907, quoted in Kenneth D. Brown, *Labour and Unemployment 1900–1914* (Totowa, NJ: Rowman & Littlefield, 1971),

p. 85; see also ibid., pp. 72–81, 88, and Harris, *Unemployment and Politics*, pp. 167–8, 178–84.

44 *Parl. Deb.*, 4, CLXXXVI, 35, 48 (13 March 1908). *Leicester Daily Post*, 10 July 1907, p. 4. By 1911 Lloyd George accepted 'the obligation of the state to find labour or sustenance', as did the oracle of new liberalism, L. T. Hobhouse, Lloyd George to Ralph Hawtrey, 7 March 1911, quoted in Harris, *Unemployment and Politics*, p. 346. Weiler, *New Liberalism*, p. 150.

45 Memoranda of 11 December 1908, 27 January, 17 April 1909, CAB 37/96/159, 37/97/17, 37/99/69.

46 Ross M. Martin, *TUC: The Growth of a Pressure Group, 1868–1976* (Oxford: Clarendon, 1980), pp. 99–102. Harris, *Unemployment and Politics*, pp. 353–5. Continued working-class suspicions limited the effectiveness of labour exchanges prior to the First World War.

47 Brown, *Labour and Unemployment*, pp. 145–59. Sydney Buxton memorandum, 22 November 1913, CAB 37/117/79. As was the case with labour exchanges, the provincial Liberal press gave little attention to unemployment insurance.

48 Churchill to Lloyd George, 20 June 1909, in Churchill, *Companion Volume II*, pp. 895–8.

49 NLF, *Proceedings* (1910), p. 23.

50 *The Times*, 16 December 1908, p. 12.

51 *Leicester Daily Post*, 10 February 1909, p. 4.

52 See memoranda analyzing the reports, AP, MSS 76, ff. 102–18; 78, ff. 5–16, 140, 169–70; 79, ff. 91–116, 146–53. Searle, *National Efficiency*, pp. 237–43.

53 *Eastern Daily Press*, 6 April, 14 October 1909, p. 5. *Leicester Daily Mercury*, 18 February 1909, p. 2; 9 April 1910, p. 4. *Leicester Daily Post*, 9 March 1909, 14 October 1910, p. 4. *British Congregationalist*, 25 February 1909, p. 157 (Horne); 20 January 1910, p. 42.

54 The evolution of the initial proposals and the modifications they underwent are discussed in Gilbert, *Evolution of National Insurance*, ch. 6. For the confusion in the drafting, see William J. Braithwaite, *Lloyd George's Ambulance Wagon: Being the Memoirs of William J. Braithwaite, 1911–1912* (London: Methuen, 1957), pp. 91–159.

55 *Leeds Mercury*, 5 May 1911, p. 4. On Liberal expectations, see Samuel to Gladstone, 14 May 1911, HGP, Add. MS 45992, f. 254; Braithwaite's diary, 29 March 1911, in Braithwaite, *Lloyd George's Ambulance Wagon*, p. 137.

56 Trevelyan to Runciman, 16 October 1911, WRP, WR 44. Asquith to Crewe, 30 November 1911 (copy), AP, MS 46, f. 193. Asquith to Elibank, 30 December 1911, EP, MS 8802, f. 363. Sir Harold Tangye to Harcourt, 13 July 1912, LHP, MS 443, f. 7.

57 There is much debate and little evidence as to how popular Liberal legislation was with the working class. Alan Clinton argues that initial hostility tended to fade as working-class organizations became involved in the administration of these measures. Alan Clinton, *The Trade Union Rank and File: Trades Councils in Britain, 1900–40* (Manchester: Manchester UP, 1977), pp. 47–9. For the opposing view, see Pelling, *Popular Politics*, ch. 1. The swing from Liberals to Uhionists in by-elections in 1912 was 4.6 per cent (or 5.3, depending on how it is measured); in 1913–14, it was 2.5 (or 2.1) per cent. P. F. Clarke, 'The electoral position of the Liberal and Labour Parties, 1910–1914', *English Historical Review*, XC, 357 (1975), p. 834.

58 *The Times*, 10 January 1906, p. 10.
59 *Parl. Deb.*, 4, CLXXXIV, 1196 (21 February 1908).
60 Pelling, *Popular Politics*, chs 1, 4, 9. Clinton, *Trades Councils*, pp. 84–9. James E. Cronin, 'Strikes 1870–1914', in Wrigley (ed.), *A History of British Industrial Relations 1875–1914* (Amherst, MA: University of Massachusetts Press, 1982), pp. 83–6. Standish Meacham, '"The Sense of an Impending Clash": English working-class unrest before the First World War', *American Historical Review*, LXXVII, 5 (1972), pp. 1343–64.
61 Van Gore, 'Rank-and-file dissent', in Wrigley (ed.), *British Industrial Relations*, pp. 64–7. Memorandum by David Shackleton, 22 July 1911, CAB 37/107/78.
62 Pease to Asquith, 12 September 1911, AP, MS 24, ff. 46–7 (emphasis is Pease's).

CHAPTER 7

1 Pease's diary, 8 January 1913, MS 39. Samuel to his mother, 16 March 1913, HSP, A/156/434. David, *Diaries of Charles Hobhouse*, p. 139 (22 June 1913). Asquith quoted in Jenkins, *Asquith*, p. 253.
2 Horne to Lloyd George, 23 June 1913, LGP, C/9/4/60. *British Congregationalist*, 26 June 1913, p. 506.
3 Liberal activists may have been more hostile to the miners than the press. Ronald Symes, C. B. Crawshaw and G. B. Hunter to Runciman, 7 March to 2 April 1912, WRP, WR 63. Joseph Henry to Gladstone, 4 May 1912, HGP, Add. MS 46038, ff. 68–71.
4 *Parl. Deb.*, 5, XXXV, 1732 (19 March 1912). Emy, *Social Politics*, pp. 258–61. Only the *Yorkshire Evening News* showed any ambiguity about including specific figures; 25 March 1912, p. 2.
5 Emy, *Social Politics*, pp. 270–2. *The Times*, 4 February 1914, p. 5. The Leicester papers opposed TUC efforts to secure a national minimum of 30s per week. *Leicester Daily Mercury*, 27 April 1911, p. 4. *Leicester Daily Post*, 25 April 1913, p. 4.
6 *Leicester Daily Post*, 6 October 1909, p. 4; 26 November 1913, pp. 4, 7. *Leeds Mercury*, 29 December 1910, p. 4; *Yorkshire Evening News*, 3 November 1913, p. 4, endorsed nationalization of the railways. *Leicester Daily Mercury*, 24, 25 October 1913, p. 4; *Eastern Daily Press*, 25 October 1913, p. 4, had no difficulty accepting it if the benefits could be demonstrated.
7 *The Times*, 12 March 1914, p. 8. Buxton memorandum, 13 April 1912, CAB 37/110/62.
8 *Eastern Daily Press*, 23 April 1910, 23 February 1911, p. 5. *Methodist Recorder*, 7 April 1910, p. 3. *Leicester Daily Post*, 10 August 1910, p. 4. *British Congregationalist*, 13 November 1913, p. 922.
9 *British Congregationalist*, 17 October 1912, p. 726.
10 National Council, *Free Church Year Book* (1914), p. 129.
11 Memorandum, GP, MS [72A]. Runciman at Batley, *The Times*, 23 October 1909, p. 11. Godfrey Sherington, *English Education, Social Change and War 1911–20* (Manchester: Manchester UP, 1981), p. 3.
12 See letters by Clifford quoted in Koss, *Nonconformity*, pp. 121–2, and Sherington, *English Education*, pp. 21–2. Correspondence, *Eastern Daily Press*, 4–23 January 1912. Annual meeting of Free Church Council, *Free Church Year Book* (1912), pp. 6, 27–8. *British Congregationalist*, 6 June 1912, p. 402.
13 Councillor Gimson in *Leicester Daily Mercury*, 15 March 1913, p. 7.

Yorkshire Evening News, 18 July 1910, p. 4. *Leicester Daily Post*, 16 March 1909, p. 4. *Eastern Daily Press*, 12 March 1914, p. 7. All Liberal papers, however, also continued to endorse the basic Nonconformist position.

14 Pease memoranda, 23 May 1913, 5 May 1914, CAB 37/115/32, 33, 37/119/58. Pease to the National Union of Teachers, *The Times*, 17 March 1913, p. 40. Board of Education memorandum, January 1913, GP, MS [72A], 9.

15 Pease memoranda, 24 January, 23 May 1913, GP, MS [72A], 17; CAB 37/115/32, 33.

16 Haldane to his mother, 2 April 1913, HP, MS 5989, f. 118. Acland to Pease, [November 1913], GP, MS 90. Trevelyan minute, 31 July 1913, cited in Sherington, *English Education*, p. 34; see also pp. 37–9.

17 Nicoll to Asquith, 17 November 1913, quoted in Sherington, *English Education*, pp. 34–5. National Council, *Free Church Year Book* (1914), pp. 113–14. *Eastern Daily Press*, 11 March 1914, p. 5.

18 Lord Riddell, *More Pages from my Diary, 1908–1914* (London: Country Life, 1934), p. 71 (19 June 1912).

19 ibid., p. 64 (27 May 1912). Trevor Wilson (ed.), *The Political Diaries of C. P. Scott, 1911–1928* (Ithaca, NY: Cornell UP, 1970), pp. 69–70 (16 January 1913). In May 1913, Lloyd George was again talking of by-passing the Cabinet, though not the Prime Minister. By July, he had again changed his mind. Riddell, *Diary*, pp. 155–6, 168–9 (31 May, 9 July 1913).

20 Haldane memorandum, 21 August 1913, CAB 37/116/56. Trevelyan to Runciman, 10 September 1913, WRP, WR 82. Riddell, *Diary*, pp. 174, 181 (26 September, 16 October 1913). David, *Diaries of Charles Hobhouse*, p. 146 (17 October 1913).

21 Cabinet memorandum, 9 January 1914, CAB 37/118/5. Lloyd George at Swindon and Pwllheli, *The Times*, 23 October 1913, pp. 9–10; 23 December 1913, p. 12.

22 G. Wallace Carter to Lloyd George, 28 May 1914; Hamer to Lloyd George, 16, 21 November 1913; LGP, C/2/4/20, C/10/2/38, 48. J. Aubrey Rees to Runciman, 3 January 1913 [1914], 8 January 1914, WRP, WR 82, 135.

23 Reports to Lloyd George, 28–31 May 1914, LGP, C/2/4/20–7. Deputation to Lloyd George by the National Farmers' Union, statement by B. B. Sapwell of the Norfolk Chamber of Agriculture, *Eastern Daily Press*, 7 February 1914, p. 5; 9 March 1914, p. 8. Charles Bathurst to Andrew Bonar Law, 4 December 1913, quoted in Douglas, *Land, People and Politics*, p. 165.

24 Lloyd George to deputation from Town Tenants' League and at Middlesbrough, Holloway and Glasgow, *The Times*, 31 October 1913, p. 9; 10 November 1913, p. 4; 1 December 1913, p. 64; 5 February 1914, p. 10. Lloyd George to Asquith, 5 December 1913, AP, MS 25, ff. 63–6. Present leaseholders could not be given the same security because of existing contracts.

25 Asquith at Ladybank, George Lambert (on behalf of Lloyd George) in North Devon, Runciman to the Devon Farmers' Union, *The Times*, 7 October 1912, p. 10; 8 October 1912, p. 8; 29 November 1912, p. 10. See also *The Times*, 19 May 1911, p. 7.

26 On poor relief, see *Eastern Daily Press*, 7 January 1913, p. 5; 20 August 1913, p. 4. The government's unemployment policy contributed little to the reduction of pauperism; Gilbert, *Evolution of National Insurance*, pp. 262–3. On education, see Sherington, *English Education*, p. 4; Pease's memorandum, 13 December 1913, CAB 37/117/90.

27 Pease's diary, [30 April 1914], GP, MS 39. Bentley B. Gilbert, 'David Lloyd

George: The reform of British landholding and the Budget of 1914', *Historical Journal*, XXI, 1 (1978), pp. 127–31.

28 Gilbert, 'Budget of 1914', pp. 132–41. *Eastern Daily Press*, 9 July 1914, p. 6.

29 Holt's diary, 19 July 1914, quoted in Cameron Hazlehurst, 'Herbert Henry Asquith', in John P. Mackintosh (ed.), *British Prime Ministers in the Twentieth Century*, Vol. I: *Balfour to Chamberlain* (New York: St Martin's, 1977), p. 96. Reports to Lloyd George, 12 May to 7 June 1914, LGP, C/2/4/16, 20, 22–7; C/11/1/58, C/15/1/29.

30 Summary of proceedings of the Scottish Liberal Association, 22 October 1910, AP, MS 23, f. 298. Memoranda from Pease, Haldane, Loreburn, Robson, Samuel and Buxton, October 1910, CAB 37/103/42–6, 52. Pease's diary, 13 October, 22 November 1910, GP, MS 38.

31 A copy of the *Westminster Gazette* article is in LGP, C/15/1/13. Oswald Partington to Runciman, 14 September 1913, WRP, WR 82. Clarke, *Lancashire and the New Liberalism*, pp. 328–9. Morgan, 'The Welsh experience', pp. 302–4. McKibbin, *Evolution of the Labour Party*, pp. 54–62.

32 Cook, 'Labour and the downfall of the Liberal Party', in Sked and Cook, *Crisis and Controversy*, pp. 40–7. Bernstein, 'Three case studies', pp. 627, 636–7. McKibbin, *Evolution of the Labour Party*, p. 85. Labour's strength on the Bradford City Council did not reflect its electoral strength because most of the nominated aldermen were Liberals or Conservatives.

33 Cook, 'Labour and the downfall of the Liberal Party', in Sked and Cook, *Crisis and Controversy*, pp. 44–7, 55–63. Thompson, *Socialists, Liberals and Labour*, pp. 183–7.

34 Gregory, *Miners*, pp. 49–52 and *passim*. Thompson, *Socialists, Liberals, and Labour*, pp. 265–85. McKibbin, *Evolution of the Labour Party*, pp. 74–6, 79–80, 87.

35 *Methodist Recorder*, 22 July 1909, p. 22; 29 July 1909, p. 23; 19 May 1910, p. 3; 21 July 1910, p. 16.

36 Elibank memorandum, 16 November 1911, CAB 37/108/148. Poll of Liberal agents, cited in David Morgan, *Suffragists and Liberals: The Politics of Woman Suffrage in England* (Oxford: Blackwell, 1975), pp. 90–1. *Yorkshire Evening News*, 12 July 1910, p. 4. *Leicester Daily Mercury*, 16 February 1912, p. 4.

37 Based on lists in LHP, MS 533, ff. 157–63.

38 For the extremes, see Alfred F. Havighurst, *Radical Journalist: H. W. Massingham (1860–1924)* (London and New York: Cambridge UP, 1974), pp. 195–8; and *Yorkshire Evening News*, 28 November 1910, 19 December 1911, p. 4.

39 Scott memorandum of conversation with Haldane, 16 March 1911, quoted in John Lawrence Hammond, *C. P. Scott of the Manchester Guardian* (New York: Harcourt Brace, 1934), p. 104. Peter Rowland, *The Last Liberal Governments*, Vol. II: *Unfinished Business 1911–1914* (London; Barrie & Jenkins, 1971), pp. 156–8. Andrew Rosen, *Rise Up Women! The Militant Campaign of the Women's Social and Political Union, 1903–1914* (London and Boston: Routledge & Kegan Paul, 1974), pp. 160–3. Clarke, *Lancashire and the New Liberalism*, p. 195. NLF, *Proceedings* (1912), p. 60. The 1912 Conciliation Bill failed partly because sixteen Labour MPs were absent due to strikes.

40 Pease's diary, 22 February 1911, GP, MS 39. See estimates by Lloyd George and Elibank, *The Times*, 25 November 1911, p. 12; 27 November 1911, p. 7; a *Westminster Gazette* article, 30 December 1910, and Jesse Herbert to Pease, 11 June 1912, GP, MSS [63], [64]. The Liberals over-

estimated the impact of plural voting. See Neal Blewett, 'The franchise in the United Kingdom, 1885–1918', *Past and Present*, XXXII (1965), pp. 43–51.

41 Blewett, 'The franchise', pp. 31–43. Elibank memorandum, 16 November 1911, CAB 37/108/148. For the historical debate, see Matthew, McKibbin and Kay, 'Franchise factor', pp. 737–41; and P. F. Clarke, 'Liberals, Labour and the franchise', *English Historical Review*, XCII, 364 (1977), pp. 582–90.

42 Morgan, *Suffragists and Liberals*, pp. 94, 101. Asquith to George V, 25 January 1913 (copy), AP, MS 7, f. 7. Samuel to his mother, 26 January, 2 February 1913, HSP, A/156/427, 428. Riddell, *Diary*, p. 118 (25 January 1913).

43 Barran to Lloyd George, 1 January 1914, LGP, C/10/3/1. See letters to Lloyd George from officers of the Liberal Women's Suffrage Union, 3–26 November 1913, 7 February 1914, LGP, C/10/2/12, 45, 59; C/10/3/19; and the correspondence concerning the Liberal candidate for Cheltenham, 4 April to 29 May 1914, LGP, C/11/1/25–6, 29, 32–3, 50.

44 Pamphlet of the National Union on its electoral fund, LGP, C/11/1/68.

45 McKenna at Cardiff, *The Times*, 22 May 1913, p. 12.

46 *Parl. Deb.*, 5, XXXVIII, 1326–7 (16 May 1912).

47 *The Times*, 20 May 1912, p. 7.

48 *British Congregationalist*, 19 December 1912, p. 927; see also 6 February 1913, pp. 85–6. *The Times*, 11 December 1912, p. 10. Pease's diary, 2 December 1912, GP, MS 39.

49 NLF, *Proceedings* (1911), p. 63. *British Congregationalist*, 5 January 1911, p. 2.

50 Most recently, in Jalland, *Liberals and Ireland*, pp. 65–72, 108–13; but also in, for example, R. C. K. Ensor, *England 1870–1914* (Oxford: Clarendon, 1936), pp. 453–4.

51 Samuel to Gladstone, 23 June 1912, HGP, Add. MS 45992, ff. 268–9. Arthur Eaglestone (constituency organizer) to Pease, 12 January 1913, GP, MS 90. Memorandum by Arthur Steel-Maitland, [June?] 1914, quoted in Cameron Hazlehurst, *Politicians at War, July 1914 to May 1915: A Prologue to the Triumph of Lloyd George* (New York: Knopf, 1971), p. 29. Jalland, *Liberals and Ireland*, pp. 30, 60–1, 87–91. Bebbington, *Nonconformist Conscience*, pp. 103–4.

52 Burn to Runciman, 9 September 1911, WRP, WR 44.

53 A. T. Q. Stewart, *The Ulster Crisis* (London: Faber, 1967), pp. 219–20.

54 Bonar Law quoted in A. P. Ryan, *Mutiny at the Curragh* (London: Macmillan; New York: St Martin's, 1956), p. 51. Jenkins, *Asquith*, pp. 282–4. Stewart, *The Ulster Crisis*, pp. 136–7.

55 *British Congregationalist*, 25 January 1912, p. 61. Both the *Leeds Mercury* and the *Methodist Recorder* urged the government to conciliate Ulster while recognizing the need for Home Rule.

56 Sir Frederick Low, MP, at Norwich, *Eastern Daily Press*, 2 August 1912, p. 6. The *Leeds Mercury* was just as firm in condemning the threats of violence as those Liberals who were less sympathetic to Ulster; 13, 15 August 1912, p. 4.

57 Herbert Henry Asquith (Earl of Oxford and Asquith), *Fifty Years of Parliament*, 2 vols (London: Cassell, 1926), II, pp. 141–2. The Attorney-General concluded that there *were* grounds for prosecution; CAB 37/117/82.

58 Birrell to Asquith, 30 August 1913, AP, MS 38, ff. 122–5. *The Times*, 11 September 1913, pp. 7–8. Jenkins, *Asquith*, pp. 282–97.

59 For the positions of Cabinet members, see Jalland, *Liberals and Ireland*, pp. 158–66. The Unionists were similarly divided; ibid., pp. 145–57.

60 Smith to Seely, 25 September 1913, quoted in ibid., p. 256. *Leicester Daily Post*, 23 February 1914, p. 4. The *Daily Post* did not agree with the resolution.

61 23 September 1913, p. 3. Over the next two weeks, the *Recorder* published letters both opposing and supporting this position. See also, *Leeds Mercury* and *Leicester Daily Post*, 14 November 1913, p. 4.

62 David, *Diaries of Charles Hobhouse*, pp. 148–9 (11 November 1913). Pease's diary, 11 November 1913, GP, MS 39. Trevelyan to Runciman, 3 November 1913, WRP WR 82. Christopher Addison, MP, to Lloyd George, 10 November 1913, LGP, C/10/2/24a.

63 Lloyd George memorandum, 23 February 1914, LGP, C/20/2/7. Irish leaders to Asquith, 2 March 1914, AP, MS 39, ff. 136–9.

64 Carson quoted in Jalland, *Liberals and Ireland*, p. 203. *Leeds Mercury*, 17 March 1914, p. 4. Nicoll to Lloyd George, 14 March 1914, LGP, C/11/1/9.

65 Grey to Katherine Lyttelton, 3 April 1914, quoted in George Macaulay Trevelyan, *Grey of Fallodon: Being the Life of Sir Edward Grey, Afterwards Viscount Grey of Fallodon* (London: Longman, 1937), p. 175. Walter Robertshaw to Harcourt, 25 March 1914, LHP, MS 444, ff. 73–6. Jalland, *Liberals and Ireland*, pp. 218–33, refutes the Unionist claim that the Liberals were trying to provoke the Ulster Volunteers as a pretext for crushing them.

66 Asquith to George V, 27 April, 1 May 1914 (copies), AP, MS 7, ff. 115–18. Herbert Henry Asquith, *Letters to Venetia Stanley*, Michael and Eleanor Brock (eds) (Oxford and New York: Oxford UP, 1982), p. 59 (22 March 1914). Jalland, *Liberals and Ireland*, pp. 242, 245.

67 *Eastern Daily Press*, 21 July 1914, p. 4. *Yorkshire Evening News*, 10 July 1914, p. 6, concurred. *Leeds Mercury* and *Leicester Daily Post*, 10 July 1914, p. 4, supported concessions. *Leicester Daily Mercury*, 21 July 1914, p. 4, accepted the conference but opposed concessions. All but the *Leeds Mercury* insisted that the Bill must be passed after the conference failed.

68 *Leicester Daily Mercury*, 22, 23 July 1914, p. 7. Robert Harcourt to Lewis Harcourt, 16 July 1914, LHP, MS 681, ff. 199–200. Trevelyan to Runciman, 25 July 1914, WRP, WR 135.

69 Dangerfield, *The Strange Death of Liberal England*.

CHAPTER 8

1 Ronald Hyam, *Elgin and Churchill at the Colonial Office 1905–1908: The Watershed of the Empire-Commonwealth* (London: Macmillan; New York: St Martin's, 1968), pp. 66–82. Technically, the government promised to leave the final decision on Chinese labour to a responsible government in the Transvaal. It had no intention, however, of allowing the system of indentured labour to continue.

2 Churchill memorandum, 2 January 1906, CAB 37/82/4. Hyam, *Elgin and Churchill*, pp. 104–36, buries the myth that Campbell-Bannerman had to persuade the Cabinet to grant the Transvaal self-government.

3 *Eastern Daily Press*, 30 July, 1 August 1906, p. 4.

4 NLF, *Proceedings* (1909), pp. 22–3.

5 Geoffrey Barker Pyrah, *Imperial Policy and South Africa*, 1902–10 (Oxford: Clarendon, 1955), ch. 4. L. M. Thompson, *The Unification of South Africa* (Oxford: Clarendon, 1960), pp. 400–32.

6 Crewe to Gladstone, 2 September 1910, HGP, Add. MS 45996, ff. 120–1.

7 Soloman memorandum, 5 April 1911, CAB 37/106/54. John Edward

Kendle, *The Colonial and Imperial Conferences 1887–1911: A Study in Imperial Organization* (London: Longman, 1967), pp. 90–7, 169–78. Australia and New Zealand tended to favour the creation of institutions to facilitate Anglo-dominion consultation.

8   Donald C. Gordon, *The Dominion Partnership in Imperial Defense, 1870–1914* (Baltimore: Johns Hopkins UP, 1965), pp. 272–8. Franklyn Arthur Johnson, *Defence by Committee: The British Committee of Imperial Defence 1885–1959* (London: Oxford UP, 1960), pp. 87–90, 106–14, 124–6.

9   Gordon, *Dominion Partnership*, pp. 225–93. McKenna memorandum, 20 July 1909, CAB 37/100/98. Churchill to Harcourt, 29 January 1912 (draft), in Churchill, *Companion Volume* II, pp. 1507–10.

10 Haldane at Brighton, *The Times*, 27 February 1909, p. 9. *Leeds Mercury*, 9 April 1907, p. 4. *Leicester Daily Mercury*, 23 July, 1912, p. 4. *Eastern Daily Press*, 31 August 1912, p. 4. Gordon, *Dominion Partnership*, pp. 265–7.

11 Morley to Lord Minto (the Viceroy), 7 October 1908, quoted in Stephen E. Koss, *John Morley at the India Office, 1905–1910* (New Haven, CT and London: Yale UP, 1969), p. 128.

12 Morley to Clarke, 18 September 1908, quoted in Koss, *Morley at the India Office*, p. 165. For Morley's views on the impact of reform, see his letters to Clarke, 3 September 1908, ibid., pp. 181–2; and to Minto, 7 May 1908, quoted in Hyam, *Elgin and Churchill*, pp. 535–6.

13 John Clifford, *The War and the Churches* (London: James Clark, 1914), pp. 10–11. Clifford reluctantly supported the First World War.

14 *Examiner*, 19 July 1906, p. 701. Also, see Horne the next year, *British Congregationalist*, 14 March 1907, p. 253.

15 Asquith to McKenna, 4 July 1908, McKP, MCKN 3/3/2A. According to Asquith, the average fell from £1 13s 5d in the 1904–5 to £1 6s 4d in 1907–9. Herbert Henry Asquith, *The Genesis of the War* (New York: George H. Doran, 1923), pp. 168–9. Howard Weinroth, 'Left-wing opposition to naval armaments in Britain before 1914', *Journal of Contemporary History*, VI, 4 (1971), pp. 104–7. *Leicester Daily Mercury*, 11 February, 3 March 1908, p. 2. *Eastern Daily Press*, 3, 11 March 1908, p. 4.

16 Fisher to McKenna, 28 July, 22 December 1908, McKP, MCKN 3/4/17, 23. Arthur J. Marder, *From Dreadnought to Scapa Flow: The Royal Navy in the Fisher Era, 1904–1919*, Vol. I: *The Road to War, 1904–1914* (London: Oxford UP, 1961), pp. 152–6, 163–4. For the divisions in the Admiralty, see Paul Haggie, 'The Royal Navy and war planning in the Fisher era', *Journal of Contemporary History*, VIII, 3 (1973), pp. 113–31; Ruddock F. Mackay, *Fisher of Kilverstone* (Oxford: Clarendon, 1973), pp. 381–410; and Jon Sumida, 'Strategy formulation as a political process: The case of the British Admiralty, 1904–1914', (paper read at the sixth Naval History Symposium, 29–30 September 1983, United States Naval Academy, Annapolis, MD).

17 Asquith to McKenna, 1 January 1909, McKP, MCKN 3/3/4C. Trevelyan, *Grey of Fallodon*, pp. 213–15.

18 Lloyd George to Asquith, 2 February 1909 (copy), LGP, C/6/11/2. Notes from the Sea Lords and Asquith to McKenna, McKP, MCKN 3/19/10, 21–5.

19 *British Congregationalist*, 29 July 1909, p. 91. A. J. A. Morris, *Radicalism Against War, 1906–1914: The Advocacy of Peace and Retrenchment* (Totowa, NJ: Rowman & Littlefield, 1972), pp. 155–65. The *Leeds Mercury* condemned the government's programme as insufficient; 17 March 1909, p. 4.

20 *Leeds Mercury*, 17, 23 January, 29 August 1911, p. 4; Hogge at the Yorkshire Liberal Federation, *Leeds Mercury*, 11 March 1911, p. 3. *Eastern Daily Press*, 10 March 1911, p.4; see also 10 March, 24 May 1910, p. 4. *Leicester Daily Mercury*, 10 March 1911, p. 4; see also 15 July 1910, p. 4.

21 *Leeds Mercury*, 15 March 1911, p. 4. Annual Report of NLF, in *Proceedings* (1912), p. 33. For the League of Peace, see Grey at the International Arbitration League, *The Times*, 18 March 1911, p. 8; Eliot Crawshay-Williams, MP, to a correspondent, and subsequent editorial, *Leicester Daily Mercury*, 17 March 1911, p. 2; 20 March 1911, p. 4. The arbitration treaty was killed by the United States Senate, British adherence to the Declaration of London by the House of Lords.

22 Haldane at the Eighty Club, *The Times*, 30 November 1912, p. 7. Viscount Haldane, *Before the War* (London: Cassell, 1920), pp. 170–5.

23 John K. Dunlop, *The Development of the British Army 1899–1914* (London: Methuen, 1938), pp. 286–7, 300. Nicholas d'Ombrain, *War Machinery and High Policy: Defence Administration in Peacetime Britain 1902–1914* (London: Oxford UP, 1973), p. 220. *Leicester Daily Post*, 18 November 1913, p. 4. J. E. B. Seely to J. A. Spender, April 1913, JSP, Add. MS 46392, ff. 99–109.

24 *British Congregationalist*, 25 July 1912, p. 526. *Yorkshire Evening News*, *Leicester Daily Mercury*, 19 March 1912, p. 2. *Leicester Daily Post*, 19 March 1912, p. 4. *Eastern Daily Press*, 12 February 1912, p. 4.

25 Churchill to Haldane, 6 May 1912, HP, MS 5909, ff. 215–16. Churchill memorandum, 15 June 1912, CAB 37/111/76. Churchill memorandum for CID, 11 July 1912, quoted in Churchill, *Young Statesman*, pp. 559–62.

26 Memoranda by Haldane, 9 May 1912, and McKenna, 3 July 1912, CAB 37/110/68, 37/111/86. Paul G. Halpern, *The Mediterranean Naval Situation 1908–1914* (Cambridge, MA: Harvard UP, 1971), pp. 20–5, 40–2, 63–76.

27 This analysis is based on the figures in E. L. Woodward, *Great Britain and the German Navy* (Hamden, CT: Archon, 1964; reprint of 1935 edn), pp. 452–3. It seems to be confirmed by Churchill's own figures. See his statement to the Commons, 6 January 1913, in ibid., p. 405; and memoranda of 28 August, 23 September 1913 in Churchill, *Companion Volume II*, pp. 1764–70, 1781–8. On the narrowest definition of the two-power standard, Woodward's figures indicate that Britain was building at a rate just short of 10 per cent above that of Germany plus the United States or Germany plus France. Keith M. Wilson, *The Policy of the Entente: Essays on the Determinants of British Foreign Policy, 1904–1914* (Cambridge: Cambridge UP, 1985), pp. 70–4, argues that Britain negotiated the entente with France primarily to avoid the pressures which the strict interpretation of the two-power standard imposed. I would like to thank Jon Sumida for suggesting this line of argument to me.

28 *The Times*, 11 November 1913, p. 10; 18 December 1913, p. 8. NLF, *Proceedings* (1913), pp. 49, 62–4. Stephen E. Koss, *Sir John Brunner, Radical Plutocrat 1842–1919* (Cambridge: Cambridge UP, 1970), pp. 264–7. Spender to Fisher, 25 January 1914, Fisher Papers, FISR 3/6/2275.

29 Simon note to Asquith, n.d., AP, MS 25, ff. 148–9. See also Beauchamp, Hobhouse, McKenna, Runciman and Simon to Asquith, 29 January 1914, AP, MS 25, ff. 170–7.

30 Churchill included most of these factors in a memorandum on 1 January 1913, in which he warned his colleagues not to expect future reductions as long as the naval race continued: CAB 37/114/11.

31 Asquith, *The Genesis of the War*, pp. 168–9. The estimated expenditure per

head for 1914–15 was £1 13s 10d, compared with £1 6s 4d in 1907–9. Foreign Office memorandum on the Hague Conference, 24 March 1914, CAB 37/119/48.

32 Scott to Leonard Courtney, September 1899, quoted in Collini, *Liberalism and Sociology*, p. 81. *Leicester Daily Mercury*, 17 June 1913.

33 Trevelyan to Runciman, 24 October 1910, WRP, WR 35. For radical approval of Grey, see Ripon to Runciman, 11 October 1908, WRP, WR 21; and Sir William Angus at the NLF, *Proceedings* (1909), p. 49.

34 Grey to Henry Newbolt, 5 January 1903, quoted in Keith Robbins, *Sir Edward Grey: A Biography of Lord Grey of Fallodon* (London: Cassell, 1971), p. 131.

35 Grey memorandum, March 1908, CAB 37/92/41. On the Congo, see S. J. S. Cookey, *Britain and the Congo Question, 1885–1913* (London: Longman, 1968).

36 Grey to President Roosevelt, 4 December 1906 (copy), EGP, FO 800/110, ff. 391–3. Grey memorandum, 20 February 1906, quoted in Eugene N. Anderson, *The First Moroccan Crisis 1904–1906* (Hamden, CT: Archon, 1966, reprint of 1930 edn), pp. 369–71.

37 George Monger, *The End of Isolation: British Foreign Policy 1900–1907* (London: Thomas Nelson, 1963), chs 9–10. Samuel R. Williamson, Jr., *The Politics of Grand Strategy: Britain and France Prepare for War, 1904–1914* (Cambridge, MA: Harvard UP, 1969), ch. 3.

38 Williamson, *Grand Strategy*, pp. 82–3. Zara S. Steiner, *Britain and the Origins of the First World War* (New York: St Martin's, 1977), pp. 128–30. Grey to Asquith, 16 April 1911 (copy), EGP, FO 800/100, ff. 236–8.

39 Quoted in A. J. P. Taylor, *The Trouble Makers: Dissent over Foreign Policy 1792–1939* (London: Hamish Hamilton, 1957), pp. 111–12.

40 Campbell-Bannerman to Grey, 8 October 1906, quoted in Trevelyan, *Grey of Fallodon*, p. 190.

41 Quoted in Beryl Williams, 'Great Britain and Russia, 1905 to the 1907 convention', in F. H. Hinsley (ed.) *British Foreign Policy under Sir Edward Grey* (Cambridge: Cambridge UP, 1977), pp. 135–6. See also Wilson, *Policy of the Entente*, pp. 75–9.

42 Henry to Gladstone, 21 June 1909, HGP, Add. MS 46037, f. 142. *Leicester Daily Mercury*, 25, 26 September 1907, p. 2, was most unambiguous in its support of the entente. *Eastern Daily Press*, 25 September 1907, p. 6, was clearly unhappy. *Leeds Mercury*, 26 September 1907, p. 4, did not trust Russia, but its objections were practical rather than moral.

43 Grey to Sir Francis Bertie, 12 November 1908, quoted in Oron James Hale, *Publicity and Diplomacy, with Special Reference to England and Germany 1890–1914* (New York and London: Appleton-Century, 1940), p. 330. The *Leeds Mercury* shared Grey's fear of Germany.

44 Grey minute, 1908, quoted in F. R. Bridge, *Great Britain and Austria–Hungary 1906–1914: A Diplomatic History* (London: Weidenfeld & Nicolson, 1972), p. 105. Paul M. Kennedy, *The Rise of Anglo-German Antagonism 1860–1914* (London: Allen & Unwin, 1980), pp. 428–30. D. W. Sweet, 'Great Britain and Germany, 1905–1911', in Hinsley, *British Foreign Policy*, pp. 217–27. Wilson, *Policy of the Entente*, chs 4 and 5, emphasizes Grey's fear of a return to isolation, with the potential of a revival of friction with France and Russia, while questioning the reality of Grey's (and others') belief in either a balance of power or a threat of German hegemony.

45 Morris, *Radicalism Against War*, pp. 183–6. In fact, Grey made clear to the Russians that Britain would not go to war in support of Serbia's claims.

46 Grey memorandum, 20 May 1911, CAB 37/107/60, summarizes the nego-
    tiations. Sweet, 'Britain and Germany', in Hinsley, *British Foreign Policy*,
    pp. 229–35. Kennedy, *Anglo-German Antagonism*, pp. 422–3.
47 Grey to Bertie, 29 July, 8 September 1911, quoted in Ima Christina Barlow,
    The Agadir Crisis (Chapel Hill, NC: University of North Carolina Press,
    1940), p. 286; and in T. P. Conwell-Evans, *Foreign Policy from a Back Bench
    1904–1918: A Study Based on the Papers of Lord Noel-Buxton* (London: Oxford
    UP, 1932), pp. 52–3.
48 Asquith to George V, 4, 19 July 1911 (copies), AP, MS 6, ff. 48–9, 56–7.
    Grey to Asquith, 19 July 1911 (copy), EGP, FO 800/100, ff. 251–3. Barlow,
    The Agadir Crisis, pp. 305–16.
49 Morley to Asquith, 27 July 1911, AP, MS 13, ff. 39–40. Loreburn to Grey,
    27 July, 26 August 1911, EGP, FO 800/99, ff. 263–4, 267–7. Of the leading
    radical newspapers, only the *Nation* was hostile to the government. Hale,
    Publicity and Diplomacy, pp. 384, 390–2. Howard S. Weinroth, 'The British
    radicals and the balance of power, 1902–1914', *Historical Journal*, XIII, 4
    (1970), pp. 674–5.
50 Correspondence between Runciman and Harcourt, 24, 26 August, 4
    September 1911, WRP, WR 44. McKenna's notes on conversation with
    Asquith, 20 October 1911, McKP, MCKN 4/2/C. On the struggle between
    the services, see d'Ombrain, *War Machinery and High Policy*, pp. 74–98.
51 Asquith to George V, 2, 16 November 1911 (copies), AP, MS 6, ff. 75–6,
    79–80. Pease's diary, 1, 15 November 1911, GP, MS 39. David, *Diaries of
    Charles Hobhouse*, pp. 107–8 (16 November 1911). Asquith to Grey, 5
    September 1911, EGP, FO 800/100, f. 260.
52 Trevelyan to Runciman, 8 July 1911, WRP, WR 44.
53 Grey at Manchester, *The Times*, 17 February 1912, p. 6. Grey to Thomas
    Hodgkin, 23 January 1912 (copy), EGP, FO 800/108, ff. 151–3. Grey to
    Spender, 24 September 1912, JSP, Add. MS 46389, ff. 19–20. D. McLean,
    'English radicals, Russia and the fate of Persia, 1907–1913', *English
    Historical Review*, XCIII, 367 (1978), pp. 342–51.
54 Asquith at the Guildhall, *The Times*, 10 November 1911, p. 10. Grey to Sir
    Arthur Nicolson, 23 September 1911, quoted in C. J. Lowe and M. L.
    Dockrill, *The Mirage of Power*, Vol. I: *British Foreign Policy 1902–14* (London
    and Boston: Routledge & Kegan Paul, 1972), p. 93.
55 *Eastern Daily Press*, 18 January 1912, p. 4. *Leicester Daily Mercury*, 28
    February 1912, p. 2. John A. Murray, 'Foreign policy debated: Sir Edward
    Grey and his critics, 1911–1912', in Lillian Parker Wallace and William C.
    Askew (eds), *Power, Public Opinion, and Diplomacy: Essays in Honor of Eber
    Malcolm Carroll by His Former Students* (Durham, NC: Duke UP, 1959),
    pp. 144–70. Hammond, *C. P. Scott*, p. 149. Havighurst, *Massingham*,
    pp. 206–8. Stephen E. Koss, *Fleet Street Radical: A. G. Gardiner and the Daily
    News* (London: Allen Lane, 1973), p. 142.
56 Harcourt, Haldane, Lloyd George and Pease wanted to try to find an
    acceptable neutrality pledge. Asquith did not, for Grey clearly would
    have resigned over the issue. Harcourt memorandum of meeting with
    Haldane and Grey, 14 March 1912, LHP, MS 442, ff. 211–14. Pease's
    diary, 29 March 1912, GP, MS 39. Asquith to Grey, 10 April 1912, EGP, FO
    800/100, ff. 275–6. Wilson, *Policy of the Entente*, pp. 35–6.
57 Richard Langhorne, 'Anglo-German negotiations concerning the future
    of the Portuguese colonies, 1911–1914', *Historical Journal*, XVI, 2 (1973),
    pp. 361–87. Maybelle Kennedy Chapman, *Great Britain and the Baghdad
    Railway* (Northampton, MA: Smith College, 1948).

58 *Leiester Daily Post*, 22 October 1912, p. 4. Asquith at the Guildhall, *The Times*, 11 November 1912, p. 10. For the new radical view of Grey, see L. T. Hobhouse to C. P. Scott, 4 June 1913, quoted in Wilson, *Diaries of C. P. Scott*, p. 89.

59 Grey in the House of Commons, 18 March 1914, in Grey, *Speeches*, p. 239. Grey to Rodd, quoted in Trevelyan, *Grey of Fallodon*, pp. 219–20.

60 Grey to Cambon, 22 November 1912, quoted in Trevelyan, *Grey of Fallodon*, pp. 139–40.

61 *Leicester Daily Post*, 5 March 1913, p. 4. See also *Eastern Daily Press*, 27 February, 16 March 1911, p. 4. Spender to Haldane, n.d. (draft), JSP, Add. MS 46390, ff. 176–80. Spender to Fisher, 25 January 1914, Fisher Papers, FISR 3/6/2275. For the justification of Spender's fears about the army, see d'Ombrain, *War Machinery and High Politics*, pp. 103–5, 215–20.

62 Steiner, *Origins*, pp. 117–23. Lowe and Dockrill, *Mirage of Power*, I, pp. 133–8. D. W. Sweet and R. T. B. Langhorne, 'Great Britain and Russia, 1907–1914', in Hinsley, *British Foreign Policy*, pp. 252–5. Steiner indicates that Grey had rejected partition proposals, Sweet and Langhorne that discussions had begun before the war.

63 Michael Eckstein, 'Sir Edward Grey and Imperial Germany in 1914', *Journal of Contemporary History*, VI, 3 (1971), pp. 121–7.

64 Asquith, *Letters to Venetia Stanley*, pp. 122–3. Haldane to his sister, 2 August 1914, HP, MS 6012, f. 48.

65 Quoted in Williamson, *Grand Strategy*, p. 352.

66 Asquith to George V, 30 July 1914 (copy), AP, MS 7, f. 151. Pease to his wife, 2 August 1914, GP, MS 521. Samuel to his wife, 2 August 1914, HSP, A/157/697. Harcourt to F. G. Thomas, 5 August 1914 (copy), quoted in Hazlehurst, *Politicans at War*, p. 114. The treaty guaranteeing Belgian neutrality had been signed by Prussia. The Cabinet concluded that the treaty did not bind any power to act without the others.

67 Pease to his wife, 3 August 1914, GP, MS 521. Asquith, *Letters to Venetia Stanley*, pp. 139–40, 145–7 (1 and 2 August 1914). Hazlehurst, *Politicians at War*, pp. 113–17. Kennedy, *Anglo-German Antagonism*, pp. 458–62. Wilson, *Policy of the Entente*, ch. 8.

68 *Leeds Mercury*, 27 July 1914, p. 4. *Yorkshire Evening News*, 30 July 1914, p. 4. *Eastern Daily Press*, 29 July 1914, p. 4. *Leicester Daily Post*, 27 July, 1 August 1914, p. 4. *Leicester Daily Mercury*, 29, 31 July 1914, p. 4. During this crisis, the *Leeds Mercury* was not belligerent towards Germany.

69 G. M. Trevelyan to C. P. Trevelyan, 7 August 1914, TP, CPT 60. Charles resigned from the government and opposed the war. For radical views, see Morris, *Radicalism Against War*, pp. 404–7; Koss, *A. G. Gardiner*, p. 149; Woodward, *Great Britain and the German Navy*, pp. 516–17; Wilson, *Diaries of C. P. Scott*, pp. 94–9 (3, 4 August 1914).

Selected Bibliography

Manuscript Collections

Asquith Papers (Herbert Henry Asquith, Earl of Oxford and Asquith), Bodleian Library, Oxford.

Bryce Papers (James Bryce, Viscount Bryce of Dechmont), Bodleian Library, Oxford.

Burns Papers (John Burns), British Library, London.

Campbell-Bannerman Papers (Sir Henry Campbell-Bannerman), British Library, London.

Elibank Papers (Alexander Murray, Baron Murray of Elibank), National Library of Scotland, Edinburgh.

Fisher Papers (Admiral John Fisher, Baron Fisher of Kilverstone), Churchill College Library, Cambridge.

Gainford Papers (J. A. Pease, Baron Gainford of Headlam), Nuffield College Library, Oxford.

Gladstone Papers (Herbert Gladstone, Viscount Gladstone), British Library, London.

Grey Papers (Sir Edward Grey, Viscount Grey of Fallodon), Public Record Office, London.

Haldane Papers (Richard Burdon Haldane, Viscount Haldane of Cloan), National Library of Scotland, Edinburgh.

Harcourt Papers (Lewis Harcourt, Viscount Harcourt), Bodleian Library, Oxford.

Lloyd George Papers (David Lloyd George, Earl Lloyd-George of Dwyfor), House of Lords Record Office, London.

McKenna Papers (Reginald McKenna), Churchill College Library, Cambridge.

Rosebery Papers (Archibald Primrose, Earl of Rosebery), National Library of Scotland, Edinburgh.

Runciman Papers (Walter Runciman, Viscount Runciman), University of Newcastle-upon-Tyne Library, Newcastle-upon-Tyne.

Samuel Papers (Herbert Samuel, Viscount Samuel), House of Lords Record Office, London.

Spender Papers (John Alfred Spender), British Library, London.

Trevelyan Papers (Charles P. Trevelyan), University of Newcastle-upon-Tyne Library, Newcastle-upon-Tyne.

Newspapers

Baptist Times and Freeman
British Congregationalist (from October 1909, *British Congregationalist and Examiner*)
Daily Chronicle
Daily Mail

Daily News
Eastern Daily Press
Eastern Evening News
Eastern Weekly Press
Examiner
Independent
Leeds Mercury (between October 1901 and October 1907, *Leeds and Yorkshire Mercury*)
Leicester Daily Mercury
Leicester Daily Post
Methodist Recorder
The Times
Westminster Gazette
Yorkshire Evening News

Other Unpublished Sources

Cabinet Papers, Public Record Office, London.
Leeds Liberal Federation Minute Books, Sheepscar Library, Leeds.
Leicester Liberal Association Minute Books, Leicester Museum, Leicester.
Yorkshire Liberal Federation Minute Books, Sheepscar Library, Leeds.

Reference Works and Series

The Annual Register (London: Longman, 1893–1914).
The Constitutional Yearbook for 1919 (London: National Unionist Association, 1919).
The Dictionary of National Biography (Oxford: Oxford UP, 1882–1961).
Directory and Topography of the Borough of Leeds and the Whole of the Clothing District of the West Riding of Yorkshire (Sheffield: W. White, 1894).
Directory of the City of Norwich, Including its Hamlets (London: Jarrold, 1889, 1905, 1908, 1911).
Dod's Parliamentary Companion (London: Whittaker, 1895–1914).
Free Church Year Book (London: National Council of Evangelical Free Churches, 1909–1914).
Great Britain, Parliament, *Parliamentary Debates*, 4th series, Vols 1–199 (1892–1908); 5th series, Vols 1–65 (1909–1914).
Hartopp, Henry, *Roll of the Mayors of the Borough and Lord Mayors of the City of Leicester, 1209 to 1935* (Leicester: Edgar Backus, [1935]).
Kelly's Directory of Leeds (London: Kelly's Directories, 1900, 1905, 1908).
The Liberal Year Book (London: Liberal Publication Department, 1907, 1910, 1911, 1914, 1915).
National Liberal Federation, *Proceedings in Connection with the [13th-35th] Annual Meeting of the Federation* (London: Liberal Publication Department, 1891–1913).
New Directory of Norwich (Norwich: Goose & Son, 1914).
Wright's Directory of Leicester (London: Kelly's Directories, 1902, 1906, 1909).

Contemporary Works

Books

Churchill, Winston Spencer, *Liberalism and the Social Problem* (New York: Haskell House, 1973; reprint of the 1909 edn).

Clifford, John, *Socialism and the Teaching of Christ* (London: Fabian Society, 1897).

Clifford, John, *Socialism and the Churches* (London: Fabian Society, 1908).

Clifford, John, *Temperance Reform and the Ideal State* (London: Macmillan, 1914).

Clifford, John, *The War and the Churches* (London: James Clark, [1914]).

Gardiner, Alfred George, *Prophets, Priests and Kings* (London: Alstone Rivers, 1908).

Grey, Sir Edward, *Speeches on Foreign Affairs, 1904–1914*, selected with an Introduction by Paul Knaplund, PhD (Cambridge, MA: Harvard UP, 1932).

Hawkins, C. B., *Norwich: A Social Study* (London: Philip Lee Warner, 1910).

Hobhouse, L. T., *Liberalism* (London: Oxford UP, 1979; reprint of 1911 edn).

Hobson, J. A., *Imperialism: A Study* (New York: J. Pott, 1902).

Lowell, A. Lawrence, *The Government of England*, 2 vols (New York: Macmillan, 1908).

Lupton, F. M., *Housing Improvement: A Summary of Ten Years' Work in Leeds* (Leeds, 1906).

Masterman, C. F. G., *The Heart of the Empire: Discussions of Problems of Modern City Life in England*, edited with an introduction by Bentley B. Gilbert (New York: Barnes & Noble, 1973; reprint of the 1901 edn).

Masterman, C. F. G., *From the Abyss, of its Inhabitants by One of Them* (New York and London: Garland, 1980; reprint of 1902 edn).

Masterman, C. F. G., *The Condition of England* (London, Methuen, 1909).

Masterman, C. F. G., *The New Liberalism* (London: Leonard Parsons, 1920).

Masterman, C. F. G., Hodgson, W. B., *et al.*, *To Colonise England: A Plea for a Policy* (London: T. Fisher Unwin, 1907).

Ostrogorski, Moisei, *Democracy and the Organization of Political Parties*, with a Preface by the Right Hon. James Bryce, translated by Frederick Clarke, 2 vols (New York: Macmillan, 1902).

The Radical Programme, with a Preface by the Right Hon. J. Chamberlain, MP (London: Chapman and Hall, 1885).

Samuel, Herbert, *Liberalism: An Attempt to State the Principles and Proposals of Contemporary Liberalism in England* (London: Grant Richards, 1902).

Watson, Robert Spence, *The National Liberal Federation: From its Commencement to the General Election of 1906* (London: T. Fisher Unwin, 1907).

Articles

Atherley-Jones, Llewellyn Archer, 'The new liberalism', *Nineteenth Century*, XXVI, 150 (1889), pp. 186–93.

Haldane, Richard Burdon, 'The Liberal creed', *Contemporary Review*, LIV (1888), pp. 461–74.

Russell, George W. E., 'The new liberalism: A response', *Nineteenth Century*, XXVI, 151 (1889), pp. 492–9.

General Works

Cross, Colin, *The Liberals in Power (1905–1914)* (London: Barrie & Rockliff, 1963).

Ensor, R. C. K., *England, 1870–1914* (Oxford: Clarendon, 1936).

Halévy, Elie, *A History of the English People in the Nineteenth Century*; Vol. V: *Imperialism and the Rise of Labour*; Vol. VI: *The Rule of Democracy, 1905–1914*, trans E. I. Watkin (New York: Barnes & Noble, 1961).

Kennedy, Paul, *The Realities Behind Diplomacy: Background Influences on British External Policy, 1865–1980* (London: Fontana, 1981).

Perkin, Harold, *The Origins of Modern English Society, 1780–1880* (Toronto: University of Toronto Press, 1972).

Porter, Bernard, *The Lion's Share: A Short History of British Imperialism 1850–1970* (London and New York: Longman, 1975).

Pugh, Martin, *The Making of Modern British Politics 1867–1939* (Oxford: Blackwell, 1982).

Read, Donald, *Edwardian England 1901–15: Society and Politics* (London: Harrap, 1972).

Rowland, Peter, *The Last Liberal Governments*, Vol. I: *The Promised Land, 1905–1910* (London: Barrie & Rockliff, 1968).

Rowland, Peter, *The Last Liberal Governments*, Vol. II: *Unfinished Business, 1911–1914* (London: Barrie & Jenkins, 1971).

Taylor, A. J. P., *The Struggle for Mastery in Europe 1848–1918* (Oxford: Clarendon, 1954).

AUTOBIOGRAPHIES, BIOGRAPHIES, DIARIES, MEMOIRS, ETC.

Asquith, Herbert Henry, *The Genesis of the War* (New York: George H. Doran, 1923).

Asquith, Herbert Henry (Earl of Oxford and Asquith), *Fifty Years of Parliament*, 2 vols (London: Cassell, 1926).

Asquith, Herbert Henry (Earl of Oxford and Asquith), *Memories and Reflections, 1852–1927*, 2 vols (Boston: Little Brown, 1928).

Asquith, Herbert Henry, *Letters to Venetia Stanley*, selected and edited by Michael and Eleanor Brock (Oxford and New York: Oxford UP, 1982).

Asquith, Margot, *The Autobiography of Margot Asquith*, 2 vols (London: Thornton Butterworth, 1922).

Anderson, Mosa, *Noel Buxton: A Life* (London: Allen & Unwin, 1952).

Bell, George Kennedy Allin, *Randall Davidson, Archbishop of Canterbury*, 2 vols (New York: Oxford UP, 1935).

Beveridge, Lord, *Power and Influence* (London: Hodder & Stoughton, 1953).

Birrell, Augustine, *Things Past Redress* (London: Faber, 1937).

Blunt, Wilfred Scawen, *My Diaries: Being a Personal Narrative of Events, 1888–1914*, 2 vols (London: Martin Secker, 1919–20).

Bowle, John, *Viscount Samuel: A Biography* (London: Victor Gollancz, 1957).

Braithwaite, William J., *Lloyd George's Ambulance Wagon: Being the Memoirs of William J. Braithwaite, 1911–1912*, Sir Henry N. Banbury (ed.) (London: Methuen, 1957).

Brockway, Fenner, *Socialism Over Sixty Years: The Life of Jowett of Bradford (1864–1944)* (London: Allen & Unwin, 1946).

Churchill, Randolph, S., *Winston S. Churchill*, Vol. II: *1901–1914, Young Statesman* (Boston: Houghton Mifflin, 1967).

Churchill, Randolph S., *Winston S. Churchill*, Companion Vol. II: *1901–1914, Young Statesman*, 3 parts (Boston: Houghton Mifflin, 1969).

Churchill, Winston S., *The World Crisis* (New York: Scribner, 1923).

Corder, Percy, *The Life of Robert Spence Watson* (London: Headley Brothers, 1914).

Crewe, Marquess of, *Lord Rosebery*, 2 vols (London: John Murray, 1931).

David, Edward (ed.), *Inside Asquith's Cabinet: From the Diaries of Charles Hobhouse* (New York: St Martin's, 1977).

Denholm, Anthony, *Lord Ripon 1827–1909: A Political Biography* (London and Canberra: Croom Helm, 1982).

Esher, Reginald Viscount, *Journals and Letters of Reginald Viscount Esher*, Maurice V. Brett and Oliver Sylvan Balliol Brett, Third Viscount Esher (eds) 4 vols (London: Ivor Nicholson & Watson, 1934).

Fisher, H. A. L., *James Bryce (Viscount Bryce of Dechmont, O.M.)*, 2 vols (London: Macmillan, 1927).

FitzRoy, Sir Almeric, *Memoirs*, 2 vols (London: Hutchinson, [1925]).

Fraser, Peter, *Joseph Chamberlain: Radicalism and Empire, 1868–1914* (New York: A. S. Barnes, 1967).

Gardiner, Alfred George, *Life of George Cadbury* (London: Cassell, 1923).

Gardiner, Alfred George, *The Life of Sir William Harcourt*, 2 vols (New York: George H. Doran, [1923]).

Garvin, James L., *The Life of Joseph Chamberlain*, Vol. I: *1836–1885, Chamberlain and Democracy*; Vol. II: *1885–1895, Disruption and Combat* (London: Macmillan, 1932–33).

George, William, *My Brother and I* (London: Eyre & Spottiswoode, 1958).

Gooch, George Peabody, *Under Six Reigns* (London: Longman, 1958).

Grey of Fallodon, Viscount, *Twenty-Five Years, 1892–1916* (New York: Frederick A. Stokes, 1925).

Grigg, John, *The Young Lloyd George* (London: Eyre Methuen, 1973).

Grigg, John, *Lloyd George: The People's Champion, 1902–1911* (Berkeley, CA: University of California Press, 1978).

Grigg, John, *Lloyd George: From Peace to War 1912–1916* (Berkeley, CA: University of California Press, 1985).

Gwynn, Denis, *The Life of John Redmond* (Freeport, NY: Books for Libraries, 1971; reprint of 1932 edn).

Haldane of Cloan, Viscount, *An Autobiography* (London: Hodder & Stoughton, 1929).

Haldane of Cloan, Viscount, *Before the War* (London: Cassell, 1920).

Hamer, D. A., *John Morley: Liberal Intellectual in Politics* (Oxford: Clarendon, 1968).

Hammond, John Lawrence, *C. P. Scott of the Manchester Guardian* (New York: Harcourt Brace, 1934).

Havighurst, Alfred, F., *Radical Journalist: H. W. Massingham (1860–1924)* (London and New York: Cambridge UP, 1974).

Holland, Bernard, *The Life of Spencer Compton, Eighth Duke of Devonshire*, 2 vols (London: Longman, 1911).

James, Robert Rhodes, *Rosebery: A Biography of Archibald Philip, Fifth Earl of Rosebery* (New York: Macmillan, 1963).

Jenkins, Roy, *Asquith: Portrait of a Man and an Era* (New York: Dutton, 1966).

Kent, William, *John Burns: Labour's Lost Leader* (London: Williams & Norgate, 1950).

Koss, Stephen E., *Lord Haldane: Scapegoat for Liberalism* (New York and London: Columbia UP, 1969).

Koss, Stephen E., *Sir John Brunner, Radical Plutocrat 1842–1919* (Cambridge: Cambridge UP, 1970).

Koss, Stephen E., *Fleet Street Radical: A. G. Gardiner and the Daily News* (London: Allen Lane, 1973).

Koss, Stephen E., *Asquith* (New York: St Martin's, 1976).

Loreburn, Earl, *How the War Came* (London: Methuen, 1919).

Lyons, F. S. L., *John Dillon: A Biography* (London: Routledge & Kegan Paul, 1968).

Mackay, Ruddock, F., *Fisher of Kilverstone* (Oxford: Clarendon, 1973).

McKenna, Stephen, *Reginald McKenna, 1863–1943: A Memoir* (London: Eyre & Spottiswoode, 1948).

Mackintosh, John P. (ed.), *British Prime Ministers in the Twentieth Century*, Vol. I: *Balfour to Chamberlain* (New York: St Martin's, 1977).

Mallet, Sir Charles, *Herbert Gladstone: A Memoir* (London: Hutchinson, 1932).

Marchant, Sir James, *Dr. John Clifford, C. H., Life, Letters, and Reminiscences* (London: Cassell, 1924).

Masterman, Lucy, *C. F. G. Masterman: A Biography* (London: Cass, 1968; reprint of 1939 edn).

Maurice, Sir Frederick, *Haldane, 1856–1915: The Life of Viscount Haldane of Cloan, K. T., O. M.* (London: Faber, 1937).

Morley of Blackburn, John Viscount, *The Life of William Ewart Gladstone*, 3 vols (London: Macmillan, 1903).

Morley, John, *Recollections* (New York: Macmillan, 1917).

Owen, Frank, *Tempestuous Journey: Lloyd George His Life and Times* (New York: McGraw-Hill, 1955).

Pentland, Marjorie Lady, *The Right Honourable John Sinclair, Lord Pentland, G.C.S.I.* (London: Methuen, 1928).

Pope-Hennessy, James, *Lord Crewe, 1858–1945: The Likeness of a Liberal* (London: Constable, 1955).

Riddell, Lord, *More Pages from my Diary, 1908–1914* (London: Country Life, 1934).

Robbins, Keith, *Sir Edward Grey: A Biography of Lord Grey of Fallodon* (London: Cassell, 1971).

Runciman, Sir Walter, Bart., *Before the Mast – and After: The Autobiography of a Sailor and Shipowner* (London: T. Fisher Unwin, 1924).

Samuel, Herbert Viscount, *Memoirs* (London: Cresset, 1945).

Sommer, Dudley, *Haldane of Cloan, His Life and Times, 1856–1928* (London: Allen & Unwin, 1960).

Spender, John Alfred, *The Life of the Right Hon. Sir Henry Campbell-Bannerman, G. C. B.*, 2 vols (London: Hodder & Stoughton, 1923).

Spender, John Alfred, *Life, Journalism and Politics*, 2 vols (London: Cassell, 1927).

Spender, John Alfred, *Sir Robert Hudson: A Memoir* (London: Cassell, 1930).

Spender, John Alfred, and Asquith, Cyril, *Life of Herbert Henry Asquith, Lord Oxford and Asquith*, 2 vols (London: Hutchinson, 1932).

Taylor, A. J. P. (ed.), *Lloyd George: Twelve Essays* (London: Hamish Hamilton, 1971).

Trevelyan, George Macaulay, *Grey of Fallodon: Being the Life of Sir Edward Grey, Afterwards Viscount Grey of Fallodon* (London: Longman, 1937).

Webb, Beatrice, *Our Partnership*, edited by Barbara Drake and Margaret I. Cole (London: Longman, 1948).

Wedgwood, C. V., *The Last of the Radicals: Josiah Wedgwood, M.P.* (London: Jonathan Cape, 1951).

Wedgwood, Josiah, C., *Memoirs of a Fighting Life* (London: Hutchinson, 1941).

Wilson, John, *CB: A Life of Sir Henry Campbell-Bannerman* (New York: St Martin's, 1973).

Wilson, Trevor (ed.), *The Political Diaries of C. P. Scott, 1911–1928* (Ithaca, NY: Cornell UP, 1970).

Wolf, Lucien, *Life of the First Marquess of Ripon, K.G., P.C., G.C.S.I., D.C.L., Etc.*, 2 vols (London: Murray, 1921).

Works on Domestic Policy and Politics

Books

Arnot, R. Page, *The Miners: A History of the Miners' Federation of Great Britain*, Vol. I: *1889–1910* (London: Allen & Unwin, 1949).

Askwith, Lord, *Industrial Problems and Disputes* (New York: Harcourt Brace, 1921).

Bagwell, Philip S., *The Railwaymen: The History of the National Union of Railwaymen*, Vol. I (London: Allen & Unwin, 1963).

Barker, Michael, *Gladstone and Radicalism: The Reconstruction of Liberal Policy in Britain, 1885–94* (New York: Barnes & Noble, 1975).

Bealey, Frank, and Pelling, Henry, *Labour and Politics, 1900–1906: A History of the Labour Representation Committee* (London: Macmillan; New York, St Martin's, 1958).

Bebbington, D. W., *The Nonconformist Conscience: Chapel and Politics, 1870–1914* (London: Allen & Unwin, 1982).

Blewett, Neal, *The Peers, the Parties and the People: The British General Elections of 1910* (Toronto: University of Toronto Press, 1972).

Briggs, Asa, and Saville, John (eds), *Essays in Labour History 1886–1923* (Hamden, CT: Archon, 1971; reprint of 1960 edn).

Brown, Kenneth D., *Labour and Unemployment 1900–1914* (Totowa, NJ: Rowman & Littlefield, 1971).

Brown, Kenneth D. (ed.), *Essays in Anti-Labour History: Responses to the Rise of Labour in Britain* (Hamden, CT: Archon, 1974).

Bruce, Maurice, *The Coming of the Welfare State* (New York: Schocken, 1966).

Carter, Henry, *The English Temperance Movement: A Study in Objectives*, Vol. I: *The Formative Period, 1830–1899* (London: Epworth, 1933).

Clarke, P. F., *Lancashire and the New Liberalism* (Cambridge: Cambridge UP, 1971).

Clarke, P. F., *Liberals and Social Democrats* (Cambridge and New York: Cambridge UP, 1978).

Clinton, Alan, *The Trade Union Rank and File: Trades Councils in Britain, 1900–40* (Manchester: Manchester UP, 1977).

Cole, G. D. H., *British Working Class Politics, 1832–1914* (London: Labour Book Service, 1941).

Collini, Stefan, *Liberalism and Sociology: L. T. Hobhouse and Political Argument in England 1880–1914* (Cambridge: Cambridge UP, 1979).

Conacher, J. B., *The Peelites and the Party System, 1846–52* (Newton Abbot: David & Charles, 1972).

Crosby, Travis L., *Sir Robert Peel's Administration, 1841–1846* (Hamden, CT: Archon; Newton Abbot: David & Charles, 1976).

Cruickshank, Marjorie, *Church and State in English Education, 1870 to the Present Day* (New York: St Martin's, 1963).

Dangerfield, George, *The Strange Death of Liberal England 1910–1914* (New York: Capricorn, 1961; reprint of 1935 edn).

Donaldson, Frances, *The Marconi Scandal* (New York: Harcourt Brace, 1962).

Douglas, Roy, *Land, People & Politics: A History of the Land Question in the United Kingdom, 1878–1952* (New York: St Martin's, 1976).

Emy, H. V., *Liberals, Radicals and Social Politics, 1892–1914* (Cambridge: Cambridge UP, 1973).

Fergusson, Sir James, *The Curragh Incident* (London: Faber, 1964).

Fox, Alan, *A History of the National Union of Boot and Shoe Operatives, 1873–1957* (Oxford: Blackwell, 1958).

Freeden, Michael, *The New Liberalism: An Ideology of Social Reform* (Oxford: Clarendon, 1978).

Gash, Norman, *Reaction and Reconstruction in English Politics 1832–1852* (Oxford: Clarendon, 1965).

Gilbert, Bentley B., *The Evolution of National Insurance in Great Britain: The Origins of the Welfare State* (London: Michael Joseph, 1966).

Gregory, Roy, *The Miners and British Politics, 1906–1914* (Oxford: Oxford UP, 1968).

Guttsman, Wilhelm L., *The British Political Elite* (New York: Basic Books, 1963).

Gwyn, William B., *Democracy and the Cost of Politics in Britain* (London: Athelone, 1962).

Hamer, D. A., *Liberal Politics in the Age of Gladstone and Rosebery: A Study in Leadership and Policy* (Oxford: Clarendon, 1972).

Hanham, H. J., *Elections and Party Management: Politics in the Time of Disraeli and Gladstone* (London: Longman, 1959).

Harris, Jose, *Unemployment and Politics: A Study in English Social Policy, 1886–1914* (Oxford: Clarendon, 1972).

Hay, J. R., *The Origins of the Liberal Welfare Reforms 1906–1914* (London: Macmillan, 1975).

Heyck, Thomas William, *The Dimensions of British Radicalism: The Case of Ireland, 1874–95* (Urbana, Il.: University of Illinois Press, 1974).

Inglis, Kenneth Stanley, *Churches and the Working Classes in Victorian England* (London: Routledge & Kegan Paul; Toronto: University of Toronto Press, 1963).

Jalland, Patricia, *The Liberals and Ireland: The Ulster Question in British Politics to 1914* (Brighton: Harvester, 1980).

Jenkins, Roy, *Mr. Balfour's Poodle: An Account of the Struggle between the House of Lords and the Government of Mr. Asquith* (New York: Chilmark, 1954).

Kinnear, Michael, *The British Voter: An Atlas and Survey Since 1885* (Ithaca, NY: Cornell UP, 1968).

Koss, Stephen E., *Nonconformity in Modern British Politics* (Hamden, CT: Archon, 1975).

Laybourn, Keith, and Reynolds, Jack, *Liberalism and the Rise of Labour 1890–1918* (London and Sydney: Croom Helm; New York: St Martin's, 1984).

Longmate, Norman, *The Waterdrinkers: A History of Temperance* (London: Hamish Hamilton, 1968).

Lyons, F. S. L., *The Irish Parliamentary Party, 1890–1910* (London: Faber, 1951).

McBriar, A. M., *Fabian Socialism and English Politics 1884–1918* (Cambridge: Cambridge UP, 1966).

McKibbin, Ross, *The Evolution of the Labour Party, 1910–1924* (Oxford: Oxford UP, 1974).

Martin, Ross M., *TUC: The Growth of a Pressure Group, 1868–1976* (Oxford: Clarendon, 1980).

Matthew, H. C. G., *The Liberal Imperialists: The Ideas and Politics of a Post-Gladstonian Elite* (Oxford: Oxford UP, 1973).

Miller, David W., *Church, State and Nation in Ireland, 1898–1921* (Dublin: Gill and Macmillan, 1973).

Morgan, David, *Suffragists and Liberals: The Politics of Woman Suffrage in England* (Oxford: Blackwell, 1975).

Morgan, Kenneth O., *Wales in British Politics, 1868–1922* (Cardiff: University of Wales, 1970).

Morris, A. J. A. (ed.), *Edwardian Radicalism, 1900–1914: Some Aspects of British Radicalism* (London and Boston: Routledge & Kegan Paul, 1974).

Murray, Bruce K., *The People's Budget 1909/10: Lloyd George and Liberal Politics* (Oxford: Clarendon, 1980).

Pelling, Henry, *The Origins of the Labour Party, 1880–1900* (Oxford: Oxford UP, 1965).

Pelling, Henry, *Social Geography of British Elections, 1885–1910* (London: Macmillan, 1967).

Pelling, Henry, *Popular Politics and Society in Late Victorian Britain* (London: Macmillan 1979; 2nd edn).

Phelps Brown, E. H., *The Growth of British Industrial Relations: A Study from the Standpoint of 1906–14* (London: Macmillan; New York: St Martin's, 1959).

Poirier, Philip P., *The Advent of the British Labour Party* (New York: Columbia UP, 1958).

Richter, Melvin, *The Politics of Conscience: T. H. Green and his Age* (Cambridge, MA: Harvard UP, 1964).

Rosen, Andrew, *Rise Up, Women! The Militant Campaign of the Women's Social and Political Union, 1903–1914* (London and Boston: Routledge & Kegan Paul, 1974).

Rover, Constance, *Women's Suffrage and Party Politics in Britain, 1866–1914* (London: Routledge & Kegan Paul; Toronto: University of Toronto Press, 1967).

Russell, A. K., *Liberal Landslide: The General Election of 1906* (Newton Abbot: David & Charles; Hamden, CT: Archon, 1973).

Ryan, A. P., *Mutiny at the Curragh* (London: Macmillan; New York: St Martin's, 1956).

Scally, Robert J., *The Origins of the Lloyd George Coalition* (Princeton, NJ: Princeton UP, 1975).

Searle, Geoffrey, R., *The Quest for National Efficiency: A Study in British Politics and Political Thought, 1899–1914* (Berkeley, CA: University of California Press, 1971).

Semmel, Bernard, *Imperialism and Social Reform: English Social-Imperial Thought, 1895–1914* (Garden City, NY: Anchor, 1968).

Sherington, Geoffrey, *English Education, Social Change and War 1911–20* (Manchester: Manchester UP, 1981).

Sked, Alan, and Cook, Chris (eds), *Crisis and Controversy: Essays in Honour of A. J. P. Taylor* (New York: St Martin's, 1976).

Stansky, Peter, *Ambitions and Strategies: The Struggle for the Leadership of the Liberal Party in the 1890s* (Oxford: Clarendon, 1964).

Stewart, A. T. Q., *The Ulster Crisis* (London: Faber, 1967).

Sykes, Alan, *Tariff Reform in British Politics 1903–1913* (Oxford: Clarendon, 1979).

Thompson, Paul, *Socialists, Liberals and Labour: The Struggle for London, 1885–1914* (London: Routledge & Kegan Paul; Toronto: University of Toronto Press, 1967).

Vincent, John, *The Formation of the British Liberal Party* (New York: Scribner, 1966).

Wald, Kenneth, D., *Crosses on the Ballot: Patterns of British Voter Alignment Since 1885* (Princeton, NJ: Princeton UP, 1983).

Weiler, Peter, *The New Liberalism: Liberal Social Theory in Great Britain 1889–1914* (New York and London: Garland, 1982).

Wigham, Eric, *Strikes and the Government 1893–1981* (London: Macmillan, 1982).

Wrigley, Chris, *David Lloyd George and the British Labour Movement: Peace and War* (Hassocks: Harvester; New York: Barnes & Noble, 1976).

Wrigley, Chris (ed.), *A History of British Industrial Relations 1875–1914* (Amherst, MA: University of Massachusetts Press, 1982).

Articles

Auspos, Patricia, 'Radicalism, pressure groups, and party politics: From the National Education League to the National Liberal Federation', *Journal of British Studies*, XX, 1 (1980), pp. 184–204.

Bealey, Frank, 'The electoral arrangement between the Labour Representation Committee and the Liberal Party', *Journal of Modern History*, XXVIII (1956), pp. 353–73.

Bernstein, George L., 'Liberalism and the progressive alliance in the constituencies, 1900–1914: Three case studies', *Historical Journal*, XXVI, 3 (1983), pp. 617–40.

Bernstein, George L., 'Sir Henry Campbell-Bannerman and the Liberal Imperialists', *Journal of British Studies*, XXIII, 1 (1983), pp. 105–24.

Bernstein, George L., 'The limitations of the new liberalism: The politics and political thought of John Clifford', *Albion*, XVI, 1 (1984), pp. 21–39.

Blewett, Neal, 'The franchise in the United Kingdom, 1885–1918', *Past and Present*, XXXII (1965), pp. 27–56.

Clarke, P. F., 'Electoral sociology of modern Britain', *History*, LVII, 189 (1972), pp. 31–55.

Clarke, P. F., 'The progressive movement in England', *Transactions of the Royal Historical Society*, Fifth Series, XXIV (1974), pp. 159–81.

Clarke, P. F., 'The electoral position of the Liberal and Labour Parties, 1910–1914', *English Historical Review*, XC, 357 (1975), pp. 828–36.

Clarke, P. F., 'Liberals, Labour and the franchise', *English Historical Review*, XCII, 364 (1977), pp. 582–90.

Collins, Doreen, 'The introduction of old age pensions in Great Britain', *Historical Journal*, VIII, Pt. II (1965), pp. 246–59.

Cornford, James, 'The transformation of conservatism in the late nineteenth century', *Victorian Studies*, VII, 1 (1963), pp. 35–66.

Cornford, James, 'The parliamentary foundations of the Hotel Cecil', in Robert Robson (ed.) *Ideas and Institutions of Victorian Britain: Essays in Honour of George Kitson Clark* (London: G. Bell, 1967).

Emy, H. V., 'The impact of financial policy on English party politics before 1914', *Historical Journal*, XV, 1 (1972), pp. 103–31.

Gilbert, Bentley, B., 'David Lloyd George: Land, the Budget, and social reform', *American Historical Review*, LXXXI, 5 (1976), pp. 1058–66.

Gilbert, Bentley, B., 'David Lloyd George: The reform of British landholding and the Budget of 1914', *Historical Journal*, XXI, 1 (1978), pp. 117–41.

Glaser, John F., 'English Nonconformity and the decline of liberalism', *American Historical Review*, LXIII, 1 (1958), pp. 352–63.

Hepburn, A. C., 'The Irish Council Bill and the fall of Sir Antony MacDonnell, 1906–7', *Irish Historical Studies*, XVII, 68 (1971), pp. 470–98.

Herrick, Francis H., 'The origins of the National Liberal Federation', *Journal of Modern History*, XVII, 2 (1945), pp. 116–29.

Heyck, Thomas William, and Klecka, William, 'British radical MPs, 1874–1895: New evidence from discriminant analysis', *Journal of Interdisciplinary History*, IV, 2 (1973), pp. 161–84.

Howkins, Alun, 'Edwardian liberalism and industrial unrest: A class view of the decline of liberalism', *History Workshop*, IV (1977), pp. 143–61.

Jacobson, Peter D., 'Rosebery and Liberal Imperialism, 1899–1903', *Journal of British Studies*, XIII, 1 (1973), pp. 83–107.

Jalland, Patricia, 'A Liberal Chief Secretary and the Irish question: Augustine Birrell, 1907–1914', *Historical Journal*, XIX, 2 (1976), pp. 421–51.

Jalland, Patricia, 'United Kingdom devolution 1910–14: Political panacea or tactical diversion?', *English Historical Review*, XCIV, 373 (1979), pp. 757–85.

Kendle, J. E., 'The Round Table movement and "Home Rule all round"', *Historical Journal*, XI, 2 (1968), pp. 332–53.

Lloyd, T. O., 'The whip as paymaster: Herbert Gladstone and party organization', *English Historical Review*, LXXXIX, 353 (1974), pp. 785–813.

McCormick, B., and Williams, J. E., 'The miners and the eight-hour day, 1863–1910', *Economic History Review*, Second Series, XII, 2 (1959), pp. 222–38.

McCready, W., 'Home Rule and the Liberal Party, 1899–1906', *Irish Historical Studies*, XIII, 52 (1963), pp. 316–48.

McGill, Barry, 'Francis Schnadhorst and Liberal Party organization', *Journal of Modern History*, XXXIV, 1 (1962), pp. 19–39.

Matthew, H. C. G., McKibbin, R. I. and Kay, J. A., 'The franchise factor in the rise of the Labour Party', *English Historical Review*, XCI, 361 (1976), pp. 723–52.

Meacham, Standish, '"The sense of an impending clash": English working-class unrest before the First World War', *American Historical Review*, LXXVII, 5 (1972), pp. 1343–64.

Morgan, Kenneth O., 'The new liberalism and the challenge of Labour: The Welsh experience, 1885–1929', *Welsh History Review*, VI, 3 (1973), pp. 288–312.

Parry, J. P., 'Religion and the collapse of Gladstone's first government, 1870–1874', *Historical Journal*, XXV, 1 (1982), pp. 71–101.

Pelling, Henry, 'The politics of the Osborne Judgement', *Historical Journal*, XXV, 4 (1982), pp. 889–909.

Petter, Martin, 'The progressive alliance', *History*, LVIII, 192 (1973), pp. 45–59.

Phillips, G. A., 'The triple industrial alliance in 1914', *Economic History Review*, Second Series, XXIV, 1 (1971), pp. 55–67.

Pugh, Martin D., 'Yorkshire and the new liberalism', *Journal of Modern History*, L, 3 (1978), pp. D1139–55.

Purdue, A. W., 'The Liberal and Labour Parties in North-Eastern politics 1900–14: The struggle for supremacy', *International Review of Social History*, XXVI, 1 (1981), pp. 1–24.

Richards, Noel J., 'The Education Bill of 1906 and the decline of political Nonconformity', *Journal of Ecclesiastical History*, XXIII, 1 (1972), pp. 49–63.

Sires, Ronald, V., 'Labor unrest in England, 1910–1914', *Journal of Economic History*, XV, 3 (1955), pp. 246–66.

Tholfsen, Trygve R., 'The origins of the Birmingham caucus', *Historical Journal*, II (1959), pp. 161–84.

Tholfsen, Trygve, R., 'The transition to democracy in Victorian England', *International Review of Social History*, VI (1961), pp. 226–48.

Vincent, John, 'Gladstone and Ireland', *Proceedings of the British Academy*, LXIII (1977), pp. 193–238.

Weston, Corinne Comstock, 'The Liberal leadership and the Lords' veto, 1907–1910', *Historical Journal*, XI, 3 (1968), pp. 508–37.

WORKS ON DEFENCE, FOREIGN AND IMPERIAL POLICY

Books

Anderson, Eugene, N., *The First Moroccan Crisis 1904–1906* (Hamden, CT: Archon, 1966; reprint of 1930 edn).

Barlow, Ima Christina, *The Agadir Crisis* (Chapel Hill, NC: University of North Carolina Press, 1940).

Bridge, F. R., *Great Britain and Austria–Hungary 1906–1914: A Diplomatic History* (London: Weidenfeld & Nicolson, 1972).

Busch, Briton Cooper, *Britain and the Persian Gulf, 1894–1914* (Berkeley and Los Angeles, CA: University of California Press, 1967).

Chapman, Maybelle Kennedy, *Great Britain and the Baghdad Railway 1888–1914* (Northampton, MA: Smith College, 1948).

Churchill, Rogers Platt, *The Anglo-Russian Convention of 1907* (Freeport, NY: Books for Libraries, 1972; reprint of 1939 edn).

Conwell-Evans, T. P., *Foreign Policy from a Back Bench 1904–1918: A Study Based on the Papers of Lord Noel-Buxton* (London: Oxford UP, 1932).

Cookey, S. J. S., *Britain and the Congo Question, 1885–1913* (London: Longman, 1968).

d'Ombrain, Nicholas, *War Machinery and High Policy: Defence Administration in Peacetime Britain 1902–1914* (London: Oxford UP, 1973).

Dunlop, John K., *The Development of the British Army 1899–1914* (London: Methuen, 1938).

French, David, *British Economic and Strategic Planning 1905–1915* (London: Allen & Unwin, 1982).

Fry, Michael, G., *Lloyd George and Foreign Policy*, Vol. I: *The Education of a Statesman: 1890–1916* (Montreal and London: McGill-Queen's, 1977).

Gordon, Donald C., *The Dominion Partnership in Imperial Defense, 1870–1914* (Baltimore: Johns Hopkins UP, 1965).

Hale, Oron James, *Publicity and Diplomacy, with Special Reference to England and Germany 1890–1914* (New York and London: Appleton-Century, 1940).

Halpern, Paul G., *The Mediterranean Naval Situation 1908–1914* (Cambridge, MA: Harvard UP, 1971).

Hazlehurst, Cameron, *Politicians at War, July 1914 to May 1915: A Prologue to the Triumph of Lloyd George* (New York: Knopf, 1971).

Helmreich, Ernst Christian, *The Diplomacy of the Balkan Wars 1912–1913* (Cambridge, MA: Harvard, 1938).

Hinsley, F. H. (ed.), *British Foreign Policy Under Sir Edward Grey* (Cambridge: Cambridge UP, 1977).

Hyam, Ronald, *Elgin and Churchill at the Colonial Office 1905–1908: The Watershed of the Empire-Commonwealth* (London: Macmillan; New York: St Martin's, 1968).

Johnson, Franklyn Arthur, *Defence by Committee: The British Committee of Imperial Defence 1885–1959* (London: Oxford UP, 1960).

Kazemzadeh, Firuz, *Russia and Britain in Persia, 1864–1914: A Study in Imperialism* (New Haven, CT and London: Yale UP, 1968).

Kendle, John Edward, *The Colonial and Imperial Conferences 1887–1911: A Study in Imperial Organization* (London: Longman, 1967).

239

Kennedy, Paul, *The Rise of the Anglo-German Antagonism 1860–1914* (London: Allen & Unwin, 1980).

Koss, Stephen E., *John Morley at the India Office, 1905–1910* (New Haven, CT and London: Yale UP, 1969).

Koss, Stephen, E., *The Pro-Boers: The Anatomy of an Antiwar Movement* (Chicago: University of Chicago Press, 1973).

LeMay, G. H. L., *British Supremacy in South Africa 1899–1907* (Oxford: Clarendon, 1965).

Louis, Wm. Roger, and Stengers, Jean (eds), *E. D. Morel's History of the Congo Reform Movement* (Oxford: Clarendon, 1968).

Lowe, C. J., and Dockrill, M. L., *The Mirage of Power*, Vol. I: *British Foreign Policy 1902–14*; Vol. III: *The Documents, British Foreign Policy 1902–22* (London and Boston: Routledge & Kegan Paul, 1972).

Marder, Arthur, J., *From Dreadnought to Scapa Flow: The Royal Navy in the Fisher Era, 1904–1919*, Vol. I: *The Road to War, 1904–1919* (London: Oxford UP, 1961).

Monger, George, *The End of Isolation: British Foreign Policy 1900–1907* (London: Thomas Nelson, 1963).

Morris, A. J. A., *Radicalism Against War, 1906–1914: The Advocacy of Peace and Retrenchment* (Totowa, NJ: Rowman & Littlefield, 1972).

Pakenham, Thomas, *The Boer War* (New York: Random House, 1979).

Perkins, Bradford, *The Great Rapprochement: England and the United States, 1895–1914* (New York: Atheneum, 1968).

Platt, D. C. M., *Finance, Trade, and Politics in British Foreign Policy 1815–1914* (Oxford: Clarendon, 1968).

Porter, Bernard, *Critics of Empire: British Radical Attitudes to Colonialism in Africa, 1895–1914* (London: Macmillan; New York: St Martin's, 1968).

Price, Richard, *An Imperial War and the British Working Classes: Working-Class Attitudes and Reactions to the Boer War, 1899–1902* (London: Routledge & Kegan Paul; Toronto: University of Toronto Press, 1972).

Pyrah, Geoffrey Barker, *Imperial Policy and South Africa, 1902–10* (Oxford: Clarendon, 1955).

Schmitt, Bernadotte E., *The Annexation of Bosnia 1908–1909* (Cambridge: Cambridge UP, 1937).

Shannon, R. T., *Gladstone and the Bulgarian Agitation, 1876* (London: Thomas Nelson, 1963).

Steiner, Zara, S., *The Foreign Office and Foreign Policy, 1898–1914* (Cambridge: Cambridge UP, 1969).

Steiner, Zara, S., *Britain and the Origins of the First World War* (New York: St Martin's, 1977).

Taylor, A. J. P., *The Trouble Makers: Dissent over Foreign Policy 1792–1939* (London: Hamish Hamilton, 1957).

Thompson, L. M., *The Unification of South Africa, 1902–1910* (Oxford: Clarendon, 1960).

Thornton, A. P., *The Imperial Idea and its Enemies: A Study in British Power* (Garden City, NY: Anchor, 1968).

Williamson, Samuel R., Jr., *The Politics of Grand Strategy: Britain and France Prepare for War, 1904–1914* (Cambridge, MA: Harvard UP, 1969).

Wilson, Keith M., *The Policy of the Entente: Essays on the Determinants of British Foreign Policy, 1904–1914* (Cambridge: Cambridge UP, 1985).

Wolpert, Stanley, A., *Morley and India 1906–1910* (Berkeley and Los Angeles, CA: University of California Press, 1967).

Woodward, E. L., *Great Britain and the German Navy* (Hamden, CT: Archon, 1964; reprint of 1935 edn).

Articles

Cline, Catherine Ann, 'E. D. Morel and the crusade against the Foreign Office', *Journal of Modern History*, XXXIX, 2 (1967), pp. 126–37.

Cosgrave, Richard A., 'A note on Lloyd George's speech at the Mansion House, 21 July 1911, *Historical Journal*, XII, 4 (1969), pp. 698–701.

Eckstein, Michael, 'Sir Edward Grey and Imperial Germany in 1914', *Journal of Contemporary History*, VI, 3 (1971), pp. 121–31.

Eckstein, Michael, 'Some notes on Sir Edward Grey's policy in July 1914', *Historical Journal*, XV, 2 (1972), pp. 321–4.

Haggie, Paul, 'The Royal Navy and war planning in the Fisher era', *Journal of Contemporary History*, VIII, 3 (1973), pp. 113–31.

Koss, Stephen, E., 'Wesleyanism and empire', *Historical Journal*, XVIII, 1 (1975), pp. 105–18.

Langhorne, Richard, 'The naval question in Anglo-German relations, 1912–1914', *Historical Journal*, XIV, 2 (1971), pp. 359–70.

Langhorne, Richard, 'Anglo-German negotiations concerning the future of the Portuguese colonies, 1911–1914', *Historical Journal*, XVI, 2 (1973), pp. 361–87.

McLean, D., 'English radicals, Russia and the fate of Persia, 1907–1913', *English Historical Review*, XCIII, 367 (1978), pp. 338–52.

Morris, A. J. A., 'Haldane's army reforms, 1906–8: The deception of the radicals', *History*, LVI, 186 (1971), pp. 17–34.

Murray, John A., 'Foreign policy debated: Sir Edward Grey and his critics, 1911–1912', in Lillian Parker Wallace and William C. Askew (eds) *Power, Public Opinion, and Diplomacy: Essays in Honor of Eber Malcolm Carroll by his Former Students* (Durham, NC: Duke UP, 1959).

Penson, Lillian M., 'Obligations by treaty: Their place in British foreign policy, 1898–1914', in A. O. Sarkissian (ed.) *Studies in Diplomatic History and Historiography in Honour of G. P. Gooch*, C. H. (London: Longman, 1961).

Sumida, Jon, 'Strategy formulation as a political process: The case of the British Admiralty, 1904–1914' (paper read at the sixth Naval History Symposium, 29–30 September 1983, United States Naval Academy, Annapolis, MD).

Watt, D. C., 'The British reactions to the assassination at Sarajevo', *European Studies Review*, I, 3 (1971), pp. 233–47.

Weinroth, Howard S., 'The British radicals and the balance of power, 1902–1914', *Historical Journal*, XIII, 4 (1970), pp. 653–82.

Weinroth, Howard S., 'Left-wing opposition to naval armaments in Britain before 1914', *Journal of Contemporary History*, VI, 4 (1971), pp. 93–120.

Weinroth, Howard S., 'Norman Angell and *The Great Illusion*: An episode in pre-1914 pacifism', *Historical Journal*, XVII, 3 (1974), pp. 551–74.

Williams, Beryl, J., 'The strategic background to the Anglo-Russian entente of August 1907', *Historical Journal*, IX, 3 (1966), pp. 360–73.

Wilson, Keith, 'The Agadir Crisis; the Mansion House speech and the double-edgedness of agreements', *Historical Journal*, XV, 3 (1972), pp. 513–32.

Index

242

Triple Entente 181, 186, 191–2
Tripoli 168, 182, 189–90

Ulster Protestants 90, 136, 158–65,
    198
Ulster Volunteers 136, 159, 161,
    163–5
unemployment 79–82, 98–9, 123–7, 132,
    135, 138, 140–3
unemployment policies, afforestation 33,
    81, 127
  farm colonies 82, 124
  Labour Exchanges Act of 1909 105,
    125–7, 200
  public works 33, 81–2, 124, 127
  right to work 79, 81, 124–5, 200
  unemployment insurance 105, 107,
    122, 125–6
Unionists, *see* Conservative Party
United States 167, 177, 183

Vivian, Henry 126, 179

Wales 18–19, 21, 35, 38, 52, 57, 61, 64, 75,
    93, 113, 117, 123, 137, 155–7, 166
Webb, Sidney and Beatrice 32–3, 125, 128
Welsh disestablishment, *see*
    disestablishment
West Ham 65, 76, 150
West Midlands 18–20, 22, 25, 41, 116
Westminster Gazette 38, 42, 119, 149
Whigs 6–9, 34
Whittaker, Sir Thomas 93, 110
women's suffrage 136, 150–5
  Conciliation Bills 152–3
working class 1–5, 10, 18–19, 23, 26–7,
    33, 40, 53–4, 58–60, 63–72, 76–9,
    82–3, 97, 99, 103–5, 107, 112–13,
    116–17, 121–6, 129–38, 144–5, 147–8,
    154, 162, 164–5, 173, 198–201
workmen's compensation 33, 97–8, 102

Yorkshire 14, 18–19, 21–2, 60–1, 64, 69,
    75–6, 113, 123, 164
Yorkshire Evening News 145, 151, 153